FOUNDATIONS FOR
A SCIENCE OF PERSONALITY

FOUNDATIONS FOR A SCIENCE OF PERSONALITY

ANDRAS ANGYAL, M.D., PH.D.

Published for
THE COMMONWEALTH FUND
BY HARVARD UNIVERSITY PRESS

Cambridge, Massachusetts · 1967

Fifth printing

Published for
The Commonwealth Fund
By Harvard University Press
Cambridge, Massachusetts

Distributed in Great Britain
By Oxford University Press, London

MANUFACTURED IN THE UNITED STATES OF AMERICA

TO ALICE F. ANGYAL

TABLE OF CONTENTS

PREFACE

THE need for a broad theoretical frame of reference for the integration of the manifold aspects of human nature and behavior into a unified picture of man gave the incentive for the present study. It was intended to construct a consistent system embodying the principles that were thought to be fundamental for the problem of personality. What is offered here is primarily a somewhat extensive outline liable to and in need of more detailed elaboration. The applicability of this theory in formulating problems for empirical investigation and interpreting empirical data, which still needs testing, is the sole criterion by which the merit of this or of any other theory should be judged.

This book is not addressed to any particular group of specialists. It deals with general problems of personality, problems on which psychiatrists, biologists, psychologists, and social anthropologists can competently and profitably exchange views. For this reason, terms and examples that assume technical knowledge on the part of the reader have been avoided as far as possible.

In accordance with the attempt to present a theory of personality in a closely knit system, the book has been so organized that each section is based on what goes before and prepares for what follows. It would, therefore, be scarcely profitable to read selected sections; the book may best be read and considered as a whole.

Citations have been used rather sparingly, although I am well aware that many of the ideas which are here presented have definite relations to other systems of thought. However, by way of facilitating the flow of the argument, digressions to point out differences from and similarities to other theories have been largely omitted.

Two small sections of the text (pages 327–333 and 243–261) with some minor changes have been published previously. One of these sections appeared under the title "The Concept of Bionegativity" in *Psychiatry,* vol. 1, no. 3, August 1938; another, "The Structure of Wholes," was published in *Philosophy of Science,* vol. 6, no. 1, January 1939. I wish to express my thanks to the editors of these journals for permission to reprint the articles.

The greater part of the contents of this book was presented early in 1937 at the Henry Phipps Psychiatric Clinic, Johns Hopkins University, and I am grateful to the staff, and especially to Dr. Adolf Meyer, for the valuable criticisms, suggestions, and encouragement which I have received. I am indebted to the members of the Research Staff of the Worcester State Hospital for many helpful comments.

A. A.

September 1941

I. THE IDEA OF A SCIENCE OF PERSONALITY

THE HOLISTIC APPROACH

IN all sciences which deal with living organisms the need increasingly makes itself felt for a radical reorientation in their foundations. The hope that life could be expressed and understood in terms of the physical sciences has largely been given up and at the same time scepticism has begun to creep in with regard to the possibility of a science of human personality. However, between these two extreme points of view a new attitude is gradually emerging. One begins to question the very foundation of our philosophy of science, the general validity of our present concept of science, and the reasonableness of our scientific ideals. Since the physical sciences were the ones which first reached a considerable degree of maturity, it was tempting to identify science in general with the physical sciences. It is still a widely held opinion that the study of a given field of phenomena is scientific only in so far as it approaches the ideal of the physical sciences. It is, however, premature and dangerous to form the concept of science in general on the basis of the physical sciences, for such a concept is too narrow to do justice to the total field of phenomena toward which one's desire for knowledge can be directed. New and broader theoretical orientation in science may be possible after all. This revives the hope that with the aid of new and proper concepts and methods it will be possible to make an adequate study of those fields which were impenetrable for the traditional physical-scientific ways of thinking.

One possible aspect of the proper approach to the study of the organism has already been rather definitely formulated. A number of scientists feel that the main obstacle to progress in the study of the organism lies in the traditional "atomistic" or "segmental" approach. The new motto which has arisen is that "the organism is a whole and should be studied as such."

The holistic approach,[1] which in the last analysis is an Aristotelian one, is penetrating ever deeper into the biological sciences, especially those sciences which are concerned with the human organism. The "organismic" theories of Haldane, Woodger, Ritter, A. Meyer (the German biologist), Bertalanffy, Uexküll, the psychobiology of Adolf Meyer, Gestalt psychology, the personalistics of William Stern, the theory of emergent evolution, the holism of Smuts, the sociological system of O. Spann are characteristic examples of this trend.

Since the basic idea of the holistic attitude is quite generally known, it will be sufficient here to indicate its

[1] The term "holism" was borrowed from Smuts (F. C. Smuts, Holism and Evolution, New York, Macmillan, 1926). It is used here in the sense of "Gestalt," "totality," and similar expressions.

meaning with but a single example. Let us draw on a surface a horizontal line A, and an oblique line B in such a manner that the two lines intersect. One can study and describe the properties of line A and those of line B. However, a knowledge of the whole resulting from these two lines, namely of the angle which the two lines form, does not emerge from such a study. The angle is something entirely new, and its properties cannot be derived from the properties of the lines which constitute it. The lines, for example, can be measured in centimeters, but the angle must be measured in entirely new units—degrees. Generalizing then, it can be stated that the study of parts cannot explain the whole, because the whole is something different from the simple summation of its parts—a statement which has become a commonplace.

Against such considerations the objection is occasionally made that although the characteristics of a given whole may not be reducible to the attributes of the parts, they could be explained on the basis of the relationships between the parts. The problem, however, is much more complex than it would seem. We shall see (Chapter VIII) that the connection of parts within the frame of a whole is of a very specific kind and that this specific holistic connection cannot be resolved into relations. The novel character of wholes remains, even if it is translated into terms of logic.

The application of the holistic principle to the study of human beings has far-reaching implications. We have a number of sciences *related to* the person, but we do not have a science *of* the person. Human physiology, psychology, and sociology deal with artificially separated single aspects of the human organism, but, in spite of some promising starts, there does not as yet exist a science which studies the human person in his totality. If we admit that the human being is more than the mere aggregation of physiological, psychological, and social functions, that is, if the person as a whole has attributes which are neither the sum of the attributes of the parts nor deducible from the attributes of the parts, we must give up the hope that knowledge of the total person will ever emerge from segmental studies. Just as complete information concerning the two lines which form an angle does not give us any knowledge about the angle itself, so knowledge of physiology, psychology, and sociology cannot result in a science of the total person. This means that, for the study of the total person, there is needed not a mere combination of the results of those sciences which study single aspects of the person, but an *entirely new science.*

The need for such a basic science is keenly felt in psychiatry. Psychiatry is evidently an applied science, but of what basic science is it the application? Is it applied physiology? Applied psychology? Applied sociology? The psychiatrist may take one of these possibilities according to his personal preference or scientific bias but he is short-sighted indeed if he does not see that the other approaches cannot be legitimately excluded. One might say that psychiatry should not be the application of any one science, but a combined application of many sciences, such as physiology, psychology, sociology, and perhaps others. However, for the reason previously mentioned, one cannot hope that the combination of segmental approaches would overcome the difficulty. Such a combination would give only the sum of the knowledge gained by studying partial aspects but would not tell anything directly with regard to the person as such.

It is paradoxical, but unfortunately true, that psychiatry is the application of a basic science which does not as yet exist. Because of this lack of an adequate scientific foundation the psychiatrist has to deal with problems of aberrations of behavior to a large extent on a practical or "common sense" basis. Practical necessities of the moment may justify this procedure, but if psychiatry is to become more than a mere collection of rule-of-thumb principles, it needs a firm scientific foundation. An ideal psychiatry would be a well-founded science of the "abnormally" behaving person. This, however, presupposes a basic science dealing with the "normally" functioning person, in other words, a science of personality. The scope of a science of personality is, of course, much wider than to furnish a basis for psychiatry alone. It would have a central significance and serve as the foundation for all those sciences which deal with human beings from one or another specialized point of view.

The desirability of such a basic science has been expressed by many students in recent years. "Anthropology" would be a fitting name for it, were it not already reserved for a more specialized discipline. The same holds for the expression "human biology." The hybrid word "personology" has also been proposed. More appropriate is Adolf Meyer's term "ergasiology" and William Stern's "personalistics." However, since these latter two terms connote rather specific theoretical positions, it is preferable to use the more neutral expression, "science of personality."

POSSIBILITY AND VALUE OF A THEORY OF PERSONALITY

If the desirability of a science of personality is admitted, one could still ask whether or not the data available at present suffice to construct such a science. With reference to this question it should be remarked that new theories do not necessarily presuppose the discovery of new facts but sometimes only the seeing of old facts in a new light; for instance, the observed factual material for Newton's system was available long before the theory was formulated. The same thing is true of a large number of other scientific systems. In principle, at least, it is possible to found a theory of personality on the basis of our present knowledge of facts.

There is, of course, a considerable difference between establishing the theoretical foundation of a new science and building up a science in all its detail. There are problems which can be disentangled by intellectual operations alone after comprehending the old facts in a new way, but there are other problems which cannot be solved by any amount of thinking, and require new factual material. The purpose of the present study is to outline the general theoretical basis for a science of personality, while particulars are being left to later empirical studies. In spite of the fact that the present theory was formulated primarily to provide a working basis for psychiatry, specific problems, such as schizophrenia, delinquency, and suicide, will not be considered here. This study deals with general principles only and is intended to form the framework of a building which can be filled in with concrete material only by means of specific empirical investigations.

The utility of a theory consists essentially in that it serves as a guide, as a point of reference, for empirical studies, which otherwise are likely to result in an utterly chaotic and incoherent mass of data. The utility of a good theory is twofold: it allows us to question nature intelligently and offers a background for the interpretation of empirical data.

The accumulation and organization of knowledge in a planned study may be compared to the process of biological differentiation. Developmental processes go, as a rule, from an initial diffuse state to a state of greater differentiation, in which the parts become more distinct and gain more individuality. This is followed by a kind of synthetic process where the parts become again deeply imbedded in the whole. Consequently the whole itself becomes more organized and more definite.

It seems wise to follow the way of this natural biological evolution in our attempt to gain more knowledge of personality. First of all, we must obtain a picture, however vague, of the total organism. The conceptualization of this first envisagement forms the theory which may serve as a starting point. The theory at this stage is little articulated. It does not allow us to explain any specific detail phenomenon. Its utility lies elsewhere. As some parts begin to differentiate themselves out of a diffuse organismic state, so out of a very general theoretical background more definite part problems emerge. This is one of the advantages of theory: it allows for the formulation of specific problems.

Once the problem is set it has to be checked against facts. When a body of empirical data has thus been accumulated, the need for a theoretical background, in which it can be "imbedded," again arises. One needs some sort of general picture to determine the meaning of the facts; one needs a general theoretical background to which to relate the single datum. This is the second use of a theory, namely, as a basis for interpretation.

By the process of successive differentiation and synthesis, by positing problems and interpreting data, the theory which we attempt to evolve has already a moderate degree of distinctness. It still has to go, however, through many stages of differentiation, that is, formulation of more specific problems and an imbedding by more extensive empirical information before it may become sufficiently definite and practically useful. Its value, if any, lies in accomplishing a few necessary initial steps.

One may ask, however, with some justification: What guarantee does one have that the general theory so built up is correct? Error, of course, is possible with regard to general theories just as much as with regard to statements about details. All that one can require of a theory is self-consistency. The final test seems to be its "imbedding capacity," its agreement with the facts.

One must always reckon with the possibility that pseudo-problems may be posited on the basis of false theories, or that facts may be interpreted wrongly in an attempt to fit them into a preconceived scheme, thereby delaying the progress of knowledge. If, however, to avoid this danger one sets to work without any theory with the expectation that the facts by themselves will lead to a theory, one is greatly mistaken. Fact and theory are inseparable. Psychological studies show clearly that even such a relatively simple phenomenon as the perception of an external object involves a greater or less degree of interpretation. The so-called "apperceptive mass" is always there and gives a definite coloring to the observation. No scientific work is possible without theoretical assumptions, even if the investigator is not always aware of them. Since hypotheses cannot be eliminated from scientific work, it is certainly more reasonable to admit their presence and consider them critically than to work with implicit, unexamined hypotheses which, because not consciously recognized, are likely to conceal gross errors.

A further advantage of general theory as compared to single hypotheses is its systematic character. It is relatively easy to find a fitting explanation for a limited group of phenomena. One expects more from a general theory. It has to cover a large field, and the various ramifications of the theory have to be consistent with each other, that is, free from internal contradictions. A theory is supposed to unify the field; poorly related hypotheses are more likely to break it up into fragments.

Lastly, the economizing value of theories should also be mentioned. Especially in the last few decades literature in all sciences has increased so enormously that the student can barely keep up with developments in his special field, not to speak of those in the related sciences. I do not think that in any field knowledge becomes so vast as to pass the comprehension of a single individual. Not the quantity but the disorderliness of data defeats comprehension. If one continues to assemble facts in a more or less blind and poorly directed manner and neglects theoretical synthesis, the effort necessarily has to end in confusion. Imagine that physical mechanics were in the same state as are the humanistic sciences today. Periodicals would be filled with articles on such subjects as the path taken by a pound of iron thrown with such and such force at an angle of 17 degrees from the horizontal, or the speed of an egg-shaped body rolling along a surface inclined at 62 degrees. A mass of information of this sort would be almost impossible to retain, while the elements of mechanics can be learned in a relatively short time, and the questions treated in the hypothetical articles we have suggested can be answered without further exploration on the basis of this condensed knowledge. It is not implied that the science of personality can ever be made as simple as mechanics; it is claimed only that broad and adequate theories accomplish a substantial and time-saving simplification in any field of knowledge.

It has already been pointed out that the present theory has to be supplemented by empirical investigations. There is also another direction in which it may be extended. Like all other theory, this one, too, has certain philosophical implications. The examination of such implications, although interesting, will not be attempted in this study, except for a few remarks indicating the philosophical relevance of certain features of the theory.

THE PROBLEM OF ANALYSIS IN RELATION TO THE HOLISTIC APPROACH

It is not the purpose of this study to defend or justify once more the holistic approach to the study of the organism and to repeat unnecessarily arguments already presented by numerous authors. It seems desirable, however, to discuss briefly one objection which is often raised against it. Some state that wholes, as such, cannot be studied since scientific investigation presupposes the analysis of the whole into parts, which then makes possible the study of the interrelationships among parts.

It is, however, a misconception that the holistic type of study excludes analysis. Analysis consists in a concrete or abstractive division of an object into smaller units. One can, however, make divisions in many different ways, depending upon the principle according to which the division is made. It is true that such division may destroy the whole if the principle of the division is extraneous to the nature of the given whole, but there is a method of analysis which is perfectly adapted to the study of wholes, a method which does not destroy the object studied but, on the contrary, brings its structure into clearer relief. Let us clarify this point.

Suppose one wishes to study a given whole, be it an animal, a plant, or even an inanimate object which exhibits some of the characteristics of wholes, for example, a building. One can divide such wholes in at least four different ways. 1) One can "cut" the object into pieces *at random*. The result of such division will be a number of *fragments*. 2) One can divide the whole *according to a certain previously fixed principle* which does not take into account the intrinsic nature of that given whole but is extraneous to it. An illustration of this type of division would be the division of a tree into inch cubes. 3) One can "divide" by *abstraction,* by which is meant the resolution of objects into a number of *distinguishable properties,* for example, color, weight, consistency, etc. The result of such analysis will be a number of *features.* 4) One can divide the whole *according to its structural articulation.* Wholes, in the technical sense of the word, are never entirely undifferentiated, but are always structured and articulated into parts. This characteristic distinguishes them from homogeneous masses and from chaotic aggregations. The multiplicity of parts is just as characteristic of wholes as the unity which holds them together. The whole is never structureless but is a true *unitas multiplex,* as the philosopher would say. The division of the whole into smaller units can be made, therefore, in such a way that the line of division coincides with the structural articulation of the whole itself, and thus *the lines of division are prescribed by the structure of the whole itself.*

The parts which will be obtained by such division are real holistic units. Such is, for example, the division of a building into corridors, rooms, windows, and doors. The study of such *parts* will be at the same time a study of the characteristics of the *whole.* The door, for example, in such a study is not regarded simply as a quadrangular wooden board but in relation to its function and adequacy *as a door of the building,* that is, as an integral part of a whole. The statement would, for instance, be made that the door is something which alternatively permits the connection and separation of a room from another or from the outside—a statement which would be impossible if the door were considered in itself and not as a part of a building. In this type of analysis one starts out with a vague, but necessary, preliminary picture of the whole. This picture becomes more definite if in the course of analysis one succeeds in determining with greater precision the role of the parts in the total scheme.

Wholes are characterized by being organized according to a main principle to which all the part structures and part functions are subordinated. In a holistic type of study we do not ask what attributes the part possesses when it is considered separated from the whole. Rather do we ask what the given part contributes to the actualization of that leading principle of organization which constitutes the essence of the given whole.

A truly holistic analysis of personality into its internally determined parts has never been made. The conventional way of analysis consists in the division of the personality by abstraction into various aspects—the physiological, the psychological, and the social—and then in a search for units in the artificially defined fields. In such analysis one will find, of course, only psychological or physiological units or units of socially defined behavior patterns, but not true parts of the integrated organism. The holistic division of the personality cuts across the conventional classification, and the units obtained by holistic analysis do not coincide with physiological or psychological units. For example, what is considered as a unit physiologically may belong to more than one part of the personality and vice versa.

REQUISITES FOR A HOLISTIC THEORY OF PERSONALITY

Without minimizing the significance of the various attempts to apply the holistic approach to the problem of personality, one must admit that a science of personality or even a well-founded theory of personality on a holistic basis is yet to be developed. Some fundamental characteristics which one is justified in demanding from any holistic theory of personality may be pointed out.

1. The existing views which emphasize the holistic character of the personality are *too general*. The statement that "the personality is a whole" has a negative rather than a positive implication. It has been said with regard to the Gestalt theory that it lives by antithesis to so-called "atomism." This statement holds true to a large extent of all holistic approaches. Much of the literature on the subject is taken up by arguments to prove the inadequacy of the atomistic approach in explaining the structure and function of the organism. These discussions have served well the purpose of breaking up the conventional mechanistic-atomistic attitude toward biological science. What is needed most at the present time,

however, are contributions of a *more positive* character. It is not sufficient to point out the inadequacy of the old attitude; one must indicate how to build up a more adequate system on the new basis.

Relatively little is to be gained from the recognition of the holistic character of personality if one does not proceed to a formulation of more specific propositions with regard to organization, functioning, and the laws which govern the organism. The first requisite of a holistic theory of personality would be that of *more specific and positive formulations* of the subject-matter. It has been pointed out in the preceding section that the possibility of specific formulations is rather limited at present. This, however, does not preclude the usefulness of efforts in this direction.

2. It is often demanded of the holistic type of study that no aspect of the personality should be neglected and that one should collect all available data concerning the psychological and the physiological state of the organism, its social background, and so on. The question arises, however, whether such data can be integrated at all, and if that is possible, what method of synthesis should be applied. An example will clarify this point. Let us suppose that we are confronted with a patient who suffers from some sort of personality disorder. We make a careful physical examination and we find that the patient suffers from some metabolic disturbance. In viewing the mental aspect, we find, let us say, a delusion

of persecution as the outstanding symptom. From the social history we get the information that the patient came to the United States at the age of twelve, which probably entailed difficult problems of adjustment to a new situation. Let us suppose in addition that he had a very cruel father and an overprotective mother. The problem arises as to how to make a meaningful whole out of such heterogeneous material. Metabolic disturbances, delusions of persecution, adaptation to a cultural change, a cruel father and an overprotective mother in the family situation do not seem to belong to the same universe of discourse. It is difficult to envisage how such apparently heterogeneous data can be synthesized. Furthermore, the significance of these data for the condition in question being obscure, one does not know that any of them is other than adventitious to the case *qua* case.

One may say either that the data referring to artificially separated aspects of personality cannot be utilized at all in holistic studies so that one must provide facts of a new type for such purpose, or that one is forced to devise a method of synthesis which would make possible the unification of apparently heterogeneous material under a common heading. The problem of synthesis can be illustrated in an example used by K. Bühler.[2] When a geographer is confronted with the problem of preparing a map of a new terrain, he begins his work by taking from various vantage points a number of photographs of

[2] K. Bühler, Die Krise der Psychologie, Jena, Fischer, 1927.

the place which is to be mapped out. But his goal is far from being achieved at this stage. The pictures which he has obtained, although referring to various aspects of the same object, represent quite heterogeneous material; they may even be entirely unlike each other. They cannot be simply fitted together. A collection of such data tells very little to the layman regarding the morphology of the given terrain, and yet it constitutes a body of data for the expert wishing to draw a precise map of the region, because he has developed a *definite method of synthesis.* He is able to transfer into a common scheme the data contained in the various pictures. The transference of the data does not consist simply in adding them together; it involves a *reinterpretation according to definite rules.* A datum contained in one picture will be inscribed into the common scheme in a way entirely different from the way the same datum contained in a picture obtained from another vantage point is utilized. The problem of synthesis, for the student of personality, is even more complicated. The data which the geographer has to unify belong at least to the same order of phenomena, whereas the data with which the student of personality deals belong apparently to very different orders.

The second requisite, with regard to a holistic theory of personality, is therefore that it should either (a) give up utilizing facts referring to single aspects and *provide new facts* which are adequate for such study; or (b) *devise a method of synthesis* of segmental data. I believe that a holistic science of personality requires new types of facts, but I will try to show later that the synthesis of segmental data in a holistic scheme is to some extent also possible and useful.

3. A holistic theory of personality should not borrow its concepts from either physiology or psychology but should *develop its own set of concepts.* The holistic theory of personality deals with facts referring to the integrated organism before any abstractive separation of the mental and the organic aspects has occurred. The description of such facts in physiological or psychological terms causes only confusion. The concepts and terms in which we describe facts referring to the total organism must be—to use an expression of William Stern[3]—psychophysically neutral. The precise formulation of this new set of concepts is one of the most important tasks of a holistic theory of personality.

[3] W. Stern, Studien zur Personwissenschaft, I: Personalistik als Wissenschaft, Leipzig, Barth, 1930.

II. THE TREND TOWARD INCREASED AUTONOMY

THE ORGANISM AS A DYNAMIC WHOLE

SOME phenomena of nature exist in the form of static structures, others in the form of reversible or irreversible processes. Examples of the first are geometrical forms, of the second, waterfall, wind, combustion, etc. The existential form of the organism is dynamic. This has been formulated by Jennings in his much quoted statement that "The organism is a process." In the last analysis, "organism" and "life" are identical concepts. The first term places the emphasis on the structural, the second on the dynamic aspect. The two aspects are inseparable from each other. The essential characteristics of the organism are, however, more clearly revealed in its function than in its morphological features. The morphological structure is subordinated to the functional organization which has a logical primacy over it. If one calls a dead animal an "organism" one implies previous function, since without this implication a corpse is obviously only a morphological pattern. Each organ is—as the word implies—a tool of the organism. The heart of the dead animal can be called a tool only with regard to its previous function. When one speaks of any organ it is always implied that it has a function in the total economy of the organism—even though our knowledge of this function may on occasion be quite inadequate—otherwise it would not deserve the name of an organ.

One has to study life as a dynamic whole. In every whole there is a leading principle according to which it is organized. Thus the necessity arises of defining the leading principle of organization of the biological total process. The problem can be stated as follows: *What is the general pattern which the organismic total process follows?* An adequate definition of the general pattern of the biological total process is not only of great theoretical interest but has far-reaching consequences for the actual study of the organism. Every organismic part process is a manifestation of the dynamism of the total organism. The part processes gain their meaning from the general pattern of functional organization and can be correctly understood only in the context of this organization.

THE HYPOTHESIS OF IMMANENCE

In spite of the differences in the way in which various students define life, there is an element which is common to almost all the existing definitions—a common theoretical nucleus which could be conveniently called the "immanence theory of life." This can be roughly stated in the following way:

One might view the organism as consisting of a number of parts or organs which have specific functions. These functions lead beyond the organ itself. Thus, for instance, the main function of the lungs is to provide oxygen and to eliminate certain gaseous waste products. The lungs, however, do not provide oxygen only for their own tissues, but also for the tissues of the other organs. The same thing holds with regard to the other organs of the body. The heart irrigates with blood not only its own tissues, but all the tissues of the body. Thus we find between the different parts of a living organism relations of the type shown in Figure 1.

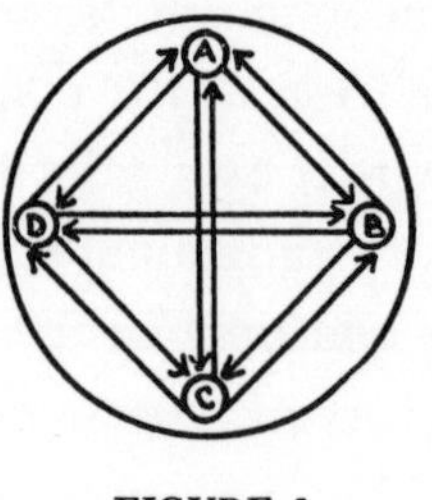

FIGURE 1

Organ A works for organs A, B, C, and D. The entire meaning of the function of organ A is to maintain itself and organs B, C, and D in a condition in which they can fulfill efficiently their specific functions. The function of organ B in return is to maintain in good functional condition itself and the organs A, C, and D—and so forth.

This would be a process taking place within a closed

circle. It would not seem to lead anywhere and it would be comparable to a wheel turning on its own axis without progressing. Within the circle the function of each organ can be defined by what it accomplishes for the rest of the organism. However, a functional definition of the total life process seems impossible from this point of view and life as a whole appears as functionally meaningless.

The "immanence hypothesis" is not a point of view which has actually been maintained by anyone in the crude form outlined here, which is almost a caricature. It is, however, the theoretical nucleus implicitly contained in most existing definitions and not a straw man which has been set up arbitrarily for the sake of argument. R. Ehrenberg refers to this implicit point of view when he writes: "There is hardly a biologist who would doubt that this [assimilation-dissimilation] is a—though not always perfect—circular process, that assimilation reestablishes a previous state which has been altered by dissimilation. The conception of life as an oscillation about a position of equilibrium, as repeated disturbances and reestablishments of an equilibrium . . . is certainly the most widely held conception."[1] In every theory which postulates the maintenance of equilibrium or self-preservation and survival, as the general trend of

[1] R. Ehrenberg, Theoretische Biologie vom Standpunkte der Irreversibilität des elementaren Lebensvorganges, Berlin, Springer, 1923, p. 10.

the life process, the hypothesis of immanence is always implicit. The assumption in all such theories is that the life process forms a closed circle which does not lead beyond the sum total of the part function. Such a point of view may, therefore, justly be called an immanence hypothesis or a "closed-circle hypothesis" of life.

This viewpoint was once commented upon satirically by a humorist who remarked: "Scientists have found out that the ears are for hearing, the eyes for seeing, the lungs for breathing, the hands for grasping, the feet for walking; they should now take just a little step further and find out what the whole man is for." The problem stated in this way is a philosophical one; but if we formulate the problem in a somewhat different way and ask: What is the general trend in the total dynamism of the organism? What is the direction in which the total life process evolves? What is the organism aiming at, in its total function?—then we have a legitimate scientific problem, which a theory of the total organism should answer. The solution of this question in terms of the hypothesis of immanence would be a *biological nihilism*. The entire functional meaning of the single part process is to "keep going" the rest of the "machinery" which has then no function, no direction, no aim. According to such a view the life process would have the pattern of a logical vicious circle: the part processes have the function to maintain life; and life is an aggregation of these part processes.

THE TREND TOWARD AUTONOMY

A PRELIMINARY DEFINITION OF THE GENERAL DYNAMIC TREND OF THE ORGANISM

In the theory represented schematically in Figure 1 some highly significant facts have been neglected. A little reflection will show that life, in all its forms—be it in the plant or animal world—is not a completely closed circle of processes. The circle is open at two points (Figure 2). These are: *assimilation* (intake), on the one side, and *production,* on the other. These terms need some clarification.

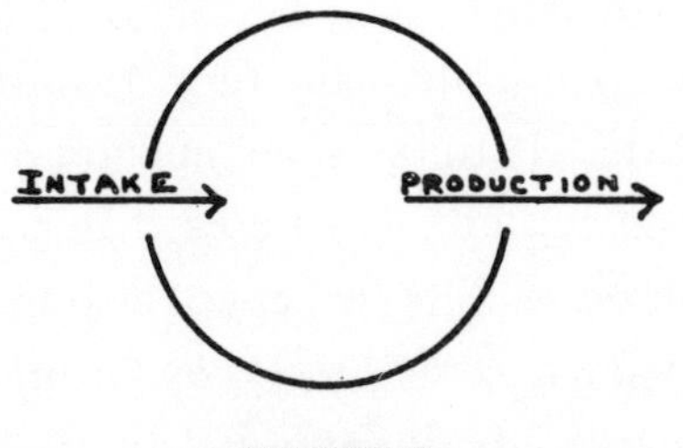

FIGURE 2

The most primitive form of assimilation, common to every organism, is a material one: that is, assimilation of food or nutrition. It is a stream of material (food substances, oxygen, carbon dioxide) flowing from the environment into the organism, a stream which is maintained and directed by the activity of the organism itself. Nutrition means more than merely an infiltration of certain substances from the surroundings into the organism. The substances on the way undergo a progressive transformation under the moulding influences of the organism until complete assimilation has taken place. This is a profound metamorphosis, a transformation of environmental matter into "living matter." A consideration of the phenomenon of assimilation makes it obvious that life cannot be considered as a process entirely enclosed within the limits of the organism. The organism reaches out into the surrounding world, draws material from it, and transforms this material into functioning parts of the organismic system. The life process has an outward direction and thus transcends the pattern of a closed circle.

I wish to emphasize that the term "assimilation" does not refer exclusively to the phenomenon of assimilation of food substances, but will be used in this study in a much broader sense. The concept of assimilation, in general, can be defined as *the process by means of which any factor which is originally external to the organism becomes a functional part of it.* The assimilation of food substances was selected as an example because, for a definition of life processes in general, only those factors can be taken into account which are common to all living beings. Assimilation of food is only one example of a more general phenomenon. Some other forms will be mentioned later.

The second break in the scheme (Figure 2) is represented by production. Each living being creates something which transcends its own limits. In order to exemplify the creativeness of the organism we may point to the fact of reproduction, that is, the production of a new organism, as a general example of processes common to all living beings.[2] With regard to reproduction the implications of the closed-circle theory of life do not hold any longer. The function of reproduction cannot be defined by "what it accomplishes for the rest of the organism." In fact, it does not serve any intra-individual purpose but it points and leads beyond the individual organism itself. Further examples of production are muscular and mental activities with their corresponding products.

The biological meaning of assimilation and production can be synthesized into a single principle. Assimilation is a continuous transformation of environmental things into functioning parts of the living organism; it is not enclosed within the limits of the organism but is a process which points beyond these limits. It draws incessantly new material from the outside world, transforming alien objects into functional parts of its own. Thus the organism *expands* at the expense of its surroundings. The expansion may be a material one as in the case of bodily growth, or a psychological one as in the case of the assimilation of experiences which result

[2] The phenomenon of reproduction, besides being an example of the creativeness of the organism, has a great significance for the theory of the total organism from another point of view as well. It is an example of the integration of the individual into superindividual units. This aspect of the problem will be taken up in Chapter VI.

in mental growth, or a functional one as when one acquires skill, with a resulting increase of efficiency in dealing with the environment, and so forth.

The organism also expands through its creativeness. Instruments invented by man extend the capabilities of the organism beyond their original limits. There are a great number of devices which broaden and refine our sensory capacities, as, for instance, the microscope, the telescope, and the telephone. The invention of writing extended our capacity to "record" whatever we wish to a degree which memory alone could never achieve. Various machines and labor-saving devices add tremendously to our muscular capacities. Our natural weapons are vastly increased by the addition of artificial weapons. The various implements which we use are almost like organs added to those which we originally possess. Other examples: there are organic mechanisms which protect us from the unfavorable influences of climatic conditions. However, we support these organic mechanisms powerfully by artificial means (habitations, clothes, and so forth). These examples could be multiplied almost indefinitely. The products of the activities of the organism have a middle position between environment and organism. Such products differ from other objects of the environment in that they are integrated with the total activity of the organism, by carrying out important part functions in the biological total process. In other words, the organism with the help of its products extends itself into the external world by converting a large range of external objects into tools which—to a certain extent—become integral parts of the organismic total process.

The process of reproduction is somewhat different. Here the progeny usually achieves sooner or later an independent existence and no longer plays any part in the life of the mother organism. But since, in reproducing itself, the organism increases the number of individuals of its own kind, this phenomenon may also be assigned to the category of expansion.

As a first approximation we may define life as *a process of self-expansion*. The dynamism of the total organism does not follow the pattern of a closed circle, but is a process which evolves in a *definite direction*. The total process can be divided into two phases: a) the centripetal stream of assimilation which draws material from the environment into the organism, and continues thence as b) a centrifugal outflow of production. All partial functions of the organism are subordinated to this general trend, and may be divided into two groups: functions concerned with assimilation and functions concerned with production. The respiratory and digestive organs stand in the service of assimilation. The environmental raw material is remoulded by mechanical and chemical methods which make it more and more similar to the material of the organism itself. It is then carried by lymphatics and blood vessels to the cells where the final assimilation, the metamorphosis of the environmental objects into the functioning parts of the organism, is completed. From here on the productive or creative phase of the organismic total process starts, maintained by the function of nervous, muscular, and generative "effectors." Although part of this activity turns back and supports a further assimilation of raw material, another part results in products as a "net profit." Nervous and chemical systems of coordination (for example, the endocrines) ensure the harmonious working of the organism.

There is, in addition, a third group of accessory functions which do not contribute directly to the main stream of the organismic total process, but safeguard it against disturbing influences. Instances of such functions are the elimination of unassimilable material and of harmful by-products of the life process in the form of urine and feces, sweat, etc.

From the point of view which has been developed here one can easily discover the fallacies contained in the closed-circle theory of life. For instance, A. von Tschermak[3] defines life as a two-directional process. On one side there is a storing-up of matter and energy, on the other side a dispersal of matter and energy; on the one side, anabolism, and on the other, catabolism.

The error in such a definition is that it seems to identify catabolism with dispersion of matter and energy, and that it considers such dispersion as the twin of the

[3] A. von Tschermak, Allgemeine Physiologie, Berlin, Springer, 1924, p. 4.

process of anabolism. The biological function of catabolism, however, is not energy dispersion, but energy mobilization. When anabolism is completed, the next step in the biological total process is not dispersion but productive utilization of energy, which is mobilized by catabolism. The dispersion of matter and energy, their escape from the organismic system, is only the unavoidable by-product of living, an epiphenomenon. The energy which is stored up by the organism is not wasted but, at least in part, used for productive activity.

The physiologist, of course, is well aware of the process of assimilation through which environmental things are taken in and transformed into functioning parts of the biological organization. He is equally aware of the productivity of living beings. The physiologist, however, *qua* physiologist, focuses his attention upon intra-organismic functional relationships. Such a limitation of the field has its value from the point of view of division of labor, but the definition of life conceived from a purely intra-organismic point of view affords too narrow a basis for a science of personality. If one neglects the inwardly and outwardly directed stream of assimilation and production, or if one does not account for it sufficiently in one's theory, the essential self-transcending character of the functional pattern of living, naturally, does not reveal itself.

According to our point of view the life process does not take place *within* the organism, but *between the or-*

ganism and the environment. If one defines life as a process of self-expansion, the factor "environment" is already implicit in the definition. The organism cannot expand within itself; it can expand only in a medium which is originally external to it, the environment. The life process embraces both organism and environment. Organism and environment are the two indispensable poles of a single process—life. The thesis that life is a process which takes place between individual and environment is discussed in greater detail in Chapter IV.

DEFINITION OF THE BIOLOGICAL TOTAL PROCESS AS A TREND TOWARD INCREASED AUTONOMY

A consideration of the phenomena of assimilation and production gave occasion to point out the self-transcending, or progressive, character of life. It has been suggested that the pattern of the biological total process may be defined provisionally as a trend toward self-expansion. This definition is, however, presented only as a first approximation. In order to reach a more precise formulation we will now consider another aspect of the biological total process.

One of the essential features of living organisms, whereby they differ from any other object in nature, is what we might call their *autonomy*. By this is meant that the organism does not represent merely an inactive point, in which various causal chains intersect—as mechanistic philosophy assumes—but is, to a large extent, a *self-governing* entity. The biological process is not a resultant of external forces, but is, in part, governed by specifically biological endogenous factors. The organism itself is, to a large extent, the cause of its functions, that is, it is endowed with spontaneity. We could also say that the organism possesses a certain degree of "freedom," if we use the term in the sense of Spinoza and call free that which acts according to its own inherent nature, according to its intrinsic law, and not under the compulsion of exogenous forces.

The organism lives in a world in which things happen according to laws which are heteronomous from the point of view of the organism.[4] The organism is subjected to the laws of the physical world just as is any other object of nature, with the exception that it can oppose self-determination to external determination. When an animal has been dropped from a height it follows the law of gravitation like any other body. In such instance the organism takes part in a mechanical happening *simply as a mass and not as an organism.* In many instances, however, such physical happenings will not be determined entirely by the law of gravitation and by the mass of the organism. The result will be modified by influences which originate from within the organism. A

[4] The term "autonomous" is used in this discussion to mean "governed from inside"; and "heteronomous" to mean "governed from outside."

cat also falls according to the law of gravity, but it will land on its feet whatever the position of its body at the beginning of the fall. By means of an endogenous factor, the so-called righting reflexes, the cat modifies the mechanical process and manages to land on its feet.

If we take as an example a chemical influence on the organism we will find conditions analogous to that described in the previous example. When one puts a drop of sulphuric acid on the skin, the skin will be burned. This is a process which is not different in its character from chemical processes which take place outside of the body. The process going on in the affected area, however, will soon be modified by influences originating within the organism (inflammation, healing of the wound) which tend to repair the damage and reestablish a state which is favorable for the organism.

It would probably be generally agreed that without autonomy, without self-government, the life process could not be understood. Selection, choice, self-regulation, adaptation, regeneration are phenomena which logically imply an autonomy of the organism. Selection, that is, the search for certain environmental conditions and the avoidance of other conditions, is only possible in a being capable of self-directed activity. The various functions usually comprised under the term "self-regulation" are another group of phenomena which clearly demonstrate the autonomy of the organism. Good instances of self-regulation are those functions which make it possible to maintain "homeostasis" (Cannon[5]), as heat regulation in the warm-blooded animals which enables them to maintain a fairly constant temperature of the body in spite of considerable changes in the temperature of the environment.

The various phenomena of adaptation in the field of sensory functions are further examples of the self-directed activity of the organism. Adaptation in the sensory field is the ability of the organism to modify the function of its sense organs according to the demands of the situation. The eyes, for instance, would be a very poor optic apparatus indeed without the capacity of accommodation for distance and of adaptation to light and darkness. Phenomena of adaptation are present in varying degrees in all sense organs.

There does not exist a single life process which could be understood without the autonomy of the organism. We may take, for instance, the process of assimilation. How could an organism, without self-directed action, manage to build up from food substances, the chemical constitution of which varies between broad limits, a protoplasm which is specific for the given species and even for the given individual?

Even such relatively simple phenomena as tropisms are unexplainable without this capacity. A plant responds to the force of gravitation by sending its roots downward, but in response to the same force of gravita-

[5] W. B. Cannon, The Wisdom of the Body, New York, Norton, 1932.

tion it sends its stem upward and the branches sideways (positive, negative, and diagonal geotropism). Thus we deal here with a true stimulus-response relationship which is different from a merely mechanical process.

The stimulus-response relationship in general shows very decidedly the autonomous nature of the organism. The organism does not react to external influences only as a physicochemical body, but responds, in its own specific way, as an organism. The external influence in such a case is not the mechanical cause of the reaction of the organism, but is the *stimulus* which *prompts* the response. The response is mainly determined by the intrinsic tendencies of the organism, or—applying the terminology used above—is essentially an autonomous function. In the stimulus-response relationship even the stimulus is not a simple physicochemical process. The external condition which prompts the response acts not by its properties as such but by its properties relative to the organism. The stimulus quality of an object is a relational property, that is, one which the object derives from its relation to the organism. For example, a piece of bread "in itself" is merely an object with certain chemical and physical properties. Its stimulus quality of being "food" is not an internal quality, but a quality which exists only with regard to the organism.[6] The dis-

[6] Woodger makes a useful distinction between the "relational" and "intrinsic qualities" of the parts of the whole (H. H. Woodger, The concept of organism and the relation between embryology and genetics, Quarterly Review of Biology, 5:14, 1930). I use the term relational

tinction between the mechanical cause-effect relation, on the one hand, and the biological stimulus-response process, on the other, may seem hair-splitting, but actually the difference is a very important one. We will return to this problem in Chapter VIII.

Some of the phenomena which we used as examples to illustrate the autonomy of the organism can be reproduced superficially by proper mechanical devices. This has frequently been used as an argument in support of a mechanistic conception of life. The comparison between organism and mechanical devices is not very useful. Mechanical devices have relation not only to inorganic constellations but also to the organism. They are created by man, who lends to them certain organismic features. The problem has been well discussed in a monograph by Alverdes, and he concludes that "the essential difference is that the mechanical device is characterized by *passivity,* the organism by *activity.*"[7] Alverdes' concept of activity implies autonomy.

The autonomy of the organism is not an absolute one. Self-determination is restricted by outside influences which, with respect to the organism, are heteronomous. The organism lives in a world in which processes go on

property here in a more general sense, meaning by it a quality which an object has only when it stands in a certain relation to another object. In the sentence, "A is larger than B," the word "larger" indicates a relational quality. An object in itself cannot be "larger." It can be larger only in relation to another object.

[7] F. Alverdes, Die Totalität des Lebendigen, Leipzig, Barth (Bios, vol. 3), 1935, p. 11.

independently of it. The organism asserts itself against the heteronomous surroundings. As has been pointed out, life by implication is not an intra-organismic process, but a process which takes place between the organism and its environment. Thus every single organismic part process, and also the life process as a whole, is always a *resultant of two components, autonomy and heteronomy*. A given organismic process can be expressed by the ratio a (autonomy) : h (heteronomy). If in this ratio a is reduced to zero, we no longer have an organismic process, but a physical one. If in this ratio the value of h is reduced to zero, we obtain the concept of an absolutely "free" hypothetical entity which is entirely exempt from the influences of the physical world. This would correspond to the old concept of "soul." In the realm of organismic happenings we find neither entirely heteronomous nor entirely autonomous processes. There is life only where in the ratio $a:h$ the values of both a and h are positive and greater than zero.

By using the terms "autonomy" and "heteronomy" I do not wish to express any theory with regard to the nature of the laws which govern physical and organismic happenings. I do not take here any attitude toward the problem whether organismic and physical laws are different or identical, whether the organismic laws can be derived from physical ones (materialism, mechanism), or the physical laws from organismic laws (Haldane, A. Meyer). Autonomy and heteronomy refer here only to the source out of which a process is governed. In this study, by autonomy is meant "self-government" and by heteronomy "government from the outside." Thus, for example, when two animals A and B are engaged in a fight, what animal A does to animal B is heteronomous for B, in spite of the fact that it originates from an organism.

As mentioned above, in an organismic process expressed by the ratio $a:h$, the value of a and the value of h must be positive and greater than zero. The relative values of a and h, however, vary within broad limits. The autonomous determination of the organism may play a larger role in one of its manifestations than in another. The relative values of a and h vary also from situation to situation, from individual to individual, and from one species to another. Thus if we compare, for instance, living beings of different species, we find *marked variations in the importance of autonomous and heteronomous determinations in their lives.* A few examples will be sufficient to illustrate this point. Supposing that the ground where a plant lives becomes poor in those substances which it needs as food. The plant has certain limited possibilities of struggling against this unfavorable environmental condition, for example, by changing the direction of the growth of its roots, but adaptive possibilities are limited. Under similar conditions an animal is not so dependent upon heteronomous determination. If an environment is poor in food, animals can seek food by moving to other regions. This means that in certain species the process of acquiring food is determined to a larger extent than in others by the self-government of the organism. Certain animals make themselves even more independent of the influences of the environment, as far as nutrition is concerned, by storing up their food as a provision for times of need.

We may take still another form of biological function, such as reproduction. In many kinds of plants the process of fecundation is to a large extent heteronomous. It is largely dependent on external conditions such as the action of insects and the wind. The autonomy of the organism is ensured in those cases only by structural arrangements which are adapted for such external influences. The seed is spread also by the influence of the wind and its fate depends again chiefly upon the conditions and the influences of the external world. If the seed drops upon fertile ground it can survive and grow; if it drops on a rock it perishes. In animals, on the other hand, the fecundation takes place to a large extent through autonomous determination, that is, by processes determined by the organism itself. The fertilized egg is not left to chance of external conditions; it is deposited in a protected, favorable place. In the case of other animals, a deposit of food is made near the egg which serves as nourishment of the young in the first period of their life. Other animals remain with the egg until the young are born. Certain animals care for the young after birth, often for a considerable length of time, continuing to exert a modifying influence on them. This again signifies a great progress in liberating oneself from external determination, a high degree of emancipation from environmental conditions.

I wish to emphasize that these differences between various biological processes are not mentioned in order to show that one form is more efficient than the other. It is, for example, quite possible that, in general, the reproductive process is more effective for plants than for animals. This is not the point, however. The important fact is that in the reproductive and other processes of plants external determination plays a greater, and internal determination a smaller, role than in the corresponding processes of animal life.

If one now considers the organismic total process with regard to the $a:h$ ratio, one discovers *a definite trend in the organismic total process toward an increase of the relative value of* a *in this ratio, that is, a trend toward an increase of autonomy*. This trend does not have a fixed objective but only a general direction. At each stage of the biological process the tendency is toward a situation which is characterized by a greater degree of autonomy than the preceding situation. The organism does not always succeed in progressing toward greater autonomy, and under heteronomous environmental influences may even be thrown back to a stage of diminished autonomy.

This, however, occurs through external compulsion and not by the activity of the organism.

In order to justify the preceding statement we do not need to survey all the functions of the organism. In an earlier section we have classified the various functions of the organism in two general groups: those concerned with assimilation and those concerned with production, and it will be sufficient for our purpose to consider the functions under these two groups collectively.

Assimilation was defined as a process by means of which a factor, which is originally external to the organism, becomes a functioning part of it. With regard to the organism the terms "external" and "internal" have a specific meaning. They do not refer to spatial relations, but rather are to be understood metaphorically. The term "internal" is used here to mean "belonging to the organism" and "external" to mean "not belonging to the organism." "Belonging" does not refer to coherence in space, but expresses primarily the general relation of the part to the whole. In a case of dynamic wholes, such as organisms, "belonging" or "being a part of" means that a certain factor is carrying out a partial function of the total system. If we consider this relationship with regard to the source which governs a function, we can conclude that a given function is only a partial function of the organism when it is governed by the organism itself, that is, when it becomes a manifestation of organismic autonomy.

In the process of assimilation environmental factors undergo stages of successive modification in such a way that they come more and more under the control of the organism until they are integrated with the organism and become a functioning part thereof. At the beginning of the process of assimilation the organism faces a given factor which is, as yet, entirely free from the influence of the organism (heteronomous). When the organism begins to exert its influence on this environmental factor, the resulting event can be represented dynamically by the ratio $a{:}h$ in which the relative value of a is very small. As the process continues, the influence of the organism on the occurrence, which results from the interaction of the organism and the given environmental factor, increases; that is, in the $a{:}h$ ratio a gradually becomes greater. Thus the process of assimilation can be regarded as a specific manifestation of the general dynamic trend of the organism toward increased autonomy.

The second major class of organismic functions, those concerned with production, also reflects the trend of the organism toward increase of autonomy. Production in general can be defined as the activity of the organism by means of which it creates planful changes in the environment. We have in mind primarily such things as the building of habitations, roads, bridges, machines, the fabrication and use of various tools and instruments, the domestication of plants and animals, and so forth.[8] The

[8] Certain activities which cannot be adequately characterized by

result of such activities is a transformation of the primitive surroundings into a situation in which events are more or less under the control of the organism. While in the world in general, events take place without regard to the needs of the organism, in the "cultivated" environment these events are modified by the influence of the organismic activity in such a way that they converge with the biological total process. In an uninfluenced environment, for example, the temperature changes according to the stark laws of physics, without regard to the welfare of the organism; but in human habitations, by a judicious use of physical principles, we modify the course of events by means of various devices in order to obtain a more or less constant, favorable temperature in our immediate environment. We influence planfully the flora and fauna of our surroundings by inhibiting the growth of certain species and promoting the growth or modifying the characteristics of others. The significance of science for human life is not materially different from what it is for other fields of production. The aim is to master, theoretically or practically, blind heteronomous happenings, to place them at the service of life and to eliminate disturbing influences.

No matter what example of production we take, we always discover the modifying, controlling influences of

stating that they "induce planned changes in the environment," like artistic creation or religious practice, are not considered here. They will be discussed in Chapter VI.

the organism on the events of its environment. The range of this influence may be very slight, as in the case of a budding yeast, or impressively great, as in human life; the general tendency is the same. This fact may be expressed in the terminology introduced above. In a world uninfluenced by the organism, events are—from the point of view of the organism—entirely heteronomously determined. This can be represented by the symbol *h*. When the organism begins to act on its environment, the resulting event can be expressed by the $a:h$ ratio in which the value of *a* is rather small. The tendency of the organism in its productive activity leads to an increased control of the environment, that is, to the increase of the value of *a* in the $a:h$ ratio.

Thus assimilation and production appear as different manifestations of the same general tendency of the organism. In so far as the functions of the organism are susceptible to division into functions concerned with assimilation and functions concerned with production, we may say that the general dynamic trend of the organism is toward an increase of autonomy.[9] This trend can be expressed in the following form:

$$\left(\frac{a}{h}\right)_1 \lessdot\!\!\rightarrow \left(\frac{a}{h}\right)_2$$

In apparent contradiction to this tendency we observe a large group of regressive phenomena. Successive stages

[9] It is very suggestive to assume that the tendency toward increased

in the organismic total process are not always characterized by greater autonomy. Frequently the opposite is true of individual life, as well as of phylogenetic history. The phenomena of regression seem to fall readily into two groups: passive set-back and strategic retreat. A passive set-back is analogous to the situation of a man swimming against the stream. His activity is directed toward progression in a given direction, and he actually does progress with every stroke with respect to the water in his neighborhood. At the same time, however, he is carried backward by the force of the stream with respect to the banks. The resulting movement depends on these

autonomy is not only the general dynamic trend of the individual organism but also the *primum movens* of the phylogenetic process. The phylogenetic line is a succession of individual lives. Hence it is plausible and methodologically convenient to assume that individual life processes and phylogenesis follow the same dynamic trend. Such factors as adaptation, for instance, can be regarded only as secondary for phylogenesis. Adaptation obviously does not mean that the organism changes under environmental influences, but that it changes in a way to retain its main dynamic trend in spite of interfering circumstances. Thus adaptation already presupposes a primary trend in the organismic total processes. The same consideration can be applied to many other factors which were claimed to be driving forces of phylogenesis.

The view developed here also permits us to distinguish between higher and lower levels of development. The higher level would be characterized by a high positive value of $\frac{a}{h}$ and the lower one by a smaller positive value of $\frac{a}{h}$. Of course, one cannot expect a perfect correlation between the value of the $\frac{a}{h}$ ratio and the place of a given organism or species in the phylogenetic line, since the former expresses *degrees of development* while the latter refers to an order of chronological successions, and the two, of course, do not necessarily always coincide. These remarks are made by way of a suggestion. The problem of phylogenesis is not our primary concern in this study.

two components. If the force of the stream is greater than his, he will be carried backward, but even in such a case we still can say that the man's tendency is to move upstream. We can say that the tendency of the organism is toward increased autonomy, even if actually it is carried backward by the stream of heteronomous influences with a resulting decrease of autonomy. The final result is always a victory of physical forces over the organism: aging and death.

Regression may also be a strategic move. In warfare one of the combatants may be pushed backward under the heteronomous influence of the enemy or actively retreat for strategic purposes. In neither case does the retreating group wish to be defeated. Sometimes an offensive, sometimes active retreat is the more expedient procedure. The goal itself is always *"progressive."* In human life regression may occur, as when a situation becomes untenable at a certain level of complexity and one partially retreats to a more primitive situation, usually to one which has been tried out at an earlier date.

Hypotheses concerning a kind of large-scale regression, as in the hypothesis of the death instinct, are not very convincing. Even among orthodox psychoanalysts the theory is far from being generally accepted. The facts which are attributed to the death instinct can probably be explained more plausibly on another basis.[10]

[10] There is, however, an important group of phenomena in human

The purpose of the preceding discussion was to define the general dynamic trend of the organismic total process. The results of these considerations can be summarized as follows: Life is an autonomous dynamic event which takes place between the organism and the environment. Life processes do not merely tend to preserve life but transcend the momentary status quo of the organism, expanding itself continuously and imposing its autonomous determination upon an ever increasing realm of events.

The process of expansion is limited not only by outside influences, but, obviously, also by the nature of the given organism. The capacity for expansion shows a broad phylogenetic and individual variation. The tendency toward increased autonomy is a tendency to achieve, dominate, and master the environment. It is closely related to the concept of aggression which, in its modern usage, does not necessarily imply hostility.

In the preceding discussion of the trend toward increasing autonomy the examples were so selected as to illustrate the broad biological basis of this fundamental human tendency. The attempt to trace its manifold manifestations in the life of the person would require a more detailed treatment than is possible in a theoretical outline as general as the present one. Hence we will have

life which are not based on the assertion of one's individuality, but definitely imply the restriction of one's individualistic existence. Such phenomena seem to be the manifestations of a "tendency toward homonomy" to be discussed in a later section (Chapter VI).

to limit ourselves to suggesting later (Chapter VII) only some of the specific channels through which the trend toward increased autonomy finds a concrete outlet in personal life. The operation of some such fundamental tendency in the human personality could not escape the attention of any student of man, and though it has been formulated in various ways and varying degrees of significance have been ascribed to it, it has found its way into practically all existing systems dealing with personality organization. In psychoanalysis the aggressive tendencies are second only to the libidinal urges. In Adlerian individual psychology the craving for power and for superiority is the axis of the entire personality organization. Aggressiveness, combativeness, the urge for mastery, domination, or some equivalent urge or drive or trait is assumed probably by all students of personality. All these various concepts imply that the human being has a characteristic tendency toward self-determination, that is, a tendency to resist external influences and to subordinate the heteronomous forces of the physical and social environment to its own sphere of influence. The definition of the exact relations of aggressiveness, craving for power, or similar concepts to the trend toward increased autonomy seems neither necessary nor fruitful in the present context. It seems advisable to use the concept of a trend toward increased autonomy as formulated here in preference to other concepts because it expresses the broad human tendency in question, while other concepts like craving for power refer merely to some aspect thereof.

SOME IMPLICATIONS OF THE ABOVE THEORY

It will be useful to point out certain characteristics and implications of the above considerations in order to bring into clearer relief certain basic features of our point of view. I wish to place special emphasis on the following characteristics of the theory just presented.

1. The organism is considered not as a static structure but as a *dynamic organization.* We are not primarily concerned with those static views of the organism which one may gain by means of certain neglective abstractions. It is not a question of a personal preference whether one studies a given phenomenon from a static or from a dynamic point of view. The nature of the phenomenon in question determines the adequacy of a given approach to a selected set of phenomena. Geometrical forms exist as static structures, but a waterfall, for instance, exists as a process. A structural analysis is an adequate approach to the study of static phenomena, but processes can be studied properly only from the dynamic aspect. Since the existential form of the organism is a dynamic one, it has to be studied from the dynamic point of view, that is, as a process.

2. Students of life conventionally place the emphasis in their considerations upon intra-organismic relation-

ships. Here, on the other hand, we take the view—which will be further developed in Chapter IV—that the life process does not take place *within* the organism, but between the organism and the environment. Organism and environment are considered as the two indispensable poles of the life process. The life process can be expressed dynamically by the ratio between autonomy (organism) and heteronomy (environment). Life is possible only when the value of both factors in the ratio is positive and greater than zero.

3. Life is here conceived *not* as an *immanent* but as a *self-transcending* process. It does not merely tend to preserve a given state, but also points beyond its status quo. One might argue that the extension of autonomy is only secondary, while the primary trend would be self-preservation. One might say that the drive "to be" must logically precede any other trends of the organism. This is, however, an erroneous point of view. The expression "to be" in the previous statement cannot refer to mere existence. Rather does it refer to a very specific form of existence. It obviously does not mean "to be in whatever form," as, for example, "to be dead," but it means "to be alive," "to live"; and life, if our definition is correct, is a process tending toward an increase in the autonomy of the organism.

4. The concept of autonomy is not new. It is an important issue in various biological theories, in that of Driesch, for example. The purpose of the present dis-

cussion is, however, not only to point out the autonomous nature of the organism, but to argue that the life process tends toward an *increase* of autonomy. It is furthermore assumed that such trend or tendency represents one of the basic patterns of the biological total process. The universality of this tendency of the organism does not contradict the phenomena of regression, when the organism is set back by heteronomous influences to a state of lessened autonomy or when it retreats strategically to such a state.

5. I wish to emphasize that the trend or tendency toward increased autonomy is *not an entity,* not something which *makes* the life process take a specific direction, but should be understood as a descriptive term referring to the *pattern of the life process.* This general trend is not a hypothetical entity hidden behind the scene and from there directing events, but is a general expression of the *way according to which the life process takes place.* Such a trend is not postulated as an explanatory principle but is a *descriptive generalization.*

Our formulation of this general trend is comparable to the manner in which laws are formulated in physics. The process of free fall, for instance, takes place according to a definite pattern. When the physicist states the law of free fall, he expresses in his formula the pattern of this process. His formula does not imply the assumption of any entity which "makes" the object fall. Our formulation of the basic trend of the organismic total process is exactly of the same nature: in both cases we deal with statements referring to the *pattern of a process.*

Concepts in physics have undergone in the past an evolution similar to the one biological concepts are undergoing now. For instance, causation means today something essentially different from what it meant in the past. The earlier conception implied a "force," an "entity" which made things happen, while today it means rather a constant or—to avoid objection from certain quarters in modern theoretical physics—an approximately constant pattern of successive events. The crude concepts of "entities" are due to primitive ways of thinking which tend to conceive of everything as object. We wish, however, to avoid here the not uncommon mistake of hypostatization.

6. The point of view presented in this paper is not strictly *teleological* but merely *directional.* The difference between the two concepts can be shown by considering one primary meaning of the term direction, namely, direction in space. The arrow A represents a direction in Figure 3. This direction could be defined with *regard to a goal "a"* toward which it is oriented. The teleological conception of the organismic process would mean, accordingly, that the organismic activity tends toward a certain goal or "telos," for instance, happiness or a state of equilibrium or some other objective. Reaching that goal would mean the end of the process and any future activity could aim only at the maintenance of this

final state. If teleology is defined in this way, then our point of view is not teleological.[11]

Directions can be conceived more adequately, however, if we do not define them in relation to fixed

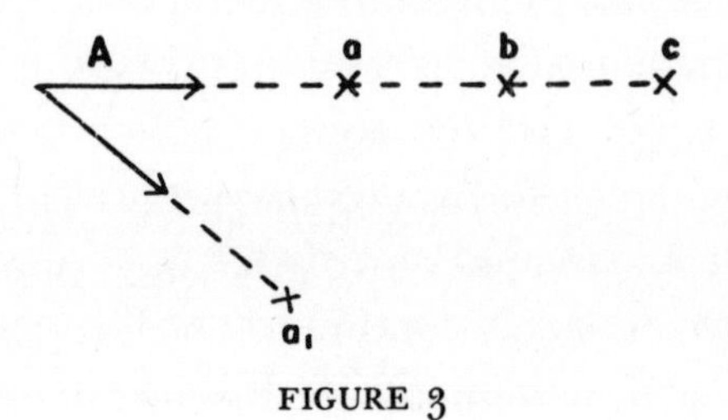

FIGURE 3

goals. In Figure 3 one can eliminate goal *a* and fit in instead *b* or *c*. The direction A will remain the same in spite of the fact that it may point toward many different goals. The objective is not specific for the direction. On the other hand, if one displaces goal *a* into the position a_1, "direction leading to *a*" will be an entirely new direction in spite of the fact that the goal toward which it points remains the same. Thus a direction (for example, A) is not defined by goals, but it is the *intrinsic pattern of a certain movement.* This is exactly what I mean by calling the general trend of the organism a directional one.

I do not want to deny, however, the teleology of the organismic activity which tends toward the attainment of fixed goals. This teleology is, however, not a primary

[11] It is only fair to point out that the much criticized "purposivists" almost never have used such a rigid and static concept of teleology.

but a secondary or derived feature of the organismic process. *It is not the goal which defines the direction, but, on the contrary, the intrinsic pattern of a direction which defines what object can become a goal.* According to our theory the directional pattern of the organismic total process is a trend toward increased autonomy. *Objects which are scattered along this direction may become secondary goals for organismic activity.*

In order to anticipate a well-taken criticism I wish to state that the tendency toward increased autonomy is important, but is not the only tendency in human beings. It appears as the sole source of human motivation only, if one considers, as we did, the organism from a solipsistic point of view, as it were; that is, when one considers it as a self-sufficient unit facing its environment. This, however, is a mere abstraction. The individual is not a closed unit, but only a relatively independent member of such superindividual units as the family and other social groupments, a participant in a culture and—in the broadest sense—a part of a cosmic order. This important aspect calls for a separate discussion. The abstraction which was implied in the previous discussion, namely, the viewing of the organism merely as an individual, is, however, useful from the didactic point of view, and will serve to demonstrate certain further aspects of the organism before entering into the discussion of the problem of the integration of the individual into superindividual organizations.

III. THE PSYCHOLOGICAL FUNCTIONS

THE SYMBOLIC CHARACTER OF PSYCHOLOGICAL PROCESSES

IN developing our point of view with regard to the general dynamic trend of the organismic total process, we resorted primarily to physiological illustrations. The purpose of the present work is, however, to advance a theory of the integrated total personality. Psychological functions play a vast role in certain species, reaching their acme in man. No theory of personality can be adequate if it does not fully take into account this important type of function. A discussion of the psychological functions of the organism is necessary also to dispel the impression that the propositions made here are based primarily on physiological facts and then that the validity of these statements for the total organism is claimed. The discussion will be restricted here to certain fundamental issues. Some other aspects will be considered later in other connections.

We advance and will attempt to justify the thesis that the function of the so-called mental process is essentially a semantic one. By this we mean that "psychological contents" function as symbols and that psychological processes are operations with these symbols.

Symbolism is based on a very particular type of relationship, if the term "relationship" applies to it at all. The characteristic feature of symbolism consists in the fact that a given A—which frequently has only a very remote primary relationship to B, and sometimes no relationship whatsoever to it—*stands for* B, it *represents* B. The symbol sometimes is an abbreviation of the primary objects, a *pars pro toto;* at other times it is something remotely related to the object. Some original connection between an object and that which becomes its symbol frequently can be traced historically. Real connections, however, are not essential or necessary for symbolism. This is clearly shown in the fact that we can construct at any time an arbitrary set of symbols which had originally no relationship to the objects for which they now stand by arbitrary definition.

Symbolism is a triadic constellation, whose terms are: the primary object, its symbol, and a third member, the subject, for whom the symbol *means* the object. The crucial factor is this third member, who has to be endowed with the capacity to connect the symbol with its referent. This implies the ability of meaning function, that is, of "mentation." If we eliminate this third member the symbolism is destroyed, and what were previously symbol and referent become unrelated objects, such as the drawing "tree" and the plant "tree."

One could object that not only for symbolism but for any sort of relationship a third member, who relates the objects, is necessary. There is, however, an important difference. A relationship such as "A is bigger than B" depends upon the reciprocal property of the relata themselves, whereas in symbolism there need not be any real connection between symbol and referent excepting the one which is more or less arbitrarily set by the connecting member.

The symbolic relationship is quite unique in that it does not occur, as far as we know, outside the psychological realm. One may rightly say that the symbolic relationship is just as general and fundamental for the humanistic sciences as the causal relationship has been for classical physics.

The immense biological importance of the symbolic function consists in the fact that it enables the individual to deal, instead of with things or with complex realities, with their simpler substitutes which are incomparably easier to manipulate. This means the saving of an enormous amount of labor and time. A further advantage of the use of symbols is that it permits the avoidance of actual contact with primary objects which often would severely damage the organism.

The characteristic feature of things psychological is their symbolic nature, which distinguishes them from all other phenomena in the world. I do not wish to state only that symbolism is a highly important characteristic of mental life, but also to emphasize that all psychological functions can be understood as processes of symbolization. Psychological activity may also be called the symbolizing function of the organism. In order to demonstrate the symbolic nature of psychological processes it is desirable to review briefly the principal groups of psychological phenomena, following for the moment the conventional classification.

SYMBOLIZATION IN PERCEPTION, IMAGINATION, AND THINKING

The person is continually engaged in some sort of interaction with his environment: taking nourishment, avoiding danger, competing with other persons, etc. Besides these more direct and obvious and gross forms of interaction there are also some more delicate ones, the so-called sensory processes, where the organism is engaged, so to say, only tangentially with the objects of its environment. This sort of contact with the environment provides the organism with a wide range of information, which may become useful on later proper occasions for adequate gross behavior.

Certain organisms have the capacity to construct, on the basis of the tangential engagements which take place in the sensory processes, perceptual mental pictures. The organism translates the physiological sensory process into perceptions of colors, sounds, tastes, odors, etc.

Mental phenomena and their relation to physiological processes are even today frequently looked upon as a sort of miracle. That conscious phenomena, such as the "raw feel" of sensation, do exist is no more miraculous than the existence of physical phenomena or anything else in the world. They are demonstrable data and beyond the domain of reasoning. Difficult problems arise only when one considers the possibility and mode of interaction between mental and physical phenomena. Since the time when Descartes so strongly postulated the dichotomy of mind and matter, it has remained a puzzling question how two supposedly widely different "substances" may influence each other. How does it happen that a physiological process in the brain produces mental processes, or how is it possible that a psychological process like volition causes the muscles to move?

This puzzle, however, exists only in so far as a psychophysical dualism is admitted. For a monistic theory the problem does not exist at all. But unfortunately, monistic theories too often evade the real issue, and, instead of evolving an integrated picture of biological reality, achieve simplification by excluding arbitrarily one or another important feature. Some authors start by pursuing a psychophysical monism and end with a clear-cut physiological monism. The other extreme, namely, psychological monism, is not too frequent in science, although an exaggeration of the "psychogenetic" point of view may occasionally approach it. It seems clear that a monistic theory is acceptable only if it is broad enough to do justice to the physiological as well as to the psychological functioning of the organism. The holistic point of view bridges the fundamentally artificial gap between mind and body by recognizing the psychophysically neutral total organism. The person is neither physiological nor psychological, but a holistic unit which implies the capacity of both physiological and psychological functioning. If one does not identify the personality with the body alone, it is not *more* miraculous that the person can produce ideas than that he can produce bile—although, in a sense, they are both miraculous enough.

For this holistic theory of personality the paradox of psychophysical interaction does not exist. We do not have to answer the question of how two such different "substances" as mind and body can act on each other, because, strictly speaking, we do not assume that such an interaction takes place. In all its manifestations, the total organism is active, but in some of these activities psychological and in some others physiological features are prevalent, and thus for practical purposes the two fields can be distinguished. Neural processes cannot produce ideas, and thoughts cannot make the muscles contract, but the total organism, the person, can do both. In response to a change in its prevalently physiological functioning, the organism may produce mental phenomena, and in response to volition the organism may produce movements. The pattern of "interaction" between psychological and physiological function is not: physiological process—psychological process, and psychological process—physiological process, but: physiological process—total organism—psychological process; and psychological process—total organism—physiological process.

By rejecting the theory of psychophysical dualism, we do not mean to deny the value of the type of research which studies the so-called "psychosomatic relations." The consideration of psychological and somatic processes always in relation to the total organism places this type of investigation on a sounder theoretical basis.

Returning to the discussion of perception, it is hoped that now it has become clearer what we meant by saying that the organism elaborates perceptual mental images on the basis of tangential engagements with the environment such as are taking place in the physiological sensory processes.

After the perceptual data are produced they are used by the organism as symbols for objects of the environment. By the term "object" I do not mean metaphysical entities, *Dinge an sich,* but "empirical objects." It is not necessary to enter into the extremely complex philosophical debate on the nature of the object. In the next chapters (IV and V) an attempt will be made to define "object" from a biological point of view and to formulate some statements with regard to the nature of the "biologically relevant object." For the present purpose it is sufficient to point out that the object is far richer in traits than the perceptual datum which indicates the object for the observer. When one sees a white bird, that which is visually given is only a white spot of a certain form; but one perceives through this the object "bird." The difference between a given object and its visual appearance is very great. When we make such statements as that the bird is an animal, that it lives, flies, eats, etc., we are obviously referring to something different from the visual datum: a white spot. The visual datum will vary if one sees the bird from the front or from the side, when it is at rest or when it is flying, but the bird will remain the same bird. The visual image is smaller from a distance and larger when seen close by; but the bird remains the same size. The visual image will be different in the sunlight than in the dusk, but we do not think in such a case that the object "bird" has changed. The white spot is merely a visual datum, while the bird has many qualities which can be experienced by means of the other senses. The object "bird" also includes meanings which, of course, cannot be *seen*. The object is incomparably richer in content than its visual appearance. On the occasion of the visual perception of an object, the visual datum is the symbol for the whole object, it indicates the object for the observer, it refers to it or—in the terminology of F. Brentano—is characterized by "intentionality" directed toward an object. The data given in perception are much simpler than the object itself. Hence the great economic value of perception for the organism.

In the process of perception the organism is not passive like a mirror which reflects the picture of the objects, but actively elaborates and constructs the perception. First of all, there is a careful perceptual selection: only certain data are used for the construction of the picture of the object, while others are omitted. Another group of phenomena from which complex perceptual elaborative activity can be inferred are those which are treated in psychology under the heading, "problems of constancy." Identical physiological sensory processes are not translated into perceptions in exactly the same way, but so that they can best fulfill their biological role, which is: to present the object adequately. A few examples may illustrate this. The brightness of a color depends, as a rule, upon the amount of diffuse light reflected per unit of surface. If one places a piece of coal in bright light and a piece of chalk in the shadow, the former may reflect more diffuse light per unit surface than the latter, but in spite of this we perceive the coal as approximately black and the chalk as approximately white. The factor of illumination is somehow taken into account, not by explicit reasoning but through the perceptual activity itself. Under medium changes of illumination we have no difficulty in distinguishing the brightness of colors, although this may not be possible under extreme or unusual conditions of illumination. Another example is the constancy of size. The size of visually perceived objects depends, on the whole, upon the visual angle at which the light rays fall upon the retina, in other words, upon the size of the retinal image. Accordingly, an object would appear smaller at a distance than from a close view. This law is, however, not valid for medium distances. If it were, a person would appear from a close view as a giant and from a few yards' distance as a dwarf. Actually, we see objects within medium limits of distance as about the same size, and one needs the painter's training and sophistication to do otherwise. In the perceptual activity, somehow, account is taken of the distance. The phenomena of constancy are of great value for the organism. Since the conditions in the environment are continually changing, without perceptual constancy one would be seriously handicapped in recognizing objects.

In elaborating perceptual pictures, not only data coming from the sensory organ which is directly involved in a given perception, but also data from other sense organs are utilized. Thus most of the spatial attributes of visual perception are based partly on kinaesthesis. In the completed visual perception the spatial attributes of "above," "below," "right," "left" appear to us visually, although we know since the famous experiment of Stratton[1] that this largely depends on kinaesthetic experiences, or rather on the coordination of vision and kinaesthesis.

These and many other examples which could be quoted from the psychological literature demonstrate

[1] G. M. Stratton, Vision without inversion of the retinal image, Psychological Review, 4:342–360, 463–481, 1897.

definitely that the organism, in the process of perception, does not reflect passively the impressions coming from the environment, but elaborates them actively in a rather intricate fashion. The work involved in the production of mental phenomena other than perceptions shows even more the active character of the translation of organismic happenings into phenomena of consciousness.

The statement that perceptions function as symbols does not imply that they are merely labels. They are just as much functions of the person as are the physiological processes. They possess an intimacy and immediate closeness to the personality. This is even more true for certain other types of experiences, such as emotions. Furthermore, in the psychological processes symbol and referent are not clearly separated, but blend with each other. A perception, for example, does not only signify the object, but the object is viewed through and in it.

It is worth while to note that symbol and referent tend to merge into each other even in the more remote and abstract types of symbolizations. An example of this has been well stated by G. Sarton: "It is only after centuries of apparently sterile but necessary quarrels and after the final establishment of the experimental method and attitude that we have slowly learned to consider words as symbols, which, as far as scientific purposes are concerned, would be usefully replaced by arbitrary signs having no signification but the one explicitly defined. The distinction between names and things is now so deeply rooted in the mind of scientifically trained men that they would find it difficult to understand how they could ever be confused, if they did not detect examples of such confusion almost every day in their own environment."[2]

Summarizing, we may distinguish two aspects in the perceptual process: the production of a type of "raw feel," perceptual pictures and the utilization of these pictures as symbols for empirical objects. The perceptions are produced by the organism on the basis of sensory processes. Perceptions are not passive reflections; the organism elaborates them actively according to certain biological needs. Perceptions, and mental phenomena in general, are not mere labels but inherent parts of the organismic total process. In mental processes there is a kind of fusion between symbol and referent. The object is not only meant, but also experienced, in the perception.

We have said that the great economical value of perception is due to the fact that it is simpler than the objects for which it stands. *Images* are still more simplified symbols and the organism is able to operate with them with still greater ease and freedom. There is a close genetic and phenomenological relation between perceptions and images. In infancy images are vivid and not markedly different from perceptions. Later, as a rule,

[2] G. Sarton, Introduction to the History of Science, Baltimore, Williams & Wilkins, 1927, vol. 1, p. 7.

they lose their vividness and become more sketchy. This apparent impoverishment of imagery is, however, not a regressive process but a positive development. This point can be illustrated by the following case. In an investigation[3] on spatial orientation, my subjects had to draw the connecting path between two given points of the city. One of the subjects did extremely poorly in this test. She was, for example, uncertain whether two main avenues, separated by only a few blocks, were parallel or perpendicular to each other. Since she had at least a good average intelligence, and since she had spent practically all her life in that city, it seemed that she must have some gross defect of imagination. A closer investigation, however, gave the following, rather unexpected result: She had a remarkable visual eidetic imagery. In the above-mentioned test situation she imagined herself standing at a given place and visualized the scenery most vividly, but had only a very hazy knowledge of the more distant parts which could not have been *seen* from that vantage point. In other words, she had a vivid image of segments of the city, but not of the relations between the various segments. In this case, in spite of her eidetic imagery, this person was not as well equipped for the ordinary tasks of imagination as is the average person who possesses only vague, schematic images, but which allow him to grasp broader connections.

[3] A. Angyal, Über die Raumlage vorgestellter Örter, Archiv für die gesamte Psychologie, 78:47–94, 1930.

The advantage of images as compared to perception does not lie in their greater simplicity only. They allow the organism to deal also with objects which are not included in the situation of the moment. They broaden the perspective and the sphere of influence of the organism over spatially distant parts of the environment and over the past (memory) and the future (planning, foresight, etc.) as well.

Symbolization is still more effective in *thought processes* because of the use of very remote, but highly condensed and simplified, symbols. A single concept stands as a substitute for a whole series of objects and relationships. The symbols involved in thought processes are representative of relation and system connections between objects. With the aid of these symbols a wide range of intellectual operations is possible which are of a high economic value for the organism.

SYMBOLIZATION IN EMOTION AND CONATION

Perceptions and images are symbols which refer primarily to the *environment.* Besides these symbols of the environment there is a wide range of psychological phenomena which indicate the states and needs of the *organism.* The sensations of pain, hunger, thirst, and other internal sensations belong to this group. The main forms of expression of the state of the organism are, however, the emotions.

For the sake of conceptual clarification certain distinctions may be useful. The term "emotion" is used with various connotations. Some writers seem to use this term to mean samples of total behavior in which emotional experiences occur. This form of behavior contains not only psychological components, but bodily reactions as well: clenching of the fist, tremor, palpitation, rapid breathing, and the like. To this total behavior we may apply the term "emotional behavior," while the term "emotion" could be reserved to denote the psychological aspect, that is, the experience of emotion. In the following discussion we are interested in the psychological aspect of emotion.

There is a great phenomenological variety of emotions. Wundt, as is well known, distinguishes three emotional dimensions: tension-relaxation, excitement-calming, and pleasantness-unpleasantness. These three dimensions probably do not suffice for an adequate characterization of the multitude of emotions, but it seems to me that they designate three, perhaps the three most important, features of emotional experience. I suspect, although I cannot as yet definitely prove, that the first two of these dimensions—tension-relaxation and excitement-calming—are of the nature of proprioception. Emotional behavior occurs whenever the organism is confronted with a biologically significant external or internal situation. The organism makes a variety of responses to such a situation. 1) It responds to the situation first of all with its neurovegetative apparatus. The proprioception of these vegetative changes would correspond to the dimension of excitement and calming. 2) The organism responds to the situation also on the neuromuscular level. Gross or incipient muscular activities take place. The perception of the changes of muscle tonus may correspond to the dimension of tension and relaxation.[4]

If our assumption is correct, then the sort of theories advanced by James and Lange may be valid if restricted to these two dimensions. It is not necessary to discuss separately the types of symbolization which take place in proprioception because the mechanism involved is approximately the same as in external perception.

These two dimensions, although they recur constantly, are not the distinctive characteristics of emotions. The really specific feature of emotion is represented by the dimension of pleasantness-unpleasantness. To this dimension the theory of James and Lange certainly does not apply. Watson's theory in which it is assumed that physiological tumescence and detumescence are the somatic basis of pleasantness and unpleasantness is much too naïve and cannot be profitably discussed here.

We consider the feeling tone of emotions as the *experience of the state and of the situation of the person un-*

[4] I make this suggestion only very tentatively. The experience of tension may not refer to muscular tension alone, but to tension in a much broader biological sense. This latter concept will be introduced and discussed in Chapter V.

der the aspect of value. The biological situations are constantly evaluated by the organism from the point of view of their significance for the life process. The emotional tone is the experience of such significances. It should be clear, however, that in emotion the significance of the biological situation is not experienced in thoughts and judgments, but in a very intimate and immediate manner, as joy and sorrow, depression and elation, or quite generally as various shadings of pleasantness and unpleasantness. It has already been pointed out with regard to perceptions that they are not to be considered as mere labels. This is true, even to a greater extent, of emotional experiences. They have a high degree of intimacy and closeness. The fact that they are elaborated and utilized by the organism as symbols of its states of welfare does not detract from this view.

Symbolization, in a sense, implies a certain degree of distance between symbol and referent. Because of the characteristic ego-closeness of emotional experiences, their symbolic nature is not as obvious as, for instance, that of perceptions. It may be useful, therefore, to clarify what is the symbol and what is the primary fact to which the emotional experience refers.

The primary fact is a situation having a positive or negative value for the person. Success, failure, a threat to one's personal security, disappointment in one's expectations, the loss of a close friend, or, on the other hand, the opening up of new opportunities, the achievement of goals, a lucky constellation of events creating a fortunate turn in one's personal affairs are examples of such situations which have a distinct positive or negative value for the person. Such ego-relevant situations are in themselves not experiences, but objective states of affairs. They are the primary facts which function as referents in the formation of a symbolic relation.

The value aspect of these objective situations is *experienced* in the form of emotion. In other words, *emotional experiences are symbols of value-laden ego-relevant facts.* This brings to the fore the processual character of emotion as an evaluative experience. It is in brief the most immediate form of personal evaluation. Value judgments may precede, accompany, or follow, but they are by no means indispensable for emotional experience (for instance, anxiety, sorrow, or experience of happiness without any reason known to the person).

These statements must be qualified in certain respects. The experience of value is not the whole of emotional experience, but merely its most characteristic specific feature, the various shadings of the feeling tone. In addition, the experience of vegetative changes and of changes in muscular tension is practically always involved. Furthermore, in certain emotional experiences such as anger or fear, conative features are present which color significantly the total experience.

The emotional coloring does not always indicate correctly the significance of a biological situation. Pleasantness does not always mean usefulness and, similarly, unpleasantness is not always a reliable indication of harmfulness. Such discrepancies arise *mainly* from the following two sources. 1) Emotions refer to and work best under *original, standard* conditions. There are poisons which have a pleasant taste, but in primitive surroundings the majority of objects with pleasant taste are useful for the organism. 2) Emotions refer primarily to the *immediate* situation and not to later consequences. The use of alcohol may be harmful to the organism, but for the moment it speeds up certain vital processes, alleviates suffering, and dissipates worry. Therefore, the emotion in such case represents correctly the immediate state of the organism.

Pleasantness and unpleasantness have a high motivating value for one's conscious activity. They are the only *immediate* guides of one's conscious behavior. It is, however, unjustified to regard the "pleasure principle" as the only or even as the main source of human behavior. The organism tends to proceed in a direction which is inherent in its nature. This direction is the measuring tape for the significance of a given state or situation. Pleasantness and unpleasantness are only crude indicators of biological significance. Pleasure may be divorced from its biological background and pursued for its own sake, but then it easily becomes almost a perversion. In Rome in the later period of the Empire it was the custom at luxurious festivities that when surfeited and gorged the participants tickled their throat with a peacock feather, thus inducing vomiting in order to be able to eat and drink more, that is, to get more "pleasure." If there existed such a simple method as a peacock feather to increase sex appetite, it would probably enjoy great popularity in our day.

The universality of the principle of pleasure seeking cannot be saved by assuming "unconscious pleasure." Those facts which are quoted as examples of unconscious pleasure seeking show only that the organism may drive toward goals in spite of the fact that they cause pain. One can assume in such cases an unconscious pleasure only if one is already convinced a priori of the universality of the pleasure principle.

Conative processes are no less symbolic in character than any other class of psychological phenomena. As has been stated, the organismic total process is characterized by a directional trend, leading from states of lesser autonomy to states of greater autonomy. This trend branches out into a number of specific manifestations, such as drives and urges, which in themselves are not psychological. The basic organismic urgency and its specific ramifications are elaborated symbolically and experienced psychologically by the organism as conscious conative processes: striving, wishing, craving, willing, etc. Both for emotional tone and for conation the primary objects are not physiological, but totalistic, organismic states and processes. In conation not only a translation of psychophysically neutral states into psychological processes takes place, but the conative processes are characterized also by a tendency to be translated into bodily activities.

THE BIOLOGICAL SIGNIFICANCE OF SYMBOLIZATION

The symbolic representations of environment and of the individual are not perfect. The psychological phenomena are not always entirely reliable indicators of the primary objects to which they refer. If one wishes to use a rather objectionable metaphor and compare symbolic elaboration to reflections in a mirror, one has to add that the "mind" is a curved mirror which reflects the object in more or less distorted pictures. Examples of distortion are illusions of perception and illusions and falsifications of memory. In the field of emotion and conation we also find distorted pictures somewhat comparable to illusions. We may experience as pleasurable a state of our organism which is harmful for its welfare and we often wish and strive for things which we do not need. Conscious intention frequently misses the real target of one's deeper urgency, a fact of which psychoanalysis is keenly aware. The "mind," the ability to have a symbolic grasp of things, is the greatest power which nature has given to some of its creatures, but it is also the deepest source of error and suffering. One of the important tasks of an organismic psychology should be to shed light on the processes of distortion brought about by the "mirror of the mind." Such knowledge might also indicate the means for correcting the imperfect pictures.

In spite of all these imperfections, the symbols represented by psychological phenomena are reliable enough to be able to fulfill in the total organism a function, the importance of which can hardly be overestimated. With the emergence of psychological functions a highly significant change occurs in the entire organization of the organismic total process. The two essential factors of the organismic total process, that is, the organism and its environment, are symbolically represented in the "mind." *The individual and the environment can now meet on the symbolic, representative ground of psychological functions.* Their encounter results in a process the dynamic structure of which is essentially identical with that of the non-psychological levels of the organismic total process. *Life is now carried out partly on a symbolic level, but without a change in its general dynamic trend.* In the psychological realm life takes place, not through the interaction of the concrete individual with a concrete environment—which is only tangential—but by the interaction of symbols representing the individual and the environment. With the growth of the symbolic function of the organism the center of gravity of life is shifted more and more toward the psychological realm.

What does enrichment through symbolic activity signify for the organism? The psychological activity has first of all the value of an important "organ."[5] It stands in the service of the primitive functions of the organism. Psychological activities are a very efficient support of the organism in such functions as acquiring food, self-defense, mating, and care of the young. Human beings who show a high development of the symbolic functions have relatively little contact with primary things. Their affairs are settled largely on the psychological level. They experience their own states and needs in symbols of emotion and conation; they obtain information, in the form of symbols, with regard to the conditions of the environment. Thus, the essential factors for the solution of most problems which man encounters are given in symbols. These problems are solved mainly with the aid of psychological operations. The handling of the concrete material is, in characteristic cases, nothing more than the realization of the end-result arrived at by psychological processes. For example, one does not start to build a house by putting stones and other materials together, but one builds it up first "in one's mind."

Symbolic functioning which originally manifests itself as a psychological phenomenon is purposely cultivated, refined, and exploited by man and thus becomes a method which is fundamental for most of man's cultural devices. Language, writing, drawing, the various

[5] "Organ" does not mean originally only a material structure. The Greek word ὄργανον means "tool" in general.

organized systems of signs, the monetary system, and the like are all based on the principle that complex realities can be replaced by simple symbols which can be manipulated with incomparably greater facility than the primary things themselves. One can realize the vast importance of the use of symbols for human culture if one thinks, for example, of the modern library which is a collection of written symbols concentrated in a relatively small space, although the referents of these symbols embrace almost the universe.

In many instances one does not stop at building up a set of symbols referring to primary objects. One goes further in the effort for economy, building up a second set of symbols as substitutes for the first set of symbols, and so on. Thus, in many cases a long chain of symbolic references is interpolated between a given symbol and the primary object. For example, the single books of the library are themselves huge collections of symbols. For further simplification the books themselves are replaced by a second set of symbols. In the catalogue a single card substitutes for a book. This secondary set of symbols not only has the value of greater simplicity, but can be arranged independently of the primary objects in convenient and multiple ways (for example, according to author and subject).

Psychological processes are of great value to the organism because they assist in an extremely useful way in satisfying its primary needs. The emergence of symbolic functions has, however, a further significance for the organism which is not less important than the economizing aspect of these processes. The emergence of psychological functions modifies significantly the whole structure of the organismic total process. Previously the general dynamic trend of the organismic total process was defined as a tendency toward increased autonomy. This tendency was illustrated with examples of prevalently physiological functions. These functions represent, however, only certain methods for the realization of the general dynamic trend of the organismic total process. Psychological functioning provides the organism with new means of expressing its inherent tendency. There are psychological ways of self-aggrandizement and self-assertion such as winning a debate, acquiring titles and honors, studying and investigating the phenomena of nature and so dominating them on a theoretical level. From the psychological process the organism obtains *new means,* new methods to achieve a greater autonomy and the possibility of a tremendous widening of the field which can be brought under the autonomous government of the organism.

THE RELATION BETWEEN PSYCHOLOGY AND THE SCIENCE OF PERSONALITY

The present study being concerned with problems of the total personality, it is not intended to enter into a discussion of any detailed psychological question, or of any other segmental aspects such as the physiological or the sociological. It seems useful, however, to point out the relationship between psychology and the study of personality, and to indicate what type of psychology might contribute most effectively to the study of personality.

The task of a holistically oriented psychology would be the study of the symbolic functions of the organism. This means the study of mental phenomena in relation to those primary personality occurrences which they symbolize. For the Wundtian type of psychology and for those psychological systems which immediately succeeded it, the subject-matter has been rather sharply defined: the study of immediate experiences, that is, of conscious phenomena. This type of psychology could be called consciousness-immanent psychology because it proposes to study the conscious phenomena as such, that is, in relative isolation from the total organism. The type of psychology which would seem most profitable for a science of personality has to be consciousness-transcendent. This psychology has to take full cognizance of the symbolic nature of mental functions and has to relate the conscious phenomena to non-symbolic personality processes. It has to consider such problems as: How accurately do perceptions present the objects? How reliable is the emotional presentation of the state and situation of the personality? What distortions can take place during the symbolic elaboration? What are the factors and conditions which may reduce or increase the amount of distortion?

The study of mental processes as consciousness-immanent phenomena is almost comparable to the study of a written text merely as script, without reference to language-content. This comparison, of course, is only partially correct. We shall have the opportunity to point out later that the mental functions form a relative autonomy within the total organism which permits to a limited extent the meaningful study of intra-psychic relations also.

Psychology, despite the earlier definition, has not restricted itself to the study of conscious phenomena alone; the earliest examples of not strictly consciousness-immanent psychology have been psychophysics and physiological psychology. Attempts have been made to correlate physical factors (as, for instance, the investigations of "Weber-Fechner's law") or physiological processes (as in the study of sensory functions) with conscious phenomena. The study of bodily changes (respiration, heart beat, etc.) in emotional states may also be mentioned here. It seems to us that the results of this type of study have not been fruitful for the following two reasons. 1) The psychological processes have been correlated directly with physical or physiological factors instead of with holistic, psychophysically neutral personality processes. 2) The relationship between the two sides of the equation has been thought of as causal or parallelistic instead of symbolic in nature. The common error has been the theory of psychophysical dualism.

Psychoanalysis has also made an attempt to broaden the field of psychological studies beyond the realm of consciousness. However, it does not recognize the universally symbolic nature of all conscious phenomena. It also fails to recognize the integrated, psychophysically neutral personality processes and instead *unconscious mental* functioning is assumed. In other words, personality processes have been psychologized and become, in psychoanalysis, unconscious *mental* functions.

An extreme opposite to consciousness-immanent psychology is behaviorism. Behaviorism can be barely called psychology at all, and not unless we wish to give the same name to disciplines so different that the one defines its subject-matter as the study of conscious phenomena, while the other does not even admit the existence of consciousness. According to certain statements, behaviorism studies the activities of the organism as a whole. If behaviorists would adhere to this principle, behaviorism would be a variety of the science of personality. The behaviorists, however, usually pay not much more than mere lip-service to the holistic principle. Actually they are physiological reductionists like Watson, or even physical reductionists like P. Weiss. Strict behaviorism is not a psychology, because it excludes mental phenomena; for the same reason neither is it an adequate study of personality.

There are other approaches in psychology, which come closer to a consciousness-transcendent type in the sense defined above. Brentano's theory of the universal intentional character of conscious phenomena may be considered as a move in this direction. Even more significant is the kind of approach which has been recently attempted by E. Brunswik in the study of perception. He proposes to study the accuracy and reliability of the perception in presenting the object rather than perceptions as mental phenomena per se.[6]

The task of a psychology which could be most useful for the study of personality would be not only to investigate the intra-psychic organization of mental processes but, recognizing the universal symbolic character of mental function, to relate it back to the holistic personality background out of which these mental processes are elaborated.

SUMMARY

Symbolism is a specifically psychological relation which presupposes a being endowed with the capacity of linking the symbol with its referent. This requires mentation.

[6] E. Brunswik, Wahrnehmung und Gegenstandswelt, Grundlegung einer Psychologie vom Gegenstand her, Leipzig, Deuticke, 1934. Brunswik's definition of the object which is presented in the perception as a *metric* object may be questionable, but his rejection of too much immanentism in psychology is very well in agreement with our point of view.

THE PSYCHOLOGICAL FUNCTIONS

Psychological activity has been considered here as the symbolizing function of the organism. The symbolization involved in perception, imagination, thinking, emotion, and conation has been briefly discussed.

The organism has the capacity to elaborate on the basis of its tangential engagements with the environment, which take place in the sensory processes, perceptual mental pictures such as colors, sounds, and tastes. These in turn function as symbols of the empirical objects.

In constructing perceptual or any other psychological data the organism is not passive like a mirror which reflects the image of the objects, but elaborates them actively in a rather complex fashion.

The economic value of perception is due to the fact that it is simpler than the objects for which it stands. Images are still more simplified symbols. They allow the organism to deal also with objects which are not included in the situation of the moment.

Symbolization is even more effective in thought processes where a single concept may stand as a substitute for a long series of objects and relationships.

In emotion various factors are involved. They contain proprioception of neuromuscular and neurovegetative processes. The specific components of emotions are, however, the feeling tones of pleasantness and unpleasantness. The feeling tone is considered as the experience of the state and situation of the person under the aspect of value. Feeling tones function as symbols which refer to the welfare of the organism.

Conative conscious processes are symbols in which the general organismic urgency and its specific ramifications are experienced.

The symbolic character of psychological phenomena does not reduce them to mere labels. They are part functions of the organism and have intimacy and personal closeness.

The conscious phenomena are not entirely reliable symbols of the primary objects to which they refer. In the process of symbolic elaboration distortions also take place frequently.

The value of symbolic processes is, first of all, economy. Symbols are simpler, can be dealt with more easily than primary objects, and also permit the subject to avoid direct contact with objects, which frequently would cause damage to the organism. Symbolic functioning is further exploited in certain cultural devices such as language, writing, monetary systems, and other organized systems of symbols.

In the psychological processes the organism obtains new means to achieve greater autonomy. Thus the field which can be brought under the autonomous government of the organism is tremendously widened.

The task of psychology which could be most useful for the study of personality would be to investigate not only the intra-psychic organization but to recognize the universal symbolic character of mental functions, and to relate them to the holistic personality background, out of which they are elaborated.

IV. ORGANISM AND ENVIRONMENT

ORGANISM AND ENVIRONMENT ARE NOT SEPARABLE AS STRUCTURES IN SPACE

ONE of the basic characteristics of the point of view which has been developed in the previous chapters is that life is not to be considered as an intra-organismic happening, but as a process which takes place *between* organism and environment. This statement may not sound quite convincing and may seem to contradict certain facts. We know, for instance, that life continues even in an encysted amoeba in spite of the fact that it is separated from its external environment. In order to make our point of view clear, it is necessary to define precisely the concepts of organism and environment and their interrelationship. These concepts are of basic importance for the present theory. In the process of clarification of concepts some of the previous statements will have to be amplified. At the same time the way will also be prepared for carrying the discussion one step further.

I do not know of any serious attempt to draw the line of demarcation between individual and environment, that is, of an attempt to answer the question of where the individual ends and the environment begins. This question is usually dismissed with the semi-jocular statement that the individual is within the skin and the environment is outside of it.

Any attempt to make a morphological separation of organism and environment fails and necessarily leads to endless, hair-splitting dialectic. It will, however, be useful to go into this dialectic to some extent, not because one might expect positive results, but because it will demonstrate that the consideration of organism and environment as structures in space is not a workable point of view.

Taking literally the statement that the organism is within the body surface and the environment outside of it, one has to consider, for example, that one should accordingly call the food before ingestion a part of the environment and after ingestion a part of the organism. It would be very strange logic, however, to regard an object at one time as environment and at another time as part of the organism merely because it is located in some internal cavity of the body, such as the stomach. Thus, the criterion for being part of the environment or of the organism would merely concern the location of an object in space. The fundamental difference between organism and environment—a difference we feel exists—would thus be almost completely nullified. Is it not more logical to regard the content of the gastrointestinal tract as environment rather than as part of the organism, that is, as an insinuation of the environment into the body? The same question may be asked with regard to the air contained within the lungs. To take another example, should we regard urine, when it is in the bladder, as a part of the organism and after it passes the urethral orifice as part of the environment? It, therefore, appears that one is not true to the facts when one states that the organism is a massive structure contained within the external body surface. Rather, it appears that the environment penetrates the organism at various points and occupies a considerable portion of the space contained within the body surface.

Examples such as those just mentioned indicate only that certain parts which are located in the internal spaces of the organism may belong to the environment, but they do not exclude the possibility of drawing a line of separation in space between organism and environment. Such considerations, however, as have been made with regard to the contents of the gastrointestinal tract, of the air spaces of the lungs, and of the contents of the bladder, can be made also with regard to other regions of the body structure. Are, for example, blood and lymph still environment, or are they already parts of the organism? One may regard the nutritive substances contained in the lumen of the intestines as environment; but are not the same substances still to be regarded as environment when they are absorbed and passed from the intestines into the current of lymph and blood? The blood has been called "internal environment" by Claude Bernard. Does it make any essential difference that the same substance is no longer in the intestines, but is flowing in the cardiovascular bed? Does an environmental object become organism merely by the passage from one space to another? Would it not be rather justifiable to call the non-cellular components of the blood "environment"? But even with regard to the cellular components of the blood, there is some uncertainty as to whether they should be regarded as part of the organism or of the environment. For example, what is the difference between a phagocyte and another monocellular being, for example, a bacterium occasionally contained in the blood stream? One could say that the phagocyte belongs to the organism because it exerts a useful function in the organism. Usefulness, however, is not a sufficient criterion to decide whether something belongs to the organism or to the environment. Utilitarian relations exist also in the case of symbiosis, but we would not regard the symbiotic animal or plant as a part of its symbiont. If we take the convergence of functions to mutual usefulness as a criterion of "belongingness" to the organism, then we should be compelled to consider, for example, the *bacteria coli* in the intestines as part of the individual, since these organisms probably have a useful function in the digestion of cellulose. In that case one could state perhaps that the phagocytes belong to the organism because they originate from the organism itself, while the bacteria do not derive from the organism. But the genetic derivation itself is not an adequate criterion either. We would certainly hesitate to call the sputum a part of the organism or the egg a part of the hen.

One could carry the argument even further and ask whether the metabolically inactive intercellular substances which form a considerable part of certain tissues (bones, cartilages, and other tissues) are to be regarded as much a part of the organism as metabolically active cells. Distinctions can be also made within the cell. The cytoplasm not infrequently has been regarded as the "environment" of the nucleus. Considering the cytostructure, how should one classify, for example, those granuli of the cell body which represent an actually inactive storage of substances, or the content of those minute channels within the cell body which possibly have a function for the cell analogous to the cardiovascular bed for the macroorganism?

These examples may suffice to indicate how vague and uncertain is the theoretical distinction between environment and organism. Such vagueness and uncertainty exist, and not only because the borderline between organism and environment is not a sharp one, for such a statement would not adequately express the existing state of affairs. We shall try to show in what follows that it is, in principle, impossible to draw any line of separation in space between organism and environment because *organism and environment are not static structures separable in space, but are opposing directions in the biological total process.*

THE DYNAMIC DEFINITION OF THE RELATIONSHIP BETWEEN ORGANISM AND ENVIRONMENT

The subject-matter of biological considerations is primarily processes and only secondarily morphological structures. We have already stated (page 20) that the existential form of the organism is a dynamic one or, as Jennings states it, "The organism is a process." This requires that the organism be studied from a dynamic point of view.

As has been indicated, a *morphological* distinction between organism and environment is impossible. We must now renew our endeavor to distinguish between organism and environment and to determine the reciprocal relationship between them by *defining the concepts of organism and of the environment in dynamic terms.*

We have previously considered the life process as the resultant of autonomous and heteronomous determinations, in other words, as a resultant of self-government and outside influences. Of the total process of life a *unified system of factors* can be separated out by abstraction. However, not every moment of the life process is organized into that system. The life process in its concrete form also contains factors alien to the system, or "random" from the point of view of the system. The biological total process results from the interaction of system-determined (self-governed, autonomous) factors and factors which are alien to the system (governed from outside the system, heteronomous). The antithesis organism-environment dynamically expressed is the antithesis of autonomy-heteronomy. Organism and environment are the reification or, at most, the "structural precipitate" of autonomy and heteronomy.

In a study of biological dynamics we do not ask whether a given morphological entity is a part of the organism or of the environment. Rather, we wish to determine whether a part process occurs by virtue of autonomous (organismic) or by virtue of heteronomous (environmental) determination. Thus, for example, we do not ask whether the contents of the stomach belong to the environment or to the organism, but whether the processes going on in the lumen of the stomach are system-determined (autonomous, organismic determination) or are due to factors foreign to the system (heteronomous, environmental determination).

The answer to such questions has already been given partially. There is no biological process which is determined entirely organismically or entirely environmentally; it is always a resultant of both factors. Any biological process can be expressed by the ratio of autonomous and heteronomous government ($a:h$) active in them. The relative values of a and h, however, are very different in the various biological manifestations. For example, the processes going on in the gastrointestinal tract are, on the one hand, heteronomous, environmentally determined through the physical-chemical properties of the food but, on the other hand, they are also autonomous, organismically determined: mechanical work of the stomach and intestines, secretion of the digestive glands. In the biological processes taking place in the blood, the external determinations play a smaller role and internal determinations a larger role than in the processes of digestion. The former are organismically governed to a larger extent than the latter. In the intracellular processes the proportion is even further displaced in the direction of the organismic determination.

We cannot tell whether a structure belongs to the organism or to the environment, but we can determine *to what extent a process is respectively organismically or environmentally governed.* The dynamic relation between individual and environment may be visualized in Figure 4.

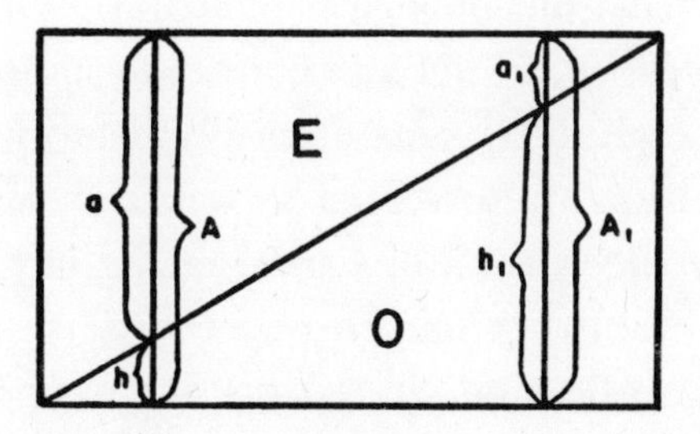

FIGURE 4

The lower triangle represents the organism (dynamically autonomous determination), the upper triangle the environment (dynamically heteronomous determination). Such vertical lines as A and A_1 represent two samples of biological processes. The proportion $a:h$ and $a_1:h_1$ is the expression of the dynamic relation between the individual and the environment in two given biological processes (A and A_1). Thus we see that although it is impossible to separate morphologically organism and environment in space, the relation between environmental and organismic determination can be defined dynamically. Such a relation is expressed in a ratio which indicates the relative potency of the two dynamic factors of which every biological process is a resultant. The relative values of the two factors vary in the various "regions" of the biological total process: in some regions the environmental determination prevails, in others the organismic government is the weightier factor. Neither of the two factors has an independent existence. They are abstracted from biological reality. Within the biological realm we do not encounter any process which would be exclusively organismically determined. The "pure organism" (represented by the right vertical side of the diagram) is not a biological reality but a concept of a theoretical limit (*theoretischer Grenzbegriff*). An organism which does not act on the environment in the direction of its specific tendency (toward increase of autonomy) is not a living organism at all. Similarly, the "pure environment," represented by the left vertical side of the diagram, is also only the concept of a theoretical limit. There is no environment without an organism. The concept "external world" must be clearly distinguished from the concept "environment." The external world can be called environment only when and in so far as it is in interaction with the organism.

In conclusion we may state that the conception of organism and environment as morphological entities which are separable in space is inadequate for the description of biological phenomena. They become fundamental biological concepts if we define them as dynamic factors. Dynamically expressed, organism is self-government and environment heteronomous influence. Every concrete biological process is a resultant of these two factors. The relationship between these two factors can be expressed theoretically in the ratio $a:h$ in which the relative values of a and h vary from case to case.

It has been pointed out in the previous considerations that the body surface is not the boundary of the organism. It has been emphasized that the organism is entirely permeated by the environment which insinuates itself into every part of it. On the other hand, the organism does not end at the body surface but penetrates into its environment. The realm of events which are influenced by the autonomy of the organism is not limited to the body but extends far beyond it. *Every process which is a resultant of the interplay of the organismic autonomy and the environmental heteronomy is part of the life process, irrespective of whether it takes place within the body or outside of it.* The biological process of feeding oneself does not begin with the chewing of one's food; the preparation of food, the raising of vegetables are also "biological" activities in the broader sense of the word. Such processes are the resultants of the autonomous activity of the organism and of heteronomous happenings in the environment and hence are, by definition, biological processes. To give other examples, locomotion by artificial means, transportation, is just as much a biological process in a broader sense as is locomotion by means of body structures; the clothing of man is just as much a part of the organism in this broader sense as the fur and feathers of the animal, artificial weapons just as much as natural weapons, and so on.[1]

The point of view I am trying to express may be made clearer by stating that in the process of building a house, for example, not only the necessary muscular and symbolic activity of the worker should be regarded as a biological process but also the progress of the construction. This process is partly governed by the organism. It is a resultant of an autonomous, organismically governed remoulding of a heteronomous environment. Our point of view can be further clarified by stating that in a worker not only the hands but also, in a certain sense, the hammer are parts of the organism. I do not intend to

[1] The term "biological" is not used here as the opposite of cultural; the term in our usage refers to cultural phenomena as well. The justification for the use of the term in this broad sense may become clear in the later parts of this discussion (Chapter VI).

disregard differences but I wish to emphasize *significant relationships* which are more than superficial analogies. Of course there are great differences between neuromuscular organs and an artificial tool, or between muscular contractions and the movements of a screw driver. The first is part of a physiological metabolic unit, the second is not. However, in one very essential respect they are alike: they carry out part functions in the organismic total process. Artificial instruments and body organs are both tools in the service of life, and *the instrumental relationship of the parts to the whole is precisely one of the essential factors which characterize certain systems called "organisms."* The term itself, "organism" (organ = tool) means a system in which the parts are the instruments, the tools of the whole.

We may state in conclusion that the life process does not take place only within the body surface, but involves a much broader realm of events. Such a broad definition of biological happenings is unconventional but necessary in order that justice be done to the problems of the total personality.

THE CONCEPT OF THE BIOSPHERE: THE SUBJECT-OBJECT DIFFERENTIATION

The broadened concept of life does not refer to an intra-organismic happening, but to a process which covers a much broader field than the body. Life involves both intrasomatic and extrasomatic happenings. The limits of life extend as far as the organism is able to exert an influence on the events in the world. In the German language there is a rather expressive term to denote the realm in which life takes place, namely, *Lebenskreis.* Accordingly I propose to call the realm in which the biological total process takes place the "biosphere,"[2] that is, the realm or sphere of life. The biosphere includes both the individual and the environment, not as interacting parts, not as constituents which have independent existence, but as aspects of a single reality which can be separated only by abstraction.

Several authors have emphasized the very intimate relationship between organism and environment. Such a relationship forms an essential point of certain biological theories (for example, those of Child and Uexküll). Here, however, a more radical attempt is being made: we regard the life process as a unitary happening, as an organized single process whereof the organism and the environment are only abstracted features. Instead of studying the "organism" and the "environment" and their interaction, we propose to study life as a unitary

[2] I introduce this term with some reluctance since the word "sphere" has a somewhat mystical taint, while the concept which I am trying to express has nothing mystical about it. On the other hand, it is known that several strictly scientific terms include the word "sphere" where the mystical coloring is entirely absent. Thus, for example, "atmosphere" brings nothing "spherical" to mind. It is also true that "sphere" literally means "globe," "ball," but it is used also in a less specific connotation to mean "field" or "realm."

whole and endeavor to describe the *organization and dynamics of the biosphere. The subject-matter of our considerations are not organismic processes and environmental influences, but biospheric occurrences in their integral reality.*

The biosphere, although an undivided unit, still is not structureless. It is differentiated along various dimensions. In the biosphere two definite directions can be distinguished: autonomous determination or organismic government and heteronomous determination or environmental government. These two directions do not exist independently but only within the biospheric happenings, in other words, as components of the biological total process. Both directions extend to the very limit of the biosphere. At one pole of the biological total process, the autonomous determination is the most potent one, and it extends to the opposite pole in the way of a gradient of decrease (see Figure 4). At the other pole the heteronomous factor is the prevailing one which extends as a gradient of decrease toward the opposite pole. The two trends are like two currents of opposing directions, inseparably united in the total dynamics of the biosphere.

According to the dominance of one or the other determinant the biosphere is roughly differentiated into two fields. Those factors which are prevalently under autonomous government constitute the organism or self or subject, while the factors which are prevalently under heteronomous government form the objects or the environment. The words "subject" and "object" express very aptly the difference which I have in mind. "Subject" is that factor which governs, "sub*jects*," the raw environment.[3] "Object" means that which is "thrown before" the subject, but also that which opposes, offers resistance, i.e., "ob*jects*" to the subject's influences. It is the non-system-determined, heteronomous factor. The differentiation of the biosphere into subject and object is the basic organization of the biosphere and forms the foundation for further structuralizations.

The single factors have no fixed position in the biosphere. Processes which, at a given moment, stand prevalently under environmental government may at the next moment come under prevalently organismic government.

Strictly speaking, one cannot generalize and state to what extent a given type of biological occurrence is organismically or environmentally governed. The exact value of this ratio can be determined only in specific instances. There is, in other words, a continuous flux between the two poles of the biosphere.

THE DERIVATION OF THE FIELD OF CERTAIN SCIENCES FROM THE BIOSPHERE BY PARENTHETIC EXCLUSIONS

The integrated totality of biospheric occurrences constitutes the world as it is lived by us. The other realms

[3] The meaning of the word "subject" is twofold. Sometimes it is used

which various segmental sciences study are derived from this total field. The fields of such sciences have no independent existence and they cannot be factually "separated" from the total context. They are derived from the total field not by *isolation,* but in such a way that we *arbitrarily disregard certain features of the biological reality.* Such a procedure can be called *"Einklammerung"* —"placing in parentheses"—a term which has been used by Husserl with a somewhat different connotation. It would not be correct to state, for example, that the phenomena which the physiologist deals with are *somatic processes in pure culture.* What the physiologist observes are certain integrated biological processes, certain biospheric occurrences; he, however, places in parentheses certain features of these occurrences.

The following scheme visualizes the derivation of the subject-matter of various segmental sciences (see page 105). The total field of integrated biological occurrences, the biosphere, forms the realm of the primary reality for us. We do not come in contact with the world in any other way than by living it. The study of biospheric occurrences in their integral reality without the parenthetic exclusion of any of their features could be called *biology* in the broad sense of the word. Such a discipline would be made up of two types of proposition. 1) Gen-

to mean that which is subjected, the *subjectum.* In certain philosophies of the Middle Ages the word was used with this connotation. At the present time the term applies almost universally to the "subjecter." The term is used here in this latter sense.

eral propositions with regard to the total field, as the statements made by us that in the biosphere there is a basic differentiation into subject and object; that a main trend of the biological total process is a trend toward increased autonomy, etc. 2) Propositions referring to single occurrences in the biological total process with emphasis on the meaning and significance which these single processes have in the biological total process.

As mentioned before, the biosphere is roughly differentiated into an autonomous factor or subject and a heteronomous factor or object of the environment. Some sciences derive their field by making parenthetic exclusions on the subject side of the biological total process, others by making similar exclusions on the object side.

A. *Derivations from the Subject.* If one studies the subject in such a way that one disregards, or places in parentheses, (a) its symbolic features and (b) its relation to the biological total process ("biospheric reference") one arrives at the concept of "somatic processes." The science which studies them is physiology. Somatic processes have no existence of their own; they are biological processes in which symbolism and relevance for the total field are disregarded. Let us take for illustration a rather simple behavior, such as weaving a basket. This activity is a biological occurrence. When the physiologist studies such an occurrence, he places in parentheses several features of this activity. First of all he *disregards the*

BIOSPHERE

SUBJECT (organism)

Parenthetic exclusion	*Subject-matter*	*Science*
a) Symbolism b) Biospheric reference	Somatic processes	Physiology
a) Somatic processes b) Biospheric reference	Mental states and processes	Psychology
Symbolism	Biospheric reference of somatic processes	Biology in the narrower sense of the word

OBJECT (environment)

Parenthetic exclusion	*Subject-matter*	*Science*
a) Symbolism b) Biospheric reference	Physical properties	Physics, chemistry
a) Physical properties b) Biospheric reference	"Ideas"	Psychology
Symbolism	Physical environment	Ecology? *Umweltslehre?*

symbolic functions which have an important role in controlling or governing such activity. That is, he excludes, or better ignores, such things as perception, memory, choice, judgment, conative functions, and cultural tradition, which without doubt play a part in such an activity as the weaving of a basket. Furthermore, he disregards the reference of this occurrence to the biological total process. Such reference has essentially two directions: namely, a subject reference and an object reference. The subject reference, in our example, is that the weaving is not unmotivated, but satisfies some need in the person. Such need, furthermore, is understandable only in the total context of the subject organization. The object reference of the occurrence consists, in our example, in that one does not simply move the fingers but is making a *basket,* transforming environmental raw material into a product. That which remains for the physiologist after such parenthetic exclusions are muscular contractions and their nervous coordination.

If one places in parentheses the somatic processes and the biological references, one obtains the concept of mental processes. The term "mental processes" is used here intentionally, instead of the term "symbolic processes." Symbolism is substitution and therefore the symbol always has a reference to something outside of itself. The symbols of psychological life refer to those realms which are beyond consciousness—that is, either to the environment or to the states of the person. Certain types of psychologies, however, deal with conscious phenomena as if they were complete in themselves, that is, the referents of these phenomena, which transcend the realm of consciousness, are disregarded. The Titchenerian type of psychology, for example, did this in a very consistent way.

If one places in parentheses only the symbolic aspect of the biological occurrences, one is in the field of biology in a narrower sense of the word. The term biology is, as a rule, not used in the broad sense given to it in these pages, namely, to denote the study of life in its integral reality. Even those biologists who have adopted the holistic way of thinking usually exclude the symbolic processes from the field. For example, Bertalanffy[4] states: "Biology is a science of the living organisms as objects of the outside world in space—while the inner world which they may have, we refer to another science, to psychology." Other biologists theoretically include psychology in the field of their studies, but in their detailed considerations the psychological factors are still largely ignored. But even in this restricted sense biology is broader than physiology since it relates the processes studied to the total life activity. Nest building, the migration of birds, and so forth lie in the field of biological consideration, while the physiologists are interested only in such activities as the coordinated changes of

[4] L. von Bertalanffy, Theoretische Biologie, Berlin, Gebrüder Bornträger, 1932, vol. 1, p. 2.

muscle contractions. Lactation is an occurrence in which the biologist is interested, while for the physiologist this represents only a secretion of the mammary glands. The subject-matter of biology, in the narrower sense, can be defined as a study of the biological reference of somatic processes.

B. *Derivations from the Environment.* Other scientific fields are derived by parenthetic exclusions of certain features of the object side of the biosphere. Objects which form the environment are factors which are mainly under heteronomous, that is non-organismic, government. The factors which ob*ject* offer a resistance to organismic determination. "Environment" is not identical with "surrounding world." The surrounding world can only be called environment when it is in *interaction with the subject,* when it actually ob*jects* to it, when it participates in biological happenings. The oxygen of the air is an environmental factor for man, while the atmospheric nitrogen is environment to a much lesser degree and approaches the concept of physical body. Environment is not a physical but a biological concept. This biological environment is the original objective (objecting) reality from which other fields may be derived by parenthetic exclusions.

If one places between parentheses the symbolic features and the biospheric reference of the biological object, one obtains the concept of physical objects, that is, matter and energy. The symbolic features of the environmental objects are, for example, their sensory qualities like color, sound, taste, etc. The physicist is not interested in colors but in light waves of various wave lengths, not in sounds but in the vibrations of air and other bodies, not in the sweetness or bitterness of the object but in its chemical structure. Classical physics disregards also the biological reference of the object. Biological objects are such things as food, enemy, hiding place, material for nest building, and also such objects as houses, furniture, books, money, and so forth. These objects do not exist as such for the physicist. For the physicist, after the parenthetic exclusion of symbolizations and of the biological reference, there remain only matter and energy.[5] The biological reference of the object points in two directions: subject reference and object reference. For example, the subject reference of food is that it serves as nourishment for the organism. Environmental objects also have certain object references which are biological in a certain sense and which are excluded in the considerations of physics. Between the objects food, plate, spoon, fork, knife, there is a biologically significant relationship which cannot be expressed in physical terms. Yet these objects are related

[5] It is interesting to note that in linguistic expressions which do not follow the artificial abstractions of science, but often remain closer to life, even the terms for abstract concepts have a strong biological taint. One says in English "it matters" or "it does not matter." Used thus, matter would be "that which matters," "that which has a biological significance."

not, as one used to state, in a logical sense, but in a biological sense, since they participate in the same biological occurrence, in the process of taking food in the conventional way of Western culture.

The parenthetic exclusion of the physical properties and of the biological references of environmental objects leaves "ideas" for the investigation of the psychologist. We do not call them symbols since their symbolic and biological references are disregarded. The field of such psychology is made up of symbols derived from both the object and subject sides of the biosphere. They are, however, not dealt with in the older type of psychology as representative, substitutive phenomena, but as phenomena having a field of their own: as consciousness-immanent phenomena.

By the parenthetic exclusion of only the symbolic feature of the subject one obtains a concept of physical environment. Certain forms of ecologies tend to restrict their studies to this aspect. They study the biological reference of the physical environment.

We, too, are making one parenthetic exclusion at present, namely, the exclusion of the social reference of the individual organism. We will reconsider our statements later with reference to social relationships.

At the present time the partial sciences are not so strongly segregated as our scheme would indicate. For example, the functional school in psychology makes efforts to take into consideration the biological reference of mental processes. Physiological psychology takes into consideration some of the physiological functions, namely, the sensory processes. In modern quantum-physics the role of the subject, the observer, is considered a rather important factor. Such a broadening of the field of partial sciences is not an entirely favorable sign. These sciences have developed their own conceptual schemes and when new factors are admitted into the originally circumscribed field one tries to force them into the old conceptual scheme which is too narrow for the broadened field. The result is a deplorable confusion of concepts. Personality phenomena are often described in merely psychological or merely physiological terms, until no scientist knows what the other scientist is talking about and one becomes uncertain even of the content of the concept one uses oneself.

The departmentalization of the biological sciences has, of course, a practical value and some kind of departmentalization will probably always be necessary. Present difficulties could be eliminated if the segmental sciences were oriented toward biology as a central field. The desirability of the biological orientation has been already pointed out with regard to psychology (page 81).

It would be rather interesting to show that not only the sciences but also various philosophical systems are based on certain parenthetic exclusions of one or more features from the total biological happening. Take, for example, idealism. Idealism makes the same parenthetic exclusions as does psychology and arrives at the concept of "idea." Philosophical idealism, however, makes a further step; it makes the idea the only true existence (ὄ ὤν) while the rest of the world is illusory, non-existing (μὴ ὤν). Thus one comes to the problem of being and appearance, *Sein und Schein, Noumenon und Phenomenon*. Realism, materialism, and other philosophies all make characteristic exclusions.

It would indeed be a fascinating task to trace the development of the various philosophical systems in order to discover what parenthetic exclusions they make of the biological total process, how they try to make abstract features absolute, how by a tremendous intellectual effort they attempt to make the system self-consistent and to account for the total field of phenomena by abstract features—which is, of course, impossible. Such a study would further an understanding of the history of philosophy from a biological point of view.

A biological orientation, that is, the considering of the biological total process instead of some abstract aspect of it as the original reality, offers very interesting possibilities for philosophy. Certain philosophies show a trend toward such an ideal (as Whitehead's philosophy).[6]

[6] The system of Klages, which is called biocentric, exaggerates the conflict between what he calls "*Geist*" and "*Seele*." The two are, for him, antagonistic forces. The *Geist*, according to Klages, penetrates from the outside (θύρατεν) into life like a wedge, causing there a fundamental split.

THE SYMBOLIC ELABORATION OF THE SUBJECT-OBJECT RELATIONSHIP: SELF-AWARENESS

It has been stated that the biosphere is roughly differentiated into a subjective component or self and an objective component or environment. In order to avoid conceptual and terminological confusion let us clarify these concepts. By subject, or self, I do not refer to a merely psychological factor but to a biological one in the broadest sense of the word. We may define the subject as a group of factors standing prevalently under autonomous government. This self is symbolically elaborated by the organism and then appears as self-awareness or consciousness of self; this is what psychologically we experience as ourselves. Thus we may define the self as the biological subject, while the symbolical representation of it we may call self-awareness or consciousness of self. Since the self-awareness is the conscious image of the biological subject, the features which can be observed in this conscious phenomenon are good diagnostic indicators of what is going on in the biological subject. Thus some of the statements which were made with regard to the subject necessarily hold true also with regard to the conscious self. For instance, it was mentioned previously that the biological subject is not restricted to psychosomatic factors, but extends far beyond the body. So also does self-awareness. Those psychologists who have studied self-awareness always stress the point that not only the perception of our body and not only our psychological activities are included in what we experience as ourselves, but also many other factors such as our clothes and our property. James, among others, gives a good description of the extension of the self-awareness over objects outside of the body.[7]

On what basis do we include "external" factors in our self-awareness? Why does our property seem to belong more to us than some other object of the environment? The reason is the same as the one which accounts for the inclusion of any factor in the biological self. My property has a closer relationship to my personality because it is subjected to my government to a larger degree than another object of the environment. One can give many examples which clearly demonstrate that we ascribe a given factor to ourselves or to the external world, respectively, on the basis of whether it is prevalently under autonomous or heteronomous government. This may be exemplified by what happens in the learning of skills. For instance, when one first learns to ride a horse, the horse seems to be a foreign object and we must make an effort to stay on it. When we become skilled, however, we feel almost one with the horse for now we are governing the process of riding.

There are differences of degree of autonomy between the various factors which we include in our self-aware-

[7] William James, The Principles of Psychology, New York, Holt, 1890, vol. 1, chapter 10.

ness; my body remains something which always belongs more intimately to me than, for example, my property. There is no absolute separation between the biological subject and the environment and, correspondingly, there is no sharp limit between the experience of the self and the outside world. There are only *degrees of ego proximity and ego distance. The degrees of ego proximity and ego distance are the symbolic expression of the gradient of autonomy and heteronomy* which was discussed previously (see Figure 4). This is another example of the reflection of the biological organization on a symbolic level.

The single factors in the biosphere have no fixed position in the subject-object dimension. There are continuous shifts to and fro between the two poles. So also on the psychological level: the same factor may at one time be ascribed to the outside world and at another time to the psychological self. When, for example, the organism loses control over a factor which usually stands under its autonomous government, this factor will be excluded from the self also on the symbolic level. A paralyzed limb does not seem to belong to ourselves to the same degree as the healthy limb over which we have complete control. Or, to give another example, in running down a hill we may want to make a sudden stop, but the body is carried further by inertia; it is experienced to a certain degree as estranged from the ego. In certain conditions the estrangement of factors which usually belong to the ego is very impressive. Such is the case, for example, with perseverations of rhythms and melodies, compulsive and obsessive experiences, states of depersonalization, and even more strikingly in the so-called "loss of ego reference" which is observed in certain forms of schizophrenia. I have discussed the latter phenomena in detail elsewhere.[8] Patients with such symptoms may experience the whole body or part of it as dead, as not belonging to the person; they feel that their thoughts and emotions do not arise from the ego, that their movements are not accompanied by a feeling of spontaneity; they experience themselves as influenced by outside forces. The term "loss of ego reference" refers to a disturbance on the symbolic level. This complex of symptoms indicates, however, that certain factors of the biological subject organization are no longer under the government of the total organism, but they have fallen out or become segregated from the biological total process. They have been segregated possibly because they are incompatible with the rest of the personality.

THE RELATIVE AUTONOMY OF THE CONSCIOUS SELF: A DISCREPANCY IN THE SUBJECT-OBJECT ORGANIZATION

With the conscious elaboration of the biological subject-object relationship, a peculiar split arises in the sub-

[8] A. Angyal, The experience of the body self in schizophrenia, Archives of Neurology and Psychiatry, 35:1029–1053, May 1936.

ject organization. It is a remarkable fact that we exclude from our self-awareness certain factors which are very important components of the subject. I do not refer here to pathological exclusions like compulsive phenomena, loss of ego reference, and the like, but to a fact which is characteristic of the human personality organization in general. One or two examples may serve for illustration. When we act under the influence of strong affects, we feel that we do not have entire control over our actions, but seem to be carried away by the affect or passion as by a foreign force. The expression "passion" has a definite reference to passivity. When we account retrospectively for such actions we may use expressions such as "I was not myself" or "I was beside myself." Another example is that state of inspiration in which ideas seem to come from the outside while one experiences oneself as a passive receiver. The words, "inspiration," *"Einfall," "Eingebung,"* refer clearly to the fact that one feels oneself passive as if ideas were "given to one." Such states have often been ascribed to supernatural forces ("divine inspiration," *"göttliche Eingebung,"* "intuition").

It is beyond doubt that affect, inspiration, and similar experiences originate from our personality, that they are activities of our organism. Why then does one not experience them as part of oneself? The important fact is that such processes—although they are determined by the autonomy of the organism—are not governed by our *will.* In order to clarify the meaning and origin of the concept of "will" we should recall that the biological total process is differentiated into an autonomous component or subject and a heteronomous component or environment. In the psychological realm the subject is elaborated symbolically as the consciousness of self. Now, it is a highly significant fact that the conscious self, which is only a part, namely, the conscious or symbolic part of the biological subject, *tends to establish its own autonomous government. What we call "will" represents the autonomous determination, the self-government of this narrower conscious or symbolic self.* The symbolic self becomes a state within a state. Thus a split is created within the subject organization.

This split is greatly aggravated by the fact that the symbolic self tends toward hegemony, tends to take over the government of the total personality, a task for which it is not qualified. It was previously mentioned that the main value of the symbolic process is an economic one. We have symbols which give us information about the environment and symbols which indicate the subject's states and needs. Many problems of living are solved, not by a direct interaction between concrete individual and concrete environment, but between symbols of the individual and symbols of the environment. Because of the high economizing value of the symbolic function, the organism tends to *utilize it to excess.* This is the source of the trend of symbolic functioning toward a hegemony over the total personality. But the psychological self is not qualified to govern the total organism. It is not qualified for the task mainly because of two reasons: first, because the conscious self is *not* an entirely *reliable* image of the subject and, secondly, because *only a small part* of the biological subject reaches the level of symbolization while a great part of it does not become conscious at all. That the symbolic elaboration in general is not a perfect one has been discussed previously. The imperfections of symbolic representations are manifested as distortions, as illusions, in the perceptual, mnemonic, emotional, and conative fields. Thus the symbolic information which we obtain with regard to ourselves—as also with regard to the environment—is not an entirely true picture of reality. Very frequently it is a highly idealized and distorted picture. Furthermore, only one part of the biological total process is represented psychologically. A greater part of it appears in hazy images or does not appear at all, as is the case for many of the functions of our internal organs. Thus when the psychological self attempts to govern the biological total process on the basis of *unreliable* and *insufficient* information, it may bring about great damage and suffering to the organism. The conscious self, when it oversteps the realm of its legitimate influence, may become a destructive factor.[9]

[9] Thus the recent anti-intellectualistic movement, which is a rebellion against the tyrannic domination of the "mind"—although it is an exaggerated point of view since it neglects the great economizing value of symbolic functions—is to a certain degree justified. A powerful ex-

The relative separation of the psychological self from the rest of the total organism justifies, to a certain degree, a distinction made by psychoanalysis, namely, that between the ego and the id. The id refers to personality functions which are not psychologically governed, which are not directed by conscious will. The ego refers to the psychological self.[10]

There is also considerable truth in the psychoanalytic theory of repression. Repression is a factor which aggravates the split between the psychological self and the rest of the personality. Repression can be defined, as a first approximation, as an inhibition of the symbolization of certain personality factors. The inhibition may be due to the incompatibility of a personality factor with the psychological self. Inhibition of symbolization, however, also arises as a useful selection between relevant and irrelevant factors (range of attention). The lack of symbolization, however, *is not merely a function of inhibition, but a more fundamental incongruity between total organism and the psychological self,* because the psychological self represents only a small part of the total organism. Only part of the biological total process is symbolized by man in his present stage of evolution.

The split between the conscious self and the total or-

ponent of this trend is Klages, who regards the mind as a factor which *disturbs* living, as a *Lebensstörung.*

[10] Some differences between my definition and the psychoanalytic one will be discussed later. For example, I do not assume an unconscious *mental* activity.

ganism becomes even more marked through the fact that not only do certain personality factors fail to reach the level of symbolization, but also that certain symbolic factors do not penetrate into the depths of the personality. They do not spread out into the total personality, but remain segregated on the symbolic level. *This phenomenon is a counterpart of repression. It is a resistance of the total personality against the acceptance of certain symbolic facts.* Although we may know quite clearly that something is not good for us or that it is unreasonable, we still cannot help doing it. This is an extremely important and difficult problem in the therapy of personality disorder. We see again and again that the patient has perfect insight on the psychological level, but this insight does not penetrate sufficiently into the personality to change his behavior. The relative segregation of the symbolic self within the organism is perhaps the most vulnerable point of the human personality organization.

SUMMARY

Organism and environment are not morphological entities which can be separated in space. It has been indicated that the consideration of the organism and environment in morphological terms leads to such logical entanglement that the concepts of organism and environment are made useless for scientific purposes. Since life is a dynamic entity it appears necessary that the two fundamental factors involved in the life process—organism and environment—be defined in dynamic terms. Thus we may speak of organismic or autonomous government, *a,* and environmental or heteronomous government, *h*. Every biological process is a resultant of these two factors and can be expressed in terms of the ratio $a:h$. The relative values of *a* and *h* differ greatly in the various manifestations of life. Exclusively organismic and exclusively environmental determinations do not exist. They are only concepts of limit. They mark the two opposite poles of life. Both types of government (environmental and organismic) extend from one pole to another in the way of a gradient of decrease.

The life process does not take place within the body alone, but includes the intrasomatic and extrasomatic happenings. Every process which results from the interplay of organismic autonomy or environmental heteronomy is a part of the life process, irrespective of whether it takes place within the body or outside of it. The realm in which the life process takes place has been termed "biosphere." Our purpose in the following chapters will be to study biospheric occurrences. The study of biospheric occurrences in their integral reality may be called biology in the broadest sense of the word. The fields of various sciences are derived from the biosphere by parenthetic exclusions.

The biosphere is roughly differentiated into subject

(organism) and object (environment). Those factors which are prevalently under autonomous determination form the subject. Those which are prevalently heteronomously determined form the environment.

When the biological subject is symbolically elaborated by the organism, it appears as self-awareness or consciousness of self. There is a strong tendency in the symbolic or conscious self to establish its own autonomy within the total organism: a state within a state. This creates a split in the personality organization which is greatly aggravated by the fact that the symbolic self tends to take over the government of the total personality, a task for which it is not qualified. The reasons why it is not so qualified are: first, that the conscious self is not an entirely reliable image of the subject and, secondly, only a small part of the biological subject reaches the level of symbolization, while a great part of it does not become conscious at all. The conscious self, by overstepping the realm of its legitimate influence, may become a destructive factor. The relative autonomy of the symbolic realm within the total organism is the most vulnerable point of the human personality organization.

V. BIOSPHERIC DYNAMICS

THE BIOSPHERE AS A SYSTEM OF TENSIONS

THE way is now prepared for the discussion of the dynamic characteristics of the biological total process. The purpose of this chapter will be to define some general terms which may be useful in the study of biospheric dynamics. The discussion of more specific dynamic characteristics will be taken up in a later chapter (VII).

In our attempt to define the main concepts which are pertinent to biological dynamics we may take as a point of departure the concept of the biosphere. Biosphere is the realm in which life takes place. The biosphere is an indivisible unit and is characterized by a bipolar organization. The subject pole is given by the tendency of the organism toward increased autonomy, that is, toward extension of organismic domination over an ever increasing field of events. The object pole is represented by the resistances in the biosphere against organismic domination. Strictly speaking, this resistance is not *directed* against the organism but is due to the fact that the object components of the biosphere are not

NOTE: The reading of this chapter may be facilitated by consulting the table on page 166, in which the concepts to be defined are systematically arranged.

organismically centralized, but are heteronomous from the point of view of the organism. The polarity of the biospheric organization is the basis for a tensional relationship between the two poles of the biosphere, between subject and object.

The trend toward increased autonomy is only a general pattern which assumes specific forms in the various concrete engagements between the individual and the environment. Thus the organism asserts its autonomy in one way when it seeks food, in another way when it fights with an enemy, and in still another way when it tries to escape danger. These are examples of biospheric occurrences, that is, specific instances of dynamic subject-object relationships.

In each biospheric occurrence we may distinguish three features: 1) the subject which tends toward some end (seeking food); 2) the object toward which the activity is directed (food); and 3) a specific dynamic relationship between the subject and object poles of the given biospheric occurrence. The specific instances of the dynamic subject-object relationships which are present in every biospheric occurrence we may call *tensions*. A biospheric occurrence can be expressed by the symbol $(s \longleftrightarrow o)$; s and o represent the subject and object poles respectively. The double arrow represents the tension between s and o. By enclosing the whole expression between parentheses we wish to indicate the unity of the biospheric occurrence in which the subjective and objective factors can be distinguished only by abstraction. The tension is not in the subject or in the object, but between the two poles of the biospheric occurrence. The concept of tension, as defined here, has not been used previously in the literature. It is therefore necessary to keep clearly in mind the definition of the term as given here and not to attribute to it other meanings. When a thirsty animal approaches the water eagerly, a tension is inherent in the process between animal and water; that is, tension is not identical either with the urge in the animal or with the "demand quality" of the water.

Tension, as defined here, is one of those "psychophysically neutral" concepts, the need for which was stressed in the first chapter. It has been pointed out there that the phenomena and characteristics of the biological total process should be described in terms which are specific for the science of the total organism and not in terms of sciences which deal with some abstract feature of the organismic activity. It is especially important to distinguish between the concepts which refer to integrated organismic happenings and those which refer exclusively to psychological, that is, symbolic, aspects, because the confusion of organismic and purely psychological concepts is a very common error. All tensions are not elaborated symbolically and experienced psychologically. Only some of them are more or less clearly symbolized, that is, consciously represented. The psychological experience of biospheric tensions could be called *interest*.

Thus we may say that between the subject and object there is a tensional state and that the organism may become aware of such tensions in the experience of an interest. The word "interest" (*inter est*) expresses rather well the concept we have in mind, namely, the experience of a significant biological relationship which *is between* the subject and the object. The concept of interest, as it is defined here, partly agrees with the common usage of this term, in spite of certain differences between our own and the general use of it. Commonly one means by interest prevalently intellectual involvements of only a moderate degree of intensity. For instance, for a situation in which life and death are under consideration, the term "interest" as commonly used is obviously too feeble, but the word in its extended sense, as here defined, can be well applied to such situations also. In spite of such deviations from the common usage, it seems preferable to adopt this term instead of coining a new one.

Interests, like psychological phenomena in general, are not independent entities. They are symbolic elaborations of biospheric tensional states; and since they reflect these tensional states they can be relied upon as fair indicators of such states. Thus, for example, in schizophrenia loss of interest is in itself a purely psychological phenomenon; it indicates, however, that the biological tensions between the subject and the objects of his environment have become less intense and less numerous, that the subject stands in biologically less significant relationships to the objects of his environment. Loss of interest indicates that the person has turned away from his environment—possibly because for one or another reason he has been unable to cope with it.

Biospheric dynamics can be described as a system of tensions. The nature and range of tensional relationships between organism and environment, hence also of the interests, change continuously. The range of tensions and interests undergoes rather typical fluctuations in the course of life. It expands at a rapid rate in childhood and usually contracts in later years. Such fluctuations of interest show marked individual variations, a fact which should be considered in compiling life histories.

Tensions are inherent in the undivided biospheric occurrence in which the subject and object factors can be separated only by abstraction. Tensions can be described, however, from various points of view. One may choose as a point of reference either the subject or the object. This involves a certain relativity comparable to the relativity in physics. A physical motion is a unitary process consisting in the change of the spatial relationship between two physical bodies. The point of reference for the description of the motion can, however, be either of the two bodies. Biological tensions viewed from the subject as a point of reference are considered as *drives.* Viewing the same tensions from the object side as the point of reference, one obtains something similar to what Kurt Lewin calls the "field forces" or "demand qualities" of environmental situations.

THE SYSTEM OF BIOSPHERIC TENSIONS VIEWED WITH THE SUBJECT AS THE POINT OF REFERENCE

A. *Drives and Cravings.* Considering biospheric tensions by taking the subject as a point of reference, such tensions appear as *drives,* for example, the drive to obtain nourishment. Drives are specific forms of expression of the self-expansive tendency of the organism. The general dynamic pattern of the organism can be considered as an undifferentiated trend in a definite direction (toward increase of autonomy). This general trend branches off into more specific channels. The specific ramifications of the general dynamic trend form the skeleton of the dynamic structure of a given organism. Such a structure is partly defined by the anatomico-physiological pattern of the given organism. The biological total process will express itself, for example, in quite different part processes in a fish, in a bird, in a mammal, although the general tendency is the same for all. Because of his anatomico-physiological structure, man will crave oxygen, food, some kind of sex expression, and so on. The general trend of the organism thus ramifies into a number of branches or channels. The whole structure can be roughly compared to a tree, the trunk being the hypothetically undifferentiated trend toward increased autonomy which branches off into primary, secondary, and tertiary tendencies (drives), culminating in the "terminal branches" of actual behavioral samples.

The channels of dynamic expression are only partly defined by the anatomico-physiological pattern of the organism. Especially in man the greater part of such channels are built up as a result of personal experiences and under the influence of social-cultural influences. Even the anatomico-physiologically defined channels are greatly modified by the superposition of personal and cultural meanings. This extremely important aspect of the personality organization will be discussed in greater detail in the next chapter.

Now the question arises: How many varieties of dynamic trends are present in man; in other words, what are the basic human drives? The question has been raised by many students of personality and has been answered in very different ways. Self-preservation and the preservation of the species have frequently been assumed to constitute the basic trends. Individual psychology assumes the will to power and the *Gemeinschaftsgefühl* as the moving forces of human behavior. Psychoanalysis traces human conduct back to basic factors: the pleasure-pain principle, the "death instinct," the reality principle. McDougall assumes some 18 basic drives ("propensities") in man.[1] James thought that their number must

[1] W. McDougall, The Energies of Man: A Study of the Fundamentals of Dynamic Psychology, London, Methuen, 1932.

be at least 1,000. In spite of their divergencies, these assumptions concerning the number of drives or trends in man are not eventually incompatible. As the general dynamic trend of the organismic total process divides and subdivides into more and more specific channels the number of these specific expressions or drives increases. The number of drives which one finds in man will mainly depend upon the level of specificity at which one makes the survey. Using the branching out of a tree as a parallel for the branching out dynamic tendencies of the organism, we may roughly represent the dynamic structure of the organism as in Figure 5.

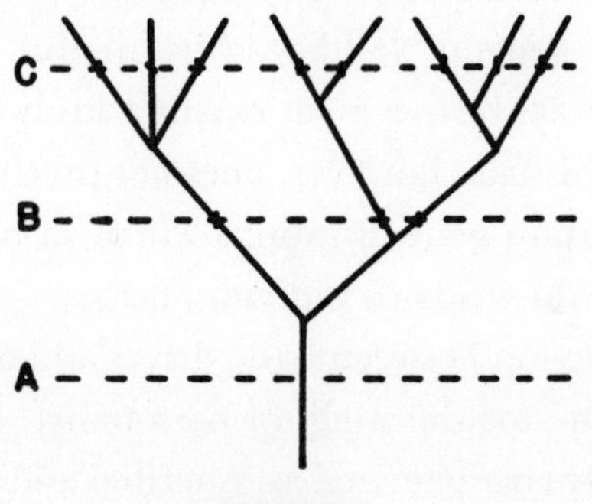

FIGURE 5

On level A one will find only a single tendency. Making a survey on level B one may find three. On level C one may count eight, and so on. On each successively higher level of specificity an increasing number of ramifications will be obtained. Thus the number of drives will depend entirely upon the level of specificity at which the survey is made, and hence these surveys will be equally correct, if the criterion on which the survey is based is kept constant. The value of such surveys, however, is very questionable. Not the enumeration of tendencies, but the correct tracing of the ramifications of the basic trend into specific channels and the study of the way in which they hang together promises insight into the structure and integration of personality. Considering the fact that the greater part of the personality structure is formed under the influence of such highly variable factors as personal experiences and social and cultural influences, we cannot hope ever to be able to describe the human personality structure in a way that would have general validity. Meaningful personality study will always be to a great extent a study of single individuals. This fact, however, does not preclude the possibility of certain generalizations which in turn serve as a compass in the study of individual cases.

The distinction between basic drives and derived ones has little value for the study of personality. Basic drives are commonly characterized as inherited and rather rigid patterns of function. We know, however, that all patterns of function—especially in man—are more or less plastic and often undergo considerable changes during the personality development. The degree of plasticity varies in different regions of the personality structure. One can roughly state that the personality structure is most plastic at the "terminal branches" (see Figure 5) while going from the "terminal branches" toward the "trunk," the structure becomes increasingly rigid. There are marked individual differences with regard to the degree of plasticity of the personality structure—a circumstance which will be considered more closely in the discussion of the integration of the personality.

Drives are the ramifications of the general dynamic trend of the organism. They are part patterns of the total dynamic pattern of the organism. The concept of drive in its present use is "psychophysiologically neutral," that is, it is a holistic concept. Drives are neither physiological nor psychological but factors which can be singled out from the organismic total process without making any abstractive distinction between psychological and physiological aspects. Drives do not always reach the level of symbolization. Sometimes, however, they are symbolically elaborated and appear in consciousness. The more or less conscious symbolic representation of drives we shall call *cravings*. We have here again a pair of concepts: the biological drives and the psychological cravings. Craving is used here as the general concept for the conscious experience of a drive while related terms like wish or desire are reserved to denote more specific forms and nuances of cravings. Thus the concept of craving will be used here as a general term for all forms of conscious conation. The phenomenon which one usually calls "will process" has—as has been indicated previously—a somewhat exceptional position among the conative functions. While drives and their symbolic representations, the cravings, refer to activities which are directed by the total organism, will processes are prevalently governed by the symbolic self, that is, by the ego.

It is not without reason that we stress the importance of a clear conceptual and terminological distinction between holistic factors and the corresponding psychological ones. There is exigent need to differentiate between the biological subject and the psychological self; between biospheric tensions and their symbolic correlates, the interests; between drives and their conscious representatives, the cravings; and between other pairs of concepts which will be introduced later. The psychologizing of holistic or organismic phenomena is probably an even more common error than their physiologizing. Psychoanalysis, through the introduction of the concept of unconscious mental activity, contributed a great deal to the psychologizing of psychophysically neutral organismic processes. According to the previous discussion, the organism may exhibit drives which are directed toward certain attainments and which can be revealed by the observation of behavior but which do not reach any symbolic elaboration, that is, of which the individual does not become conscious. Psychoanalysis speaks in such instances of "unconscious drives" and "unconscious wishes." There is no objection to the term "unconscious" drives—because they are indeed not conscious—except that the term is a negative one, since it expresses only what a factor is not, instead of stating positively what it is. The weakness of the concept becomes apparent, however, when the attribute "mental" or "psychological" is ascribed to the unconscious factor. Psychoanalysis contributed probably more to the knowledge of the total personality than any other single system, but committed a grave error by posing as a system of psychology. Psychoanalysis is rather a study of the manifestations of the integrated organism expressed in terms of mental processes, that is, in a terminology which is deceptive and inadequate for the description of such manifestations. It is not our intention to add one more objection to the numerous and often pedantic criticisms of the psychoanalytic concept of the unconscious. We wish, however, to take issue with the basic presupposition of this study, namely, that the manifestations of the integrated organism form a scientific realm of their own which is irreducible to physiology or psychology. The introduction of unconscious psychological factors does not solve the problem. To do justice to the realm of organismic activity, we need a set of new and appropriate concepts.

B. *Attitudes.* The concepts of drive and craving refer to dynamic patterns in the state of actual functioning. However, as a rule, dynamic patterns do not function continuously, but only when certain specific situations arise. Strictly speaking, then, it is not quite correct to state that an organism is characterized by certain types of drives like the drive for food or for self-defense. Such expressions refer to momentary states. The organism has no drive for food unless it is in a state of hunger and does not show defensive behavior unless there is an endangering situation present. The organism is, however, characterized by the *readiness* to certain types of behavior. This readiness is activated whenever the proper situation arises and becomes an actual drive. The readiness to behave in certain specific ways we shall call *attitude.* Thus the dynamic structure of the organism can be more adequately described as a system of attitudes than as a system of drives. The process of activation of an attitude may be called *setting.*

Attitude is another genuinely holistic concept. Attitudes are not necessarily conscious; they are active without being conscious. They may occasionally become conscious by an additional symbolic elaboration. In fact, the first investigators of attitudes—who usually studied attitudes of rather narrow range, the so-called "minor sets" —were primarily impressed with the fact that such attitudes or sets function as a rule without any apparent participation of conscious activity. The fate of "attitudes" has been the fate of holistic phenomena in general; they have been either psychologized or physiologized. Von Kries[2] made the *ad hoc* assumption that, since a set is not

[2] F. von Kries, Über die Natur gewisser mit den psychischen Vorgängen verknüpfter Gehirnzustände, Zeitschrift für Psychologie, 8:1–33, 1895.

conscious, it must be considered as some kind of brain pattern. More frequently sets have been psychologized in the usual way: they were considered as unconscious mental factors.

Minor sets (very simple attitudes) have been studied rather extensively and certain facts concerning them are already fairly well established. Von Kries gave the first detailed description of sets. He was also the one who introduced into psychology the term *Einstellung*—the German equivalent of set. Karl Marbe and his collaborators made the concept of set the central problem of their investigations and other students have also devoted a considerable amount of work to the study of sets.

An example of a minor set, the one involved in the reading of musical notes, may be mentioned. Identical notes serve as symbols for different tones according to whether the notes are written in treble or bass clef. As one takes notice of the clef one is set to read the notes in a definite way and one reads them without thinking at all of what the notes would mean in another clef and indeed without even becoming aware of the fact that one is set for a definite way of functioning. Sets exert a selective function without the aid of any conscious considerations. They admit only definite kinds from among a number of possible ways of functioning, and automatically eliminate every other possibility. They spare us the labor of choosing between various activities. Hypnosis is an impressive example of the functioning of sets. In a hypnotic state the subject is so strongly set to obey the suggestions of the experimenter that in successful experiments the suggested actions are carried out without choice and without any further consideration. Not only in the state of hypnosis, but also in everyday life one acts to a great extent in a similar fashion. For instance, if a man is asked by his table companion to pass the salt, as a rule he will not ponder whether he should do so or not, but does so almost automatically without any conscious deliberation.

Sets accomplish a very important function for the organism. They may be regarded as the key function of a highly economic arrangement in the biological organization. This arrangement makes it possible to carry out, with the aid of a relatively small number of factors, a very large variety of functions. The part structures of the organism have multiple functions. One needs only to realize the great variety of activities which can be carried out with the aid of such a relatively simple apparatus as the human hand. Given the functional multiplicity of biological part systems no single function could be carried out properly if it were not possible to set the system for a definite, required way of functioning with the temporary exclusion of all other functional possibilities. The biological arrangement allowing a multiplicity of functions may be roughly compared to certain technical devices. For instance, a typewriter is constructed in such a way as to permit the writing of both capital and small letters. Instead of having separate keys for each individual letter, one builds only half as many keys as the number of letters, assigning to each key two functions, namely, to write a small or a capital letter according to the need. This double function is made possible by means of a shifting mechanism which allows the setting of the typewriter for one or the other way of functioning.

The ease or difficulty wherewith one is able to shift from one set to another is an important personality characteristic. Zillig,[3] in her experimental studies, found marked individual differences in this respect and classified her subjects as "good and bad shifters." Such differences exist not only with regard to minor sets but also with regard to more general attitudes. The rigid personality is characterized mainly by the fixity of its attitudes. The rigidity of a personality may manifest itself, for instance, not only in perseveration of minor sets, but also in perseverance in pursuing larger goals. At the other extreme is the flighty, inconstant, loosely organized type of personality which is not able to maintain a given set for a sufficient length of time.

Attitudes and minor sets do not determine, as a rule, all details of the corresponding activities but only their general pattern. Since sets are only the patterns of activities, the actual content of such activities may vary within

[3] M. Zillig, Experimentelle Untersuchungen über Umstellbarkeit, Zeitschrift für Psychologie, 97:30, 1925.

more or less broad limits. Occasionally the set activity is carried out on entirely improper material. This, for instance, is the case in those curious forms of perseveration which can be observed in states of fatigue, physiological exhaustion, fever, and in the fore-period of sleep, the so-called hypnagogic state. If during the evening one is engaged for several hours in some type of work, for example in mathematical calculations, one frequently continues in the state of somnolence to carry out the same activity pattern even on entirely inadequate material. One may then think of events, persons, objects, and so on, in terms of mathematical calculation. It is very difficult to describe in words these strange experiences, but most people have observed them in one form or another.

Good examples of carrying out activity patterns on improper material are the phenomena which in psychoanalysis are called *Fehlhandlungen* (slips) and similar so-called "symbolic" manifestations. It is an important contribution of psychoanalysis to have discovered the value of such phenomena as aids for the detection of the presence of certain non-symbolized and rather inaccessible attitudes in the person. The psychoanalytic theory of the "mechanism" of such phenomena is, however, not convincing. It is not necessary to assume that *Fehlhandlungen* are products of intentional symbolization. *Fehlhandlungen* may arise when in the course of consciously intended activity a certain set or attitude is activated which is not symbolically elaborated, that is, which is not conscious, but impresses its pattern on the first activity. The conscious activity, which is being overlaid by a second pattern, will be more or less strongly distorted and thus a *Fehlhandlung* is produced. *Fehlhandlungen* reveal the presence of certain attitudes of a person and can be utilized as *symptoms* on the basis of which the existence of certain attitudes in a person may be inferred. It seems, however, entirely unjustified to regard the distortions which arise in *Fehlhandlungen* through the fusion of two separate activity patterns as the result of an *intention to disguise* forbidden attitudes in order to elude the "censor" and under such disguise to smuggle the forbidden attitudes into consciousness. Such a strong dramatization is not only unnecessary but is also an unpermissible psychologizing of non-mental life processes.

The situations which activate attitudes are not always quite univocally defined. Attitudes can be aroused not only by the proper situation, but also by situations which have some points of similarity in common with the proper situation. This can be illustrated, for instance, by the phenomenon which the psychoanalysts call "transference." Transference means the transfer of an attitude, which one has formed toward a certain person, to another person—frequently on the basis of quite superficial resemblances. It seems to be the rule that when one enters into new social relationships one does not immediately build up new and adequate attitudes toward a given person but uses to a large extent the old patterns which one has established in earlier social relationships with other persons. This might be one of the examples of the economizing tendency of the organism, a tendency which can be observed in all departments of personality functioning. Since the first social relationships refer usually to the parents and siblings and perhaps a few other persons who have intimate contacts with the young child, it is understandable that these first social attitudes are carried over to a quite considerable extent into the social relationships of adult life. This is quite in line with the psychoanalytic point of view. Certain further psychoanalytic implications which are related to the transfer of attitudes do not seem, however, to be warranted. One could, for instance, agree with psychoanalysis that sex difficulties in the adult male might frequently be related to the idea of incest. This occurs, however, not because he had as a child incestuous wishes toward his mother—which, of course, may also occur—but because he carries over, he transfers, the general attitude which he has built up toward his mother to a certain woman or to women in general. He sees, so to speak, the mother in the woman, and this intrusion does not permit him to form a satisfactory sexual attitude toward her.

We previously defined attitudes as activity patterns. It was indicated that they make it possible for the organism to carry out a large variety of functions with the aid of a relatively small number of factors. Thus they accomplish a highly important function for the economy of the organism. Attitudes can be set and shifted according to the demands of the situation. Attitudes define only the pattern, but not the details of the corresponding activity. They can exert their influence over a variety of contents and occasionally are carried out even on entirely improper material. Not only a single situation but a greater or smaller range of situations may activate the same attitude. All these factors are important for the knowledge of the mechanism of attitudes, but, on the whole, relatively little is known about this subject. Research in this field would seem especially desirable since the mechanism of attitudes gives considerable insight into the way the organism works and in addition one is dealing here with phenomena which lend themselves relatively easily to experimental study and to other types of empirical investigation.

THE ORGANIZATION OF ATTITUDES

The attitudes of a person are more or less closely related to each other and form a definite organization. We shall discuss the organization of attitudes in connection with the problem of personality integration and limit ourselves here to only a few general remarks.

The organization of the attitudes of a person is essentially a hierarchical one. Taking a behavioral sample of an individual we are usually able to identify it as a part manifestation of a set attitude; this attitude is again a part manifestation of a broader setting; the latter again is a part of an even broader attitude; and so on. When, for example, a servant is building a fire his single movements are organized and governed by the fact that he is set to build the fire. The whole activity of building a fire is again one of the activities in a larger set: it is one of the activities which he, as a servant, has to carry out. When he entered the job he set himself quite in general to a certain role, that is, to carry out a number of activities that are defined by the character of the job. The total setting of the job may be part of an even broader setting, for example, a means of acquiring money in order to establish a home. If we trace the connection between attitudes, starting out with the actual behavioral sample, we arrive successively at attitudes of a broader and broader range. If one carries out such an analysis on a large number of behavioral samples of the same person, one arrives at a rather limited number of very general attitudes. These few attitudes seem unquestionable, axiomatic for that given person. Such a group of *axioms of behavior* is highly characteristic of a given person and forms the basis of an active philosophy of life. Every person's attitudes can be traced back to more general attitudes leading finally to certain axioms of behavior and in this sense one could say that every person has an active philosophy of life. The term "philosophy" in this connection would be, however, somewhat deceptive. It suggests, on the one hand, intellectually formulated principles and, on the other hand, a unified and intrinsically consistent system of such principles. The personal axioms of behavior, however, need neither to be adequately formulated intellectually nor to form a self-consistent system. Axioms of behavior are not intellectual formulations but general attitudes, active principles which manifest themselves in certain characteristic, more or less consistent directions of a person's total behavior. These characteristic directions or trends of behavior allow the investigator to detect, during long-term observations, the behavioral axioms of a person. A person may know nothing of such axioms but he *behaves* according to them. They may be intellectually formulated and in such a case we may speak of maxims of personal behavior. As with other concepts, it is desirable to distinguish terminologically the holistic and the psychological aspects of attitudes, applying in this context to the holistic factor the term *axiom,* and to the psychological one, *maxim.* In the same manner we could distinguish the *"system of axioms"* from the *"philosophy of life"* (system of maxims). Personal philosophies of life may deserve more or less the name of "philosophy" according to the degree of unity and inner consistency.

There are great individual differences with respect to how well and how correctly a person knows the axioms of his behavior. A person may profess intellectually a certain philosophy of life and still behave according to entirely different principles and—what is more—may never become aware of this discrepancy. One of the typical ways of smoothing over the discrepancy between one's maxims and one's behavior is the device known as rationalization.

When in a personality study one has succeeded in tracing back the behavioral manifestations of a person to a limited number of personal axioms, the next important step is to examine the interrelation and integration of these axioms with each other. Perhaps the most important point of view for such an examination is that of the compatibility of the axioms with each other and with reality. A good compatibility of axioms among themselves and with reality, in spite of many-sided differentiations of the person, is the main characteristic of the harmonious personality. The incompatibility of axioms among themselves and/or with reality is the characteristic feature of the "discordant personality" (Adolf Meyer). Such discordances are likely to explode in the form of actual conflicts. Strong discordances may exist even in powerful personalities, but in fortunate cases they may be built into the total personality structure in such a way that they become stimulants of intensive creative activity. Discordances in a personality may be well balanced or even disappear in a higher synthesis; but they may also remain "unbalanced," a term by which one often designates, not quite without justification, personality disorder in general.

Discrepancies and conflicts do not necessarily refer to the incompatibility of axioms. They may arise also between minor attitudes. Therefore, working with personality disorders it is important to have an estimate of the depths of the discordance.

The consideration of biospheric tensions with the subject as a point of reference necessitated the differentiation of the concepts of drive and craving: drive is a tension viewed with the subject as a point of reference and craving is the conscious manifestation of a drive. From here we proceeded to the discussion of attitudes. While a drive is a feature of an actual activity, attitudes refer to potentialities, to the readiness of the organism to behave in certain ways whenever the proper situation arises. It has also been indicated that the attitudes are organized in a hierarchy culminating in axioms of behavior. These axioms form a more or less well-integrated system. This system has its conscious correlate in the philosophy of life of the individual.

THE SYSTEM OF BIOSPHERIC TENSIONS VIEWED WITH THE OBJECT AS A POINT OF REFERENCE

A. *Valences and Demand Qualities.* As an example of a biospheric occurrence we may take an animal hunting food. This process involves both the organism and the food, as well as the tension which binds them together into a single biological event. Describing this occurrence one may place the point of reference in the subject. Then one may say that the animal is *driving* to obtain food. Viewing the same occurrence with the object as the point of reference, one may say that the animal is *attracted* by the sight of food. The whole biosphere, viewed from the object pole as a point of reference, appears as a system of attractive and repulsive environmental forces acting upon the organism. In everyday thinking it is not uncommon to view life from the object side. One frequently describes environmental objects and situations as attractive, repulsive, pleasing, challenging, seductive, trying, provoking, threatening, conducive to one or another type of activity. Kurt Lewin's system of psychology is largely an attempt to describe and study behavior in terms of environmental attractive and repulsive influences, called by him "negative and positive valences," "field forces," or "demand qualities" of environmental situations.

One might gain the impression that the description of biospheric occurrences in terms of environmental attractions and repulsions was nothing more than a way of rendering pictorially certain phenomena, while the description in terms of organismic tendencies or drives is a true, factual account. One could think that it is permissible to say *metaphorically* that the food attracts the animal, but *factually,* the animal drives toward satiation.

Is one justified in stating that an object attracts or repels the organism if we take such statements literally? In what sense are such attractions and repulsions to be understood? It is clear that the "field forces" do not act on the organism in the sense of physical influences. Food does not attract the animal in the way that a magnet attracts iron. The food substance as a physical body does not exert any biological influence whatsoever on the organism. It exerts an influence only through its biological relevance. One should recall in this connection the distinction which has been made between the external world and the environment. The objects of the external world can be called environment only in so far as they participate in the biological total process, that is, in so far as they are within the boundary of the biosphere.

Lewin probably has a similar concept in mind when he repeatedly stresses the point that "field forces" are not physical forces but forces in the psychological time-space. Because of our more specific use of the term "psychological" we may say that they are forces in the biosphere. What does participation in the biosphere mean? It means that the environmental object forms the one pole of the biospheric occurrence while the other pole is represented by an organismic factor and a tensional relationship connects the two poles into an indivisible unit. The environmental factor, the "field force," affects the organism only in so far as the object is needed by the organism; for example, only the food which is needed attracts the organism. Without a corresponding drive there is no environmental attraction. But, on the other hand, without an object there is no drive. This seems at first sight contradictory to the facts. One gets hungry when the digestive activity reaches a certain phase, irrespective of whether food is present or not. The case is similar in thirst, sex, and some other spheres of activity. One should, however, consider this: hunger means physiologically a specific disturbance, a kind of stoppage in a definite phase of the nutritional total activity of the organism. Psychologically it consists of specific unpleasant sensations through which the disturbance is signaled in consciousness. Hunger, however, is not a drive, if we mean by drive the pattern and direction of an activity, but is a disturbance in the biological total process. We speak of drive only from the moment that the organism begins to do something about the disturbance. The moment that activity sets in, the organism is already involved in the bipolar tensional relationship with the object. The object might be within reach or it might only be in prospect, but biologically it is present as one pole of a tensional relationship. The object pole may be well defined, in which case the activity is definitely directed, or it may be ill defined, hazy, in which case the activity remains poorly directed and corresponds to restless behavior. But in spite of such differences, both factors must be present, so that we can truly say that there is no biologically active object of the environment without the drive, and no drive without the biologically active object. The object attracts the organism while the organism drives for it and the organism drives only for such kinds of objects as attract it by their biological relevance. Thus, if one speaks of drive the concept of the biologically relevant object is already implied, and if one speaks of environmental attraction the concept of drive is implied.

Fundamentally then the fact is that we cannot speak of drives and environmental attraction as two different phenomena: they both refer to a single phenomenon, to the biospheric occurrence viewed at times from the side of the subject and at other times from the side of the object. Neither of the two ways of considering the phenomenon has a greater justification than the other, and we cannot say that one is a realistic and the other a metaphorical description. To use one or the other type of description is a matter of convenience.

It has been pointed out previously that organismic dynamics cannot be adequately described in terms of drives alone. Besides drives which are active at a given moment we have to consider also the *potential* dynamic features of the organism, that is, its attitudes, the various forms of readiness for certain activities. On certain occasions an environmental situation first appears which appeals to an attitude in the organism and activates the attitude to the actual craving of the moment. An example: Walking on the street one discovers a coin on the road. One picks it up although in the moment immediately preceding the discovery of the coin one was not driving at the acquisition of money. In this instance there is on the subject side a readiness in the person for acquiring money whenever an appropriate situation is present, and on the object side there is the biological relevance of money which, under proper conditions, will be activated to become an actual environmental attraction. This relationship could be called a *readiness for tension*. The readiness for tension is not a property of the organism but of the biosphere. The readiness for tension viewed from the subject side is *attitude;* viewed from the object side it is *biological relevance of an environmental factor*.

The next phase in our example is the actual appearance in the situation of the biologically relevant object, which appearance is followed by the activation of the *readiness* for tension to an *actual* tension with its two aspects: drive and environmental attraction. Thus the transition from the readiness for tension to actual tension is effected in the above example by the appearance of the biologically relevant object in the momentary situation. On other occasions it is the momentary constellation of attitudes which activates tensions. In the first case it is usually more convenient to describe the process in terms of environmental attractions, in the second in terms of organismic tendencies.

The unity of a biospheric occurrence does not imply that the tensional relationship between the two poles is identical in both directions. The tension in the direction subject→object is an *activity* of the organism tending toward a general aim, to fit the environmental object into the organismic scheme (trend toward increased autonomy). The action upon the environment takes place according to a dynamic pattern inherent in the organism. The influence of the organism upon the environment is an "action," the exertion of an influence out of a centralized system.

The tension in the direction object→subject is different both from physical causation and from the action of the subject. The influence of a feeding bottle upon the child is comparable neither with the influence of the magnet upon the iron nor with the centralized, directed activity of the organism. The influence of the environmental object upon the organism consists in inducing or *prompting* the organism to respond in its own specific way.[4] The prompting influence of the biologically relevant object upon the organism is a specific category *sui generis* in the larger category of dynamic relations. The

[4] The conventional concept of dynamic relations in nature, namely, the concept of causality in the classical sense of the word, appears to be too narrow when it is applied to biological phenomena. The concept of causality refers essentially to those dynamic connections with which the physicist deals. Besides physical causality there are also other forms of dynamic relation. The autonomous activity of the organism is one example, the prompting influences of the biologically relevant object another. It is quite conceivable that all these various categories are fundamentally one. It is, however, not justifiable to select one specific group of dynamic connections—in this case physical causality—and generalize on that basis about the whole category of dynamic connections.

response of the organism is very different, for example, from the way the mechanistic theory conceived the operation of tropism. Even in reactive behavior the autonomy of the organism is an important determining factor. The concept of Lewin's "field forces" seems to have justification only in this definite sense, namely, as *prompting forces.*

If it is true that one describes in terms of drives and environmental forces not two different phenomena, nor even two different components of the same phenomenon, but the whole unitary process of biospheric occurrence, one is justified in asking whether the two methods of study are not an unnecessary duplication. The most adequate way of dealing with biospheric occurrences would be not to make either pole arbitrarily a point of reference, but to consider the whole process, so to say, from a neutral point of view. Indeed it is necessary to have such a neutral point of view always in mind when one wants to determine any basic characteristic of biospheric occurrences. Each method of study allows, however, certain simplifications and brings different features into sharp focus.

The organism may be attracted or repelled by objects of the environment without consciously experiencing such attraction or repulsion. Iodine, for example, is a biologically relevant environmental object, but the organism does not become conscious of this relevance as such. Various agents, such as microorganisms or foreign protein, prompt in the organism violent defensive processes without one's being conscious of the negative biological relevance of such agents. For the sake of terminological clearness we may apply the term *valence* to a prompting influence in the environment which acts without participation of consciousness, while we may designate the conscious experience of attractions or repulsions of an environmental situation as *demand quality*.

It is interesting to note that in the psychoanalytic system, too, there is a concept which roughly corresponds to the concept of valences and demand qualities. This is the concept of "cathexis" or "libido investment." When the psychoanalyst speaks of cathexis, or of an object being invested with libido, he means fundamentally that the object is biologically relevant for the person, that the person is interested in and attracted by certain objects. The concept of cathexis has, of course, a more specific content in psychoanalysis; I only wished to point out one common feature between this concept and the concept of environmental attractions.

B. *Biospheric Relevancies.* When biospheric dynamics were discussed from the subject side as a point of reference it was necessary to consider potential factors (attitudes) besides the actual ones (drives). The same distinction is necessary when we are discussing biospheric dynamics with the object as a point of reference. The range of biologically relevant objects is much larger than the range of the objects which are actually involved in biospheric occurrences at any given moment. We are surrounded by a large number of objects which are relevant for us but which do not function continuously as valences and demand qualities. As I survey the contents of this room I see several objects such as the telephone, the stethoscope, a paper knife, books, which are relevant to my person, although at this moment they have no demand quality for me. But at any moment, when the proper situation arises, they will gain an actual valence and will be involved in activities. For the sake of terminological clarity it seems desirable to speak of the *valence* of an object when it exerts an actual prompting influence upon the organism and of its *relevance* when the object has the potentiality to exert such influence under proper conditions. To use a simple example, we may say that food is always relevant for the organism, but it acquires valence only when the organism is in a state of hunger.

It is important to realize that the objects of the environment do not conform to some conventional definition, for example, the definition of the dictionary. They have a rich personal content. A dog is for its master not an animal of such and such a shape and color, belonging to such and such a zoological class, and so on, but has for its master a more special content by virtue of which it acquires a personal relevance for him. A watch which one received as a present is not merely a time-measuring apparatus. The object "egg" has an entirely different content for a housewife, for the embryologist, and for the person who has an allergy toward eggs. One could also say that the objects of the environment are biologically relevant not by what they are "in themselves" but by what they "mean" to the organism. Such "meaning," however, is not a mere label of the object but is incorporated into the object and forms an integral part of it. For instance, to a religious person a prayerbook not only *means* a sacred object, but *is* a sacred object. The picture of a person who is dear to one is not only a piece of paper with some colors on it representing a person. One would show, for example, a strong reluctance to damage the picture. It is as if something of the person portrayed were incorporated in the picture and in harming it one would almost feel as if one were harming the person. An antique object has a very rich content for the lover of antiques. For him the object is one which carries in itself as an integral part a past in a way somewhat similar to that in which a person carries in him his own past in form of memory. This formulation may seem akin to "magic" or "primitive" thinking, but actually we function in this way in all matters which are close to life and refrain from doing so only in highly abstract scientific speculations. This "primitive" way of thinking seems to be rather a sign of close contact with life and of personal refinement than of primitivity.

Since the term "meaning" commonly refers to sign or

symbol relations, it is advisable not to use it in this context but speak of the *content* of the biologically relevant object.

The content of the biologically relevant object is not defined by what we know about it, but in terms of the role it plays in our personality processes. *The content of the object is not defined entirely by one's ideas about the object but by one's attitudes toward the object.* Content in this definition is a holistic concept. Only a small part of that content is conscious. Some time ago I made an analysis of objects toward which one reacts with disgust or other forms of aversion,[5] and was greatly impressed by the richness of content of such objects as compared to one's ideas about them. The same thing is true with regard to other classes of objects.

It is a mistake to regard non-conscious contents as "unconscious ideas." The so-called "unconscious idea" is not an idea at all but the content which an object has for the person, the way the object "figures" in the life and conduct of a given person. The content of the object is determined by those attitudes which one builds up toward the object. The non-symbolized contents of various objects have manifold complex relationships to one another. The manifestation of such relationships is what, in psychoanalysis, is called "unconscious equation." Psychoanalysis has definitely demonstrated that non-sym-

[5] A. Angyal, Disgust and related aversions, Journal of Abnormal and Social Psychology, 36:393–412, July 1941.

bolized content also exerts considerable influence on the conscious activity. It influences, for instance, the direction of associative trends. The method of "free association" is based on this fact.

The importance of the fact that the organism does not live in the world of the physicist but in an environment which is made up of objects each with a rich, highly individualized personal content cannot be sufficiently stressed. This biological world has its own genetic history. The content of the object grows mainly through personal experience. The child has his first experiences with the objects of his surroundings, and it will depend upon the nature of these experiences what attitudes he will build up toward them, what the content of the objects will be for him. Later, further and different kinds of experiences are made, new attitudes are built around the object, and its content will be more and more enriched. Some of the attitudes may fade away, some of the contents may be obscured, but they are seldom completely lost. The early experiences seem to leave especially deep imprints. If the content of an object is formed in a certain way at an early date, further modification will be increasingly difficult. There are many good examples in psychoanalytic literature of the persistence of childhood impressions, for instance, cases where in the ideas and attitudes of adults traces of infantile theories can be detected.

Since the objects of the environment are formed under the influence of such highly variable factors as personal experiences, one may say that every person has his own personal world consisting of objects, the content of which is highly individualistic and not comparable with the content they have for another person, even if from a physical point of view the objects are identical. It is important to keep this in mind, because even now one not infrequently speaks of similarity of environments because of the physical similarity of the surroundings. In studying personality it is extremely important to obtain an estimate of the individualistic content of the personal world, at least with regard to matters which are most crucial for the person. In other words, one should aim to obtain what I propose to call the "private vocabulary" of the person.

As stated above, individuals living in the same surroundings may live in very different environments. If one built an opera house in this city, it would mean a highly significant environmental change for the lover of music. It would mean an entirely different type of environmental change for the person who gets a job in the ticket office. For many people it would mean hardly any change in the environment at all.

The environment of a person is not fixed, even if the physical surroundings remain constant. It necessarily changes with the growth and decline of interests, with the changes of attitudes or ideas or, in general, with the change in the biospheric constellation.

In addition to personal experiences, another important factor has to be considered in the formation of the personal content of objects. We have relatively little contact with the primary objects of our surroundings. We are born into a world which is already laden with rich content by cultural definition. For example, the content of the word "pig" for most people in our culture is certainly not acquired by direct experience with that animal. The objects, when the child encounters them first, are not any longer primary objects of the surroundings, but have already culturally defined contents. The child has experience mostly with such culturally defined objects and modifies their content only according to the nature of his experiences. Thus, the content of the object will, on the whole, be a blend or a resultant of cultural definitions and personal experiences.

In recapitulation, then, we may say that on the object side biological relevancies are the counterpart of attitudes. Just as under proper conditions attitudes become actual drives, so also under proper conditions the biological relevancies become activated and thus become active valences which prompt specific responses on the part of the organism. The relevance of an object depends, on the one hand, upon the structure of the organism and, on the other, upon the personalized content of the biological object. By content is meant what the object is to the organism, and how it figures in its life process. The content of an object can best be characterized by the attitudes built around the object. It is in part culturally defined and in part built up under the influence of personal experiences.

C. *Axiomatic Values.* The biological environment has a definite organization. The biologically relevant object represents a value to an organism. Some of the values are subordinated to, or are instrumental for, some more general value which again may be subordinated to even more general ones. Tracing values back to more general ones, one is finally led to a few values of broad scope which, for a given person, are unquestionable. They are, for him, values in themselves or, as I propose to call them, "axiomatic values." The axiomatic values are the counterparts of the axioms of behavior. In the same manner as the axioms of behavior of a person form a system, so also the axiomatic values are organized into a system. This system of values is a working system, but not necessarily a conscious one. It is a determinant of behavior, although the person may pass no formal judgment of value. There is often considerable discrepancy between what the person consciously considers as value and the valuations which actually determine his behavior. A person may place, for example, personal integrity very high in the scale of values and give social recognition a rather low value. His behavior, however, may indicate that he is far more strongly motivated by social recognition than by personal integrity. I had a young patient who thought that his mother was dearer to him than anything else in life and that he would be even willing to die for her. He had a phobia of being poisoned and would not touch any food unless someone else tasted it first. The person whom he most frequently asked to test the possibly poisonous food was his mother. To demonstrate such discrepancies between conscious value and values which actually determine one's behavior one does not need to refer to pathological cases. They can be observed frequently enough in the daily life of average persons.

A system of axiomatic values like a system of axioms of behavior can be analyzed from the point of view of compatibility, discordance, and degree of integration.

SUMMARY

In this chapter have been defined some of the concepts which seem to be useful in studying personality dynamics. In the table on page 166 these concepts are systematically arranged.

Tensions have been defined as specific instances of dynamic subject-object relationships. Not only actual tensions are characteristic of the dynamics of the biosphere but also tendencies or potentialities to form certain types of tensions. These potentialities were called *readiness to tension*. Tension is a holistic term and is psychophysically neutral. The conscious experiences of tensions are the *interests*.

In a biospheric occurrence subject and object are bound together by a tensional relationship as an indivisible unit. Biospheric dynamics, however, can be described by placing the point of reference arbitrarily either in the subject or in the object.

Viewed from the *subject pole as a point of reference* the biospheric tensions appear as *drives*. Drives are part patterns of the general dynamic pattern of the organism. The general dynamic pattern of the organism branches off into more specific channels in a manner which is roughly comparable to the branching of a tree. It ends in the "terminal branches" of actual samples of behavior. Drives are psychophysically neutral. The conscious experience of a drive may be called *craving*. The concepts of drive and craving refer to dynamic patterns in the state of actual functioning. Drives are not continuously active but arise from a potential state. The organism can be more exactly characterized by its *readiness* for certain types of behavior rather than by actual drives. The readiness to behave in certain specific ways has been termed *attitude*. The way of functioning of the attitudes has been discussed briefly and the high economizing value of attitudes has been pointed out. They allow the organism to carry out a large number of functions with the aid of a relatively small number of instruments.

Any sample of behavior may be regarded as the manifestation of an attitude. Attitudes may be traced back successively to more and more general ones. In so doing one arrives at a limited number of very general attitudes which are unquestionable, axiomatic for a given person. These have been called *axioms of behavior*. When such axioms are intellectually elaborated we may speak of *maxims of behavior*. The axioms of behavior form a *system of personal axioms*. The system of maxims may be called a *philosophy of life*.

Biospheric tensions *viewed from the object pole* appear as environmental attractions or repulsions; to these the terms negative and positive *valences* can be applied. The valences prompt the organism to behave in one or another way. The organism may be attracted or repelled by the valence of an environmental situation without the valence being consciously experienced. The conscious experience of a valence may be called *demand quality*. We speak of the valence of an object when it exerts an actual prompting influence upon the organism. When the object has the potentiality of exerting such influence we may speak of the *biological relevance* of the object. The objects of the environment are relevant for the person essentially by virtue of their "meaning," or better, by virtue of their "*content*." The content of the object is different from what it would be by some common definition. The content of the biologically relevant object is highly individualized and personal. In the genesis of contents, cultural definitions and personal experience are the most important factors.

The biologically relevant object represents a value for

the organism. The specific values can be traced back to successively more general ones, until one finally reaches a rather limited number of fundamental personal values. These are *axiomatic values,* values in themselves; they are unquestionable for a given person. They form the *system of axiomatic personal values.* They often contain a large share of cultural material.

System of values	Axiomatic values	Relevance	Readiness to tension	Attitude	Axioms of behavior	System of axioms
		Valence	Tension	Drive		
		Demand quality	Interest	Craving		

In the preceding table in the first horizontal row are placed potential dynamic factors; in the second the dynamic factors in the state of actual function, and in the third horizontal row the conscious correlates of dynamic factors. In the middle vertical row are given those concepts which are obtained by looking at biospheric dynamics from a neutral point of view. On the right side of the table are placed the concepts which are obtained by viewing the biospheric dynamics with the subject as the point of reference, on the left side those concepts which are obtained by viewing the same biospheric factors with the object pole as a point of reference. The symmetry of the table is due to the fact that not different but identical phenomena have been considered, with the two opposite poles as points of reference.

VI. THE TREND TOWARD HOMONOMY

THE CONCEPT OF HOMONOMY

THUS far we have discussed the biological total process from a rather solipsistic point of view. We have considered the individual organism as if it were standing alone in the world facing its environment. This abstraction facilitated the presentation of the material. The picture thus obtained shows, however, only one aspect of living. In order to penetrate deeper into the problem of personality we must go beyond a purely individualistic point of view and consider the problem of the integration of the individual into superindividual units.

The individual organism does not stand alone in the world. It derives its existence genetically from other organisms of the same type. The individual is but one member of a phylogenetic chain. An outstanding theoretical biologist, Uexküll, makes the following statement: "I believe that it cannot be doubted that each species presents a real living being with specific characteristics, but of an unusually long life duration."[1] One

[1] J. von Uexküll, Theoretische Biologie, 2d ed., Berlin, Springer, 1928, p. 182. A similar point of view is expressed also in L. von Bertalanffy, Theoretische Biologie, Berlin, Gebrüder Bornträger, 1932, vol. 1, p. 274.

may be disinclined to go as far as does Uexküll, and one may hesitate to consider the species as a sort of a more inclusive real individual—this depends upon one's criterion of individuality—but the phylogenetic integration of the individual remains a fact, nevertheless.

The human individual, besides its general phylogenetic integration, is a member of a family, a member of a social group, a participant in a culture, a part of nature, and, in the broadest sense, a part of a cosmic order. Thus a person does not lead a purely individual life, but also a family life, a social life, a cultural life, in which he participates and which he shares with others. The individual existences are at the same time co-carriers of the existence of superindividual units, somewhat in a similar way that the cells of an organism are not only the loci of cell life but participants and carriers of the life of the total organism.

Life, even on the somatic level, is not a purely individualistic process. There are also certain interindividual somatic processes of which copulation is a good example. A striking example of intra-individual physiology is the relationship between child and mother during the intra-uterine life of the former. During this period the physiology of child and mother are intimately connected. A great number of processes take place in the mother organism which are biologically understandable only with reference to another organism, the child. Even after birth there still remains a close physiological tie between mother and child: the process of lactation. The secretion of the mammary glands when regarded as an intra-organismic process is biologically meaningless. It gains a biological significance only with reference to the nutrition of the child. The postnatal parent-child relationship well illustrates interhuman integration. The closeness of the ties between parent and offspring depends on the degree of maturation of the latter at birth, which varies greatly from one species to another. The so-called lower animals are, as a rule, highly matured at birth, while higher animals, man especially, are born at a very early stage of maturation. A young chicken, for instance, shortly after hatching walks, feeds itself, and in many other respects behaves in a manner which is characteristic for the species. The human child, on the contrary, is born very immature. The greater part of maturation takes place after birth. This process does not depend on the child alone, but is possible only with parental aid. After birth the child could not survive and develop further by its own resources alone. Parental care is a natural component of the maturation process. One could figuratively say that parental care is "counted upon" by nature; it is a biologically necessary arrangement. The process of extra-uterine maturation, including parental assistance, has a biological importance for the development of the child equal to that of any of the physiological processes of the intra-uterine development.

Parental care includes not only aids for the physiological needs of the child, but also the establishment of certain basic behavior patterns, the transmission of language, and socialization. These, too, are biological facts in a broader sense—they are necessary for the life of the individual in a human community. In the process of socialization the young individual is aided not only by the family group, but also by other persons with whom he comes in contact, by the community at large, and by social institutions.

The integration of the individual into the social group, the assimilation of its culture, of its written and unwritten codes, are just as essential for the personality development and personality organization as any of the physiological functions. Thus it appears that personality is a larger unit than a mere individual organism, because it also includes those factors through which it functions as a participant in the superindividual units of society and culture.

The integration of the individual into superindividual units is not restricted to membership in a phylogenetic succession, in a family, a society, and a culture. Man in his religious attitude experiences himself as a member of a meaningful cosmic order. Ethical and esthetic attitudes as well as numerous forms of everyday behavior seem to transcend the scope of a strictly individualistic life, and a definite trend toward superindividual goals is discernible in them.

The direction and range of sharing may greatly vary.

One person may turn toward religion, another toward some social unit, but one has to have some object for one's homonomous tendency. One may be identified with the human race or go even further and include all living beings as St. Francis of Assisi did. The range of identification and sharing may be on the other hand quite restricted. One may be antisocial to the larger community but highly loyal to the gang. There are people who are ready to make every sacrifice for a small group, a family, or even a single person, and are even prepared to kill the outsider in the interest of that small group.

The objective existence of superindividual wholes is a problem for philosophy and as students of personality we need not be concerned with such problems. Whether the world as a whole actually represents a meaningful organization, or whether there is an ethical order in the world, or even whether or not a social group can be regarded as a true unitary whole with "emergent" qualities, is immaterial for a science of personality. For the study of personality it is important only to recognize that man's attitudes are to a large extent oriented toward superindividual units. Since such attitudes represent a powerful source of human motivation, they are vitally important factors in personality organization, irrespective of whether the superindividual wholes may be revealed by philosophical analysis to be real or fictitious.

The attitude of the person toward the superindividual units of which he feels himself a part, or wishes to become a part, is very different from the self-assertive tendency (the trend toward increased autonomy) which has been discussed in the previous chapters. While the trend toward increased autonomy aims at the domination of the surroundings, the characteristic attitude toward superindividual wholes is rather a kind of submerging or subordination of one's individuality in the service of superindividual goals. In this latter trend a person seeks union with larger units and wishes to share and participate in something which he regards as being greater than his individual self. This principle reminds one of the concept of Eros, the great uniting principle, except that the Eros of the ancient Greeks was thought of as a cosmic force, while the concept which we are formulating here refers exclusively to personality occurrences. For this principle we propose the term *"trend toward homonomy,"* that is, a trend to be in harmony with superindividual units, the social group, nature, God, ethical world order, or whatever the person's formulation of it may be. I wish again to emphasize that for the present purpose it is entirely immaterial whether such formulations are founded in reality or whether they are illusory. The particular formulation of a given person is not of immediate importance in this context. Only the fact that a trend toward homonomy is easily discernible in everyone's life is important. I do not mean by this only that everybody has some moments in his life when he thinks of "higher things." If such attitudes were only exceptional phenomena, they would be of interest only as *curiosa,* and they would have little significance for the study of personality. I hope, however, that the discussions in the following chapters will show with sufficient clarity that the trend toward homonomy penetrates the whole realm of human life. Pure manifestations of this trend may be rare, but in combination with other trends it is a practically constant co-determinant of behavior. The trend toward homonomy, because of its combination with other tendencies, may be obscured and distorted, but it is my contention that without it human behavior cannot be understood.

The trend toward increased autonomy and the trend toward homonomy seem to form a dichotomy of diametrically opposed forces. The first trend is distinctly individualistic. It is a self-assertion of the organism, it tends to master and govern the environmental happenings, it aims at achievement and conquest. In the trend toward homonomy the emphasis is displaced from the individual to the collective, to superindividual wholes in which the person tends to submerge himself. The goals of the homonomous trends are sharing, participation, union.

The antagonism between the two principles is probably only apparent. While the organism in its autonomous trend extends its influence over increasingly large fields of events, in its homonomous trend, although submerging itself in superindividual wholes, it does not destroy itself. On the contrary, by identifying oneself with and experiencing oneself as part of superindividual wholes, one expands beyond the narrower individual self. Thus, for instance, merging into a social group does not mean the loss of one's personality, but means its broadening beyond purely individualistic limits.

The two trends may be regarded as two phases of a more inclusive process. In the trend toward increased autonomy the biologically chaotic items of the environment are fitted into the organization of the individual's life, while in the homonomous tendency the individual seeks to fit himself into even larger organizations.

The dynamics of the autonomous and homonomous aspects of behavior, however, are sufficiently different from one another to deserve separate discussion. Unfortunately, too little scientifically useful information is available at present concerning man's homonomous attitudes and behavior to allow generalizations. Certain points of distinction, however, can be at least briefly indicated.

The autonomous trend expresses itself in a variety of cravings. For the homonomous tendencies, on the other hand, the concept of craving is not quite adequate and it seems that "longing" would be a more appropriate term for such tendencies. One does not say that a person is craving for human contact, friendship, love, beauty, or that a religious person is craving for God, but says that one is "longing" for it. The goal of autonomous craving is always taking possession, domination, mastery of the object or, in general, the subordination of outside factors to the organism. In homonomous expression, on the other hand, the person wishes to unite himself with, to belong to, to share and participate in the object of his longing.

The homonomous trend is directed toward the environment. Environment is the totality of those factors within the biosphere which do not follow the organism's determination, which are not centralized, do not depend upon the organism, but are "random" from the point of view of the individual. The environment from the point of view of the organism is largely a chaos, and the autonomous tendency of the organism is to organize these factors and to coordinate them with the organism which acts as a governing center. The object of the homonomous trend, on the contrary, is not the environment, not a collection of random and alien factors, but meaningful wholes of which he feels himself to be a part or wishes to become a part.

Autonomous behavior is characteristically restless and drives toward advancement, while homonomous behavior has a more peaceful character and aims at permanency. The gratification of cravings is short-lived and is soon followed by renewed craving and one wishes it to be so. One does not merely wish to be satiated; one also wants to get hungry again. People usually do not wish lasting satiation—even less an everlasting one—but they do want, for instance, lasting friendship or love. The autonomous behavior reminds one of the continuously changing, becoming world of Heraclitus, while homonomous behavior is rather reminiscent of the world picture of Plato.

In autonomous behavior the individual is *stimulated* by situations and *responds* to them; homonomous behavior, on the other hand, proceeds by *impressions* and *expressions*. The clearest examples of impression and expression are to be found in esthetic enjoyment and in esthetic creativeness. A satisfactory distinction between stimulus-response, on the one hand, and impression-expression, on the other, is still wanting. One of the distinguishing features between stimulus and impression seems to be that the first stirs up some form of self-assertive activity, while the latter has rather the character of a *resonance:* it is the experience of harmony or of the correspondence of one's person with that which impresses one. Thus, for example, a tree standing alone in a meadow may cause a deep esthetic impression in an individual because it corresponds to his inner loneliness. Such a connection need not be conscious to the person. The death of nature in autumn may awaken forebodings of one's own death. Through the correspondences between that which is outside and that which is inside, one's individual problem is, so to say, extended into the realm of the superindividual and in this way a certain kind of unity between man and nature is experienced.

Response is directed toward moulding and conquering the environment, while expression tends to repeat, to present in some tangible form, relationships between the individual and the superindividual. Even in very primitive forms of artistic expression where the main purpose seems to be an imitation or duplication of the object, a superindividual trend is detectable. To imitate means to create an object which should resemble or represent some other object, to mirror one thing in another, to create some inner unity between the *discreta* and thus break down individualistic limits.

Common observation and various investigations in personality problems show with sufficient clarity that man's behavior in general is determined only to a rather slight extent by intellect and is to a very large extent non-rational. On examining the differences between autonomous and homonomous behavior it appears that in autonomous behavior rationalistic supports are utilized to a considerable extent, while homonomous behavior is more deeply rooted in man's non-rational nature. In driving toward achievement man is led to a great extent by knowledge and he wishes to have proofs and certainty as guiding factors. On the other hand, in his homonomous behavior the person is guided essentially by non-rational factors—for instance, faith. The non-rational character of homonomous behavior makes it an especially difficult object of study. The difficulty lies not alone in the nature of the subject-matter—the non-rationality of phenomena does not preclude the possibility of study—but also in the prevalent bias of our day when everything which does not fit into an intellectualistic frame is likely to be looked upon as mysticism. But even though one sets aside every metaphysical problem concerning man's homonomous behavior, the trend toward homonomy as a source of profound motivation for human behavior may not be ignored. The overwhelming factual evidence compels its consideration.

The trend toward homonomy is manifest in common, everyday behavior, but can best be studied in the realm of social, artistic, and religious attitudes. Even in these fields, however, the trend toward homonomy does not manifest itself in "pure culture," but is intermingled with other elements. Taking, for instance, any religion as defined in the historical religious codes, it can be easily seen that it contains elements which have very different origins and character. Religion contains, besides its homonomous features—the sharing in a meaningful cosmic order—many other elements, such as science, law, cosmology, and a great deal of magic. The magical element is, for instance, fairly evident in many forms of prayer. Magic is an attempt to coerce or bribe (by offerings) or to persuade the supernatural forces to do what one wants of them. Those forms of prayer in which one wishes to obtain something are somewhat reminiscent of magical practices. There are, on the other hand, also certain other forms of prayer which express more clearly the trend toward homonomy. Nor are artistic pursuits and social behavior pure expressions of the trend toward homonomy. They contain many other elements. The forms in which the trend expresses itself are manifold. A rather intellectualistic expression is what Spinoza called a consideration *"sub specie aeternitatis,"* that is, the consideration of an individual fact not as it is in itself but as it appears in a cosmic perspective. An emotional expression of the trend toward homonomy is a feeling of union. As an extreme example of the latter, there may be mentioned states described as ecstasies or as experiences of mystic union. Such states are, of course, exceptional and are mentioned only as the extreme form of expression of a very common trend.

The prevalence of autonomous or of homonomous tendencies, respectively, is quite characteristic of a given person and might possibly serve as a basis for typological differentiations. One person is almost exclusively motivated in his behavior by the goal of self-expansion, ego-maximation, personal achievement. Another person's behavior is to a larger extent determined by social, religious, artistic, and similar attitudes characterized by the subordination of one's personal ambitions to superindividual, or social, goals. The culminations of such types are—to mention again only the very extremes—the creative artist, the saint, and the hero.

A certain degree of homonomous expression is absolutely necessary for normal adjustment. Self-centeredness, being wrapped up in oneself, inability to "loosen up," to get out of oneself, is a well-recognized characteristic of many forms of personality disorder. In such persons there seems to be a fear of self-abandonment, as if the "loosening up" would involve the peril of losing oneself or the destruction of the self. One wonders whether expressions like "I feel all tied up in a knot," which one occasionally hears from acute schizophrenic patients, do not refer to precisely this factor. The lack of ability for self-abandonment shows clearly its deleterious effects on social adjustments, especially sex adjustment.

The merging into superindividual wholes, the sharing and participation in larger units, is a powerful support of mental health. By a homonomous attitude, that is, by experiencing oneself as a small part of the world, one's personal sufferings and troubles are considerably reduced. One is then able to see one's own problem in a universal perspective and in a more or less correct proportion. Not the gravity of one's difficulties alone is responsible for upsetting the functioning of personality, but also the lack of a sense of proportion. A person may be so much wrapped up in himself and so isolated from everything leading beyond his individuality that his own individual being is the whole world for him, and whatever happens in this individual sphere—since there is nothing which matters beyond this—assumes gigantic proportions. An example of this can be seen in certain forms of schizophrenic disorder, in which the disorganization of the person is experienced as a cosmic catastrophe.

Through the subordination of one's individual cravings to superindividual goals the person may derive an extraordinary strength which enables him to display heroism and lends him courage to endure pain and to face even death. One is often impressed by the endurance, efficiency, and courage of some social leaders. Such qualities, however, may not be ascribed only to the individual make-up of the person. They are derived, to a large extent, from identification with the group. One to whom the safety of a group is entrusted may be able to do things of which he would be incapable when pursuing purely individualistic aims.

By way of a summary our point of view may be restated thus: besides a trend toward self-expansion, increased autonomy, a second trend has also to be examined for an understanding of human behavior. This trend, which we call the trend toward homonomy, is based on the experience of being a part of meaningful superindividual wholes such as the family, social group, meaningful world order. The person's homonomous attitude toward such superindividual entities consists in a tendency to submerge himself, participate, and share in those larger units and to conform to them.

Some objective evidence was mentioned in support of the integration of the individual into superindividual formations. The functions of procreation show that man's behavior, even on the somatic level, is not merely an individualistic affair but is explicable by definitely interindividual somatic processes. The objective existence of superindividual wholes, however, is a metaphysical problem and not a matter of immediate interest for an empirical scientist. For the student of personality the only important fact is that the trend toward homonomy —the tendency to conform to, unite with, participate in, and fit into superindividual wholes—is a powerful motivating force in behavior, irrespective of whether philosophical analysis affirms the objective existence of superindividual units or proves them to be illusory. Artistic, religious, and social behavior may serve as comparatively pure examples of the trend toward homonomy. The trend toward homonomy appears in numerous forms of common, everyday behavior but usually occurs in an intricate interconnection with other tendencies which derive from the self-expansive trend. Thus homonomous manifestations frequently appear greatly distorted.

The analysis of artistic and religious behavior would involve too many problems for the specialist and cannot be attempted here. We wish, however, to discuss briefly and in a general way some aspects of social behavior because of its great significance for the study of personality.

SOCIAL INTEGRATION

As a matter of convenience we may consider certain general features of social organization by describing it on two more or less arbitrarily selected planes: the symbiotic and the cultural level. It should be understood, however, that no particular weight is attached to this distinction. Its purpose is to facilitate our presentation. An attempt to differentiate too sharply between these two aspects of actual social behavior may, on the other hand, be rather artificial.

A. *The Symbiotic Level.* The simplest level of social integration is one which could be called the "symbiotic level." On this level society is a cooperative organization. The activities of human beings have become so complex that no single person is able to provide what he considers the necessities of life on his own account. Many human activities and the products of such activities are not the results of an individual undertaking but of the coordinated efforts of many individuals. The building of a bridge, the production of a book, or agricultural production are results of coordinated efforts, each individual doing his share in a specialized, segmental way. Such organization is based on the principle of division of labor. Since, in such a system, a single individual does not produce as large a variety of things as is needed by him, but overproduces in some specialized field, the necessity arises for a distribution of goods or exchange of values. The undisturbed running of such an organization has to be ensured by certain codes (laws) which regulate the behavior of the individual within this organization. In order to make such regulations effective they must be supported by a sufficient power of enforcement. Thus it may be said that social organization on the symbiotic level is based on division of labor and exchange of values, and is regulated by codes which are supported by a power of enforcement.

The structure of this system as such, that is, the study of institutions, is a direct topic not for the student of personality but for students of sociology, economics, technology, law, and the like. Personality problems arise, however, when we consider the individual's behavior within such a system and the problem of social adjustment on this level. The interhuman relationships on a symbiotic level are, by definition, not very deep. In such interaction mechanical devices could be and actually often are substituted for the individual. Even on this level, however, the actual behavior is not quite so simple as it would be by definition. Even so simple a situation as purchasing merchandise may involve more than a simple exchange of values. Other interhuman relations like sympathy, antipathy, confidence, distrust may be involved. Man, merely as a participant in economic organization, the *homo economicus,* is only a fiction.

Man's participation in a symbiotic social organization would be possible also without any homonomous tendencies. Division of labor and exchange of values are only practical means for obtaining what one thinks necessary for oneself. Personality problems arise in connection with the integration of the individual into the economic organization: problems of adjustment, of establishing one's place in the economic system, and so on. Theoretically these problems are rather simple, but practically they are very important. In this organization one has to allow a place for the production of sufficient exchange value. One has to have some occupation, the products of which can be "sold" to others. In order to obtain this, one has to struggle against difficulties which may lie in outside circumstances or in the person. Working capacity may be impaired because of physical handicaps or personality difficulties. Impairment of working capacity through personality difficulties is a common practical problem in psychiatric practice.

One can appreciate readily the importance of occupational behavior if one considers that the average person is engaged during the greater part of the day in exactly such activities. Good occupational adjustment requires that one's work should not only supply one with sufficient exchange value but should also satisfy some other needs of the person. Occupation should be a well-integrated part of the total personality organization. It has been repeatedly shown, for instance, that—quite apart from material gain—work can be more efficiently done if it has some inner meaning for the person.

A symbiotic relationship may degenerate and become a one-sided, or parasitic, relationship, and it may become a problem for the student of personality, especially for the psychiatrist. He may have to deal with parasitic attitudes, especially in certain forms of psychopathic personality. He may also have to face the problem of the "host" and to deal with the motives which lead a person to tolerate parasitic ties. The practical problems which may arise on the symbiotic level with regard to adjustment are numerous, but, as has been said before, they are of a relatively small theoretical interest.

The symbiotic integration not only provides a regulated method of production and exchange, but also offers possible outlets for various human tendencies. It gives outlets for such autonomous tendencies as competition, control of others, striving for higher places in the symbiotic structure, which apart from the material gain carry the advantages or prestige of higher rank. Homonomous tendencies may also express themselves in this system. In a symbiotic working group, loyalties, identification with the group, and similar tendencies may arise.

B. *The Cultural Aspect of Interhuman Integration.*[2] Interhuman behavior can be studied with considerably greater profit on the level of cultural integration than on

[2] In the academic year 1932–1933 the writer was a member of a research group studying the problem "Impact of culture on personality" which was sponsored by the Rockefeller Foundation. The group was composed of students of various scientific fields such as psychology, cultural anthropology, sociology, criminology, and psychiatry and was under the scientific direction of the late Dr. E. Sapir of Yale University. If I succeeded in gaining any insight into the problem of culture and personality I owe it in a great degree to this year of study and especially to Dr. Sapir. The point of view expressed in this paragraph follows rather closely that of Dr. Sapir in some respects, even if occasionally I may have paraphrased it.

the merely symbiotic level. Culture can be defined as an organized body of behavior patterns which is transmitted by social inheritance, that is, by tradition, and which is characteristic of a given area or group of people. Culture as such is a mere abstraction which becomes reality only when the individual participates in it; it exists only in the actual behavior of people. Culture as such is a subject of study for the cultural anthropologist, while for the student of personality it is a subject of study only in so far as it manifests itself in actual behavior.

Every culture is characterized by a number of generalized and rather definite attitudes, of socially approved or disapproved (tabooed) ways of doing things. Culturally sanctioned or disapproved behavior patterns form partly written but mostly unwritten cultural codes.

The cultural definition of doing things "properly" or "improperly" extends to practically all spheres of life. Cultural determinations are superimposed also on the primary physical functions such as sex, food intake, and excretory functions. Sex behavior, for instance, is to a large measure culturally patterned in every society. Culture defines the modes of courtship, proper or improper ways of intercourse, and regulates intermarriage by an often highly complicated system of laws and taboos. It defines what kind of behavior is proper to men and to women respectively. It may emphasize the differences between the sexes in the way of clothing, occupation, and etiquette. In certain Western cultures drinking, smoking, the use of certain words are permitted to men, but strongly tabooed for women. Differences of temperament, degrees of independence, and other personality qualities which one frequently considers as the biologically distinguishing characteristics of the sexes are to a great extent the results of cultural training. Even where real biological differences are present they may be grossly exaggerated, occasionally diminished, or in some other way modified by cultural influences.

Food intake is another physiological function which is greatly influenced by cultural patterns. Dietary restrictions are present almost everywhere. Many people may not be even aware of the number of culturally defined dietary habits in our Western culture. Many people in our culture would certainly refuse to drink the milk or eat the meat of a horse, while drinking the milk or eating the meat of the cow is regarded as proper. We have many rules regarding what is and what is not eatable which have no biological basis whatsoever. In some European cultures it is considered highly improper to start the first meal of the day with fruit, while in England or America that is the proper thing to do. Even such a thing as whether a certain mixture of foodstuffs is "tasty" or not is not entirely biologically determined, but is to a large extent a result of culturally defined habits. In some cultures a mixture of sweet things with meat would be regarded as disgusting; in others it is considered "tasty." The psychologists David and Rosa Katz[3] made the following experiment. For a certain period of time they allowed their children to take from the food placed on the table whatever they wanted and to mix it as they wished. The children made and ate with apparent delight mixtures which to an adult European would be abhorrent.

The evaluation of certain minor physiological manifestations varies greatly from culture to culture. For instance, belching in the presence of others is a very improper act in the Western culture. If that happens the proper thing to do in Europe is to feign that one hadn't noticed it and the European finds it quite improper when, for instance, an American excuses himself on such an occasion, since by so doing he calls attention to a fact which should be allowed to pass unnoticed. On the other hand, in India belching is a very proper way of paying a compliment to the host for the excellence of the food. In Turkey a similar compliment is paid by making frequent smacking noises which in Western society would be regarded as bad manners. Also the excretory functions as well as many other physical functions are patterned by cultural influences.

Cultural rules and restrictions refer not only to primarily physiological functions but to a greater extent even to the modes of social intercourse. One could point

[3] D. Katz and R. Katz, Psychologische Untersuchungen über Hunger und Appetit, Archiv für die gesamte Psychologie, 65:269–320, July 1928.

to innumerable examples concerning, for instance, the codes of etiquette in various cultures.

As in the individual, so also in culture attitudes can be traced back to certain unquestionable axioms of behavior. A culturally determined behavior axiom is, for instance, the general acceptance of magic in certain societies. The basic axioms of a culture form a more or less integrated philosophy of life which is characteristic for a given society. Such cultural philosophies of life can be roughly characterized by certain leading principles. If, for instance, one had to point out some of the leading principles of American culture one would have to consider such points as: a philosophy of self-help, the ideal of the self-made man—an ideal which historically is probably a derivation of the pioneer attitude. As further characteristics one could mention an essentially optimistic attitude toward life ("prosperity is just around the corner") and a strong faith in progress; an overvaluation of visible greatness, which is expressed not only in such objects as the skyscrapers of New York but also, for instance, in the Rotarian slogan of "bigger and better things"; a high valuation of achievement mainly in terms of practical, visible results. The American attitude toward life can be characterized, at least roughly, by these and some other points. The leading idea of life in India may be a special form of self-perfection. It is possible to work out the leading attitudes of various cultures and thus roughly characterize the various regional philosophies of life, and thus to obtain a kind of cultural typology.

As in the individual, so also in cultures there may be considerable discrepancies between the attitudes which actually govern behavior and the awareness or intellectual formulation of such attitudes. The present writer had the opportunity to observe such discrepancies in an international group of students where once the task was put to each member to describe the leading principles of his own culture. Thus one heard that the ideals of Chinese life were loyalty to friend, family, and state; that the social structure in China would follow the family structure, the head of the state being the head of this large family and loyalty being the real tie in such an organization. One heard that a sense of honor is the leading principle of Japanese life. In another cultural group bravery was said to be the moving spirit of the people. In every case the generalization sounded too good to be true. It is an intellectual formulation—a rationalization rather than an active principle. Cultures have their own rationalizations. One may, for instance, consider the multitude of cultural rationalizations justifying racial hatred or the aggression of one nation against another. Rationalizations, however, are not merely ineffectual ideas; they may have secondarily a strong motivating power. Even if it were not true, for example, that the Japanese are led in their behavior by a sense of honor and this were only a rationalization of other traits, still it may become a secondary source of motivation. A demagogue, for instance, could probably count on most success by appealing to the sense of honor of the Japanese, to the loyalty of the Chinese, to the bravery of the Iroquois.

Culture defines the *meaning* of objects and of various forms of behavior and by such definitions lends them positive or negative values. Culture defines what form of behavior is worthy and what is reprehensible. Thus, the various cultures have their own system of values which are added to or superimposed on primary biological values and become forces of attraction or repulsion respectively to the individual. One seeks or avoids many things, not because of their primary physiological relevance for the organism, but because they are culturally proclaimed as desirable or undesirable. Out of sheer physiological need no one would, for instance, wear such an uncomfortable object as a top hat. One may have a special liking for caviar or some other expensive food, not primarily because of the satisfaction of a physiological need, but because it symbolizes social and economic status. It is interesting to note how intimately physiological and cultural significance may blend so that in the end the desirability of an expensive food may appear to the person a true physiological attraction: he may find it especially tasty.

Cultures, like individuals, have what we have called (page 160) figuratively a "private vocabulary." It is much easier to understand the behavior of people of one's own culture than that of members of other cultures because one "speaks the same language." It is well known that one of the most common sources of error in anthropological studies is the tendency to interpret the behavior of other people in terms of one's own culture.

It is the great merit of modern cultural anthropology to have demonstrated the relativity of cultures. For instance, a given behavior may in one culture be considered as an expression of thrift and valued as a virtue, while in another culture an apparently very similar behavior may be considered avarice and be condemned. In general one can state that whatever cultural pattern one examines one finds that it is not generally valid for the human race, but varies greatly from one culture to another. Insight into the relativity of cultures warns us not to regard all forms of behavior as direct expressions of man's biological nature, and gives us a practical lesson in tolerance. This insight, however, should not be exaggerated; it would be false to regard behavior as entirely the product of culture. There is no such dissociation between man's biological nature and his culture. All culturally determined behavior patterns must give some outlet to man's fundamental tendencies in spite of the fact that the *form of expression* may be culturally determined and may show great variation from one culture to another.

The knowledge of cultural relativity teaches us to be cautious in making judgments concerning the various manifestations of behavior. The unsophisticated person is apt to regard the behavior which is customary in his own culture as the only "proper" behavior possible. Even in anthropological research not long ago a naïvely evolutionistic point of view was quite common. One used to distinguish between primitive and more highly developed cultures, implying thereby that the latter was better and more perfected than the former. Although such a view is untenable, it would be unjustifiable to go to the other extreme and deny that certain behavior patterns are more adequate than others. One behavior pattern may be more in agreement with man's nature than another.

The basic cultural attitudes which make up the philosophy of a culture may be rather closely integrated with each other, or may show a considerable degree of discrepancy. Cultures may vary in the number and intensity of the conflicts that they make possible. If, for instance, the positive evaluation and the condemnation of premarital sex relations coexist in a given culture, that culture is not well integrated in that particular respect and presents a source of conflict. Cultures usually contain also a smaller or larger number of behavior patterns which are distinctly contrary to man's nature and therefore unhealthy. Such unhealthy attitudes can be traced to various sources. Frequently they are based on false beliefs or theories. For instance, the use of excreta in primitive medical practice may be based on the theory of homeopathy, the principle of driving out one evil through the agency of another. Other unhealthy elements in culture can be understood on a historical basis. In the course of time an originally useful practice may lose its significance, but it may still persist afterward as an incongruous factor in culture.

Cultures change very slowly. If a cultural pattern is outmoded and has lost its significance, it is not as a rule dropped at once but may persist and usually gains a new function which is entirely different from the original one. For example, the collar was originally a part of the warrior's equipment, a protection for the throat; today this function is entirely lost. In the meantime the collar has taken on a different meaning as an object of ornamentation and as a symbol of social status.

Culture becomes significant for the study of personality in two different respects. First, the relation of the person to culture presents a problem of adjustment. As social structure on the symbiotic level, so also culture on a different level is an organization in which one has to live, in which one has to find one's place, with which one has to get along. Briefly, culture on this level is an external factor, a medium to which one has to adjust. It is true that the cultural codes are mostly unwritten mores, folkways, and the like, and many of them lack a legal power of enforcement. They have, however, an unofficial but none the less strong compulsiveness. The common penalty for offending cultural codes is relative or complete ostracism. This punishment is severe enough since it frustrates a deep-seated trend of personality, the trend toward homonomy, the trend to belong to, to participate and share in society.

Besides the problem of adjustment, culture becomes significant for the person in still another and more intimate fashion. Culture does not remain merely an outside factor with which one has to get along. Cultural patterns are also assimilated by and integrated with the total personality. They become internal factors, a part of the person. The person thus acquires an individual culture, his personal standards and definitions of doing things in the proper and improper ways.

One of the most important problems of personality in relation to culture is the problem of determining the ways in which the broader culture is assimilated, how it becomes part of the personality. The culture of an area, Western culture, for instance, is only an abstract and very general frame. Within the broader cultures there are more specific, narrower cultural units, cultures of smaller groups of people, such as the culture of the "four hundred," of the gang, of the family.

The culture of the family is extremely important for personality studies because this is the mediating link through which the broader regional culture reaches the child. This is the culture which will become fundamental for the person, although later it will be modified through the influences of the school, the street, and so on. Each family has its own cultural atmosphere, specific values, meanings, approved and disapproved ways of doing things, ideals and taboos, unwritten rules defining order of rank and other relations between the members of the family. Family culture, although it follows rather closely the lines determined by the broader regional culture, is more concrete and more specific than the latter.

Cultural patterns become even more concrete and more specific when they are assimilated by the individual. Since culture is assimilated by the individual and becomes a vital part of his personality, we may rightly speak of the "culture of the individual." This aspect of the personality roughly corresponds to what in psychoanalysis is called "the super-ego." The psychoanalytic evaluation of the significance of the super-ego in the personality organization differs, however, in some respects from the present concept. The super-ego in psychoanalysis is not considered as a primary factor of personality, but something which is imposed on it artificially. In psychoanalysis the super-ego seems to be more or less a necessary evil which, even though it facilitates social existence, is rather a disturbing factor in the personality organization. Contrary to this we claim that the assimilated cultural patterns, that is, the super-ego, correspond to very basic needs of the person because they allow the expression of homonomous tendencies.

The significance of culture for the person is twofold. First, it has utilitarian economic significance. It is a great advantage that the individual does not have to work out standards of behavior for each department of life by himself, but gets them ready-made by social inheritance. A more important function of culture is that it provides an outlet for one's homonomous trend. The common culture binds people together. It provides possibilities for belonging to and participating in a group. This need is not a luxury or a superstructure, but a part of man's very nature.

As pointed out, culture has a twofold relevance for the personality: as a complex of environmental factors to which one has to adjust and as a part of the personality organization. With regard to the latter aspect, important problems such as the integration of the personal culture, the super-ego, with the rest of the personality and the changes in one's personal culture in the course of life will have to be considered.

The influence of change of culture has been studied mainly by sociologists, for instance in connection with the problem of immigration. In such studies many important facts have been established. It was shown, for instance, that the first generation of immigrants is, on the whole, a fairly well-adjusted group, while in the second generation maladjustment is a frequent occurrence. The explanation is sought in the fact that the children of immigrants are not sufficiently firmly rooted in the old culture and have not sufficiently assimilated the new.

Change of cultural milieu occurs not only in the case

of migration, but is a general feature of personality development. The person comes in contact successively with groups of people of various cultural standards and is continuously exposed to these influences. It is a widely held opinion that strict standards, that is, standards which strongly limit free instinctual expression, are harmful to the personality. One has to consider, however, that the shift from strict to looser standards may also be traumatic for the person and be causative of maladjustment. It is not an infrequent occurrence that a girl from a cultural milieu with rigid sex codes after being transplanted into an environment where sex codes are more liberal may superficially accept the new codes in order to be "like the others," but consequently she may break down with a neurosis. Thus one sees that shifts from strict to liberal cultural standards, or vice versa, have their dangers.

The factor of acculturalization makes a person out of a human organism. The term personality derives from the Latin *persona:* an individual carrying out a role. We carry out a role in the social organization, we represent parts with specific functions in the symbiotic organization of society and our special part in more complex social relationships. Personality is a holistic quality because the individual derives it from the relationship to society or to other superordinate wholes of which he is a part. The qualities of leader or follower, a good or a bad reputation, an agreeable or a disagreeable personality are not properties of the individual as such but properties relative to others. To a large extent we participate in society not with our individual selves but with our "social selves," not with that which we are in ourselves but what we mean to others. If one reviews the terms which one uses to characterize a person, one will find that a large percentage of them refer to characteristics of the social self. May[4] defines personality as "what the others think of us." Lange-Eichbaum[5] in his study of genius holds a similar point of view. Since it is the social self which enters into social relationships, one can understand why people make so much effort in order to establish a satisfactory social self: to win reputation, fame, prestige, and the like. To restrict the term personality to the social self does not seem practical, however, because the latter is intimately connected with other factors. We use the term personality to denote the total organism when, as in man, the latter includes the social self and other factors which bind the individual into superindividual relationships.

THE SUBJECT-MATTER OF SOCIAL PSYCHOLOGY

The study of the social aspect of the personality is still in its beginnings. Most of what passes today as social psy-

[4] M. A. May, The foundations of personality, *in* P. S. Achilles, ed., Psychology at Work, New York, Whittlesey House, McGraw-Hill, 1932.

[5] W. Lange-Eichbaum, Genie, Irrsinn und Ruhm, Munich, Reinhardt, 1928.

chology touches only on the periphery of the social aspect of man. If one surveys the articles in the journals devoted to this topic one finds that a great percentage of them are concerned either with problems of racial differences (for instance, a comparative study of the intelligence of white and Negro children), or with the study of public opinion (for instance, what college students think of some political change). It would, however, be more important to know what is going on between people in actual social intercourse. Some of the problems which may be of great interest in understanding interhuman relations may be mentioned here.

It seems, first of all, that we need to know more about the motivations and attitudes involved in interhuman behavior. Motivations for social behavior derive either from autonomous or homonomous sources. Usually both types of factors are involved and intricately interconnected in various proportions in any given interhuman relation. The degree of autonomous and of homonomous motivations respectively can serve as a fairly satisfactory criterion for a preliminary classification.

There are interhuman relationships in which the other person is regarded like the rest of the environment, something which has to be conquered, dominated, and used for one's own purposes. Such relationships are based on autonomous attitudes. An extreme form of it is slavery. In a milder form such a tendency constitutes one aspect of many interhuman relations. Such attitudes do not necessarily involve obvious cruelty to the other person. The other person is useful to one just as a domestic animal, from which one can gain some profit, is useful. The value of the other person is an instrumental one: he is worth as much as the use that can be made of him.

A somewhat more socialized form of interhuman relationships is that in which one still wants to obtain something from the other person, but something which only socialized beings, persons, can give. Such is the case, for instance, when a person is trying to obtain recognition or fame, to be admired by others. Such an attitude is still quite egocentric. The other person is only one's public, a possible admirer, somebody from whom one may obtain recognition. The good which one wants to obtain is, however, a *social* good: things which have a value because of the valuation given them by others. Somewhat more emphasis is placed here upon the other person, who is no longer a quasi-physical tool, but a giver of values. Although the trend toward increased autonomy still prevails, a recognition of superindividual —in this case, social—values is definitely involved in such attitudes.

The homonomous tendency is the dominating factor in forms of interhuman relationships where the other person is recognized to be a value in himself. This involves identification with the other person or with a group of persons. Such an attitude may go so far that the other person or group of persons, or an ideal for which the group stands, may become more important to one and have a greater motivating power than one's individual needs.

Only certain stages of social behavior have been indicated here. The finer shadings have to be worked out empirically.

The gradation of social attitudes ranging from a more autonomous to a more homonomous form may be applied to topically different interhuman relationships. Take, for instance, sex behavior. On the level where the other person represents an instrumental value for the satisfaction of one's individualistic needs, sex behavior is not much more than a masturbatory equivalent. On the second level, one may expect from the other person the gratification of somewhat more socialized needs—to be admired, to be appreciated as a male—but the emphasis is still on one's own person. Finally there is the mature sex attitude as a clear expression of the trend toward homonomy based on the idea of sharing, union, and self-abandonment.

Another group of problems which need to be carefully studied for the understanding of interhuman relations includes the methods and techniques employed in social intercourse. Such studies would require a fine psychological analysis because the most important means of social intercourse are of a very subtle and elusive kind. The outstanding fact here seems to be that social intercourse does not use many frank manifest expressions, but proceeds essentially by hints and implications. In social intercourse overt verbal expressions with their manifest meanings often serve only as the lines between which one may read significant meanings. This is true not only with regard to speech, but also with regard to gestures and actions. It is astonishing how much skill the average person has in expressing himself and understanding others in this semiconscious subtle way of communication by innuendo. There are individual differences in this skill, which one might call "social intelligence," an ability which is related only loosely, if at all, to general intelligence.

A further task of social psychology would be to study the structure of typical interhuman associations and group situations involving two or more people. Here again the study of the family is of prime importance because of its great influence on shaping personalities.

SUMMARY

Human behavior cannot be adequately understood solely as a manifestation of the trend toward increased autonomy. There is a second trend, a trend toward homonomy, in which the person seeks to share and to participate in, and to fit into or conform with superindividual units, such as the family, social groups, meaningful world order, and so forth.

THE TREND TOWARD HOMONOMY

As an objective evidence of the integration of individual into superindividual units we mentioned the processes concerned with procreation. The objective existence of superindividual wholes, however, is a metaphysical problem with which the empirical scientist need not be particularly concerned. For the student of personality, the only important fact is that the tendency to share and participate in something which the person regards as greater than his individual self is a powerful motivating source of behavior.

The trend toward homonomy appears in many forms of everyday behavior, but always in intricate connection with other tendencies. It is thus frequently considerably obscured. Relatively pure manifestations of the trend toward homonomy are certain forms of artistic, religious, and social behavior.

In social behavior we may distinguish between various levels or aspects. On the symbiotic level social structure is based on division of labor and exchange of values; these are regulated by legal codes which are supported by some sort of enforcing power. The structure of social organization is not a direct topic for personality studies. Personality problems arise when the adjustment of the individual to the social organization is considered. The symbiotic social organization is based to a large extent on the trend toward increased autonomy, but it offers some outlet also for the person's homonomous tendencies.

Interpersonal behavior can be better studied at the level of cultural integration. Culture is an organized body of behavior patterns which is transmitted through tradition, and which is characteristic of a given group of people. Culture defines what are "proper" and what are "improper" ways of behavior. Cultural sanctions and taboos are superimposed also on primary physiological functions, but to an even larger extent they refer to modes of interpersonal relationships. Just as with the individual person, we may speak of the axioms of behavior and of axiomatic values by which a given culture is characterized and which form the philosophy of a given culture.

Cultures are relative. We can, however, distinguish between more or less well-integrated cultures, and also between cultures which conform to a greater or less degree to man's nature.

The advantage of culture lies partly in providing standards of behavior and partly in securing an outlet for one's tendency toward homonomy.

Culture has a twofold relevance for the personality: first, it is a complex of environmental factors to which one has to adjust; second, it is assimilated by the individual and becomes an important part of the personality. The psychoanalytic term for this part of personality is "super-ego."

Three groups of problems have been suggested as the most important topics for social psychology. 1) The study of the attitudes involved in interhuman relationships. The proportion between autonomous and homonomous motivations respectively may serve as a satisfactory criterion for a first classification. 2) The study of the techniques of social intercourse. The outstanding fact about this point seems to be that in social behavior manifest expressions are of only secondary importance, as compared with hints and implications. 3) The study of typical interhuman associations and typical group situations.

VII. SPECIFIC DYNAMIC TRENDS

THE present theory assumes that human activity shapes itself according to a broad double pattern: the trend toward increased autonomy and the trend toward homonomy. Some general concepts useful in describing personality dynamics, such as tensions, drives, attitudes, axioms of behavior, environmental attractions and values, have been defined. These concepts, however, refer only to classes of phenomena and do not include any specific content. A tendency toward increased autonomy, for instance, cannot appear as such, but only in more specific manifestations. Thus the question arises as to the specific forms in which the basic tendencies of the human being express themselves.

Attempts have been made by several authors to compile a list of human trends, basic drives, instincts, or wishes. We contend that the life pattern in man has such a great variety of specific expressions which may differ substantially from person to person that it would be futile to attempt to draw up a complete inventory, for which general validity could be claimed for every person. Generalization being, however, one of the main objectives of science, it will be worth while to investigate whether there are not at least some fields of the total personality in which a certain degree of generalization is possible.

STRUCTURALLY DEFINED FUNCTIONS

I. The first group of phenomena with regard to which generalizations can be made is represented by those functions which are defined by the structural features of the human body. Since body structure is fairly uniform in the human race, the corresponding functions are relatively the same. The greatest uniformity occurs in those functions which go under the name of metabolic processes and reflexes (both of the vegetative and of the central nervous system). These are highly standardized and relatively rigid functions.

II. Another group of relatively uniform functions which depend directly upon the physiological organization are certain standard reactions to standard needs and to recurring typical forms of distresses.

II A. *Standard Reactions to Standard Needs.* Here, in order to avoid the coining of a new word, we employ the term "need" although it will be used in a much narrower and in a more specific sense than is usual. The organism in its various functions is dependent upon the resources of the environment. Need is a biospheric constellation in which the environmental factor which is necessary to carry out the given function is absent or insufficient. Thus food is a necessary environmental factor for the metabolic functions. When the usable raw material is diminished within the organism, a specific need situation—the state of hunger—arises. This necessitates certain steps aiming at the relief of this situation, that is, the introduction of new food material.

The needs of the person are manifold and variable. There are, however, a few standard need situations which recur regularly. The recurrence of such situations is necessary in consequence of the physiological organization of man. They arise from the organismic function itself. Living involves, for instance, the using up of food material; thus the introduction of new food material becomes necessary at certain intervals. The need situation is created by the organism itself.

In human beings there are probably only two types of physiologically defined groups of "instinctive" activities aiming at the satisfaction of need situations, namely, food and sex. Activities related to these needs may be analyzed according to three aspects. First, we may consider the arising of the need situation which grows out of the activity of the organism. Second, attention may be given to one feature or to a group of features of the need situation which signals to the organism the presence of the need; for instance, the constrictions of the stomach (hunger pangs) which signal the need to the organism. Third, one may discuss the activities which are carried out for the satisfaction of the need. The latter are only partially standardized and usually show individual variation.

The need for food and the activities associated with it fall into various subgroups. First, there is a differentiation with regard to solid food and liquids. These two differ from each other with regard to the specific need situation, the signalling conditions (hunger and thirst), and also with regard to the kinds of activities which lead to satisfaction. Richter[1] has recently shown that this form of behavior includes even more specific differentiations. Animals have certain specific appetites corresponding to needs of the organism for specific substances (calcium, proteins, sugar, and so on). It is probable that such differentiation exists also in man.

It is interesting to note that functions concerned with the intake of solid and fluid food are generally considered as "instincts," while the functions concerned with the oxygen intake are not. This is due to the fact that oxygen is practically always present in the environment and the intake of oxygen can be carried out by means of highly standardized functions which are almost at the reflex level. Under ordinary circumstances there is no condition which signals to the individual the need for oxygen. When, however, there is a lack of oxygen in the environment, activities arise which come close to the "instinctive": the need for oxygen is signalled by air hunger and definite non-reflex activities are carried out

[1] C. P. Richter, L. E. Holt, and B. Barelare, Nutritional requirements for normal growth and reproduction in rats studied by the self-selection method, American Journal of Physiology, 122:734–744, June 1938.

to satisfy the need. For instance, one holds firmly with the hands to some object to give a better support for the muscles of the shoulder and chest for the movements of voluntary respiration.

The other function of this group is the sexual one. The need situation here arises also from the organism's own activity. It is signalled to the organism by means of specific sensations. The mode of satisfaction is, however, only approximately standardized. Sex has a very special position among the standard need satisfactions. It has by definition interpersonal implications. Furthermore, a highly complex symbolic structure is often superimposed on the primary sex functions.

II B. *Standard Reactions to Standard Distress Situations.* While needs are such "open" organismic constellations for the closure of which certain environmental factors are necessary, distress situations are those constellations in which some factor interferes with and disturbs the function of the organism. These disturbing factors have to be eliminated or removed, or else the organism has to get out of the distressing situation. On the other hand, the organism tends to remain in "comfortable" situations, that is, it persists in a surrounding in which its activities can best be carried out. (Note: comfort = *con + fors,* a force working *with* the organism.) We may say that needs refer to environmental opportunities, distresses to environmental contraventions.

Distress situations may vary in degree from relatively

harmless disturbances to serious danger situations which threaten the existence of the organism. Some of the distress situations are created by the organismic function itself, like distress constellations for the excretory functions, fatigue, somnolence, and the like. Other distress situations arise from the outside, like hurting or otherwise irritating substances, too high or too low environmental temperature. The activities which aim at the removal of the distressing factor and the methods of getting out of the distressing situation may be highly standardized; that is, they may be on the reflex level or close to it, or else there may be plastic and variable forms of behavior. Standardized warding-off reactions are, for instance, blinking at the approach of an object toward the eyes, coughing when the respiratory tract is irritated, resting in case of fatigue and somnolence. To this class belong also the excretory functions, some of the methods of coping with high and low environmental temperature, and so forth.

II C. *Auxiliary Functions.* The standard needs mentioned above cannot always be easily satisfied. Likewise, coping with distress situations may necessitate complex reactions. Various activities may intervene between the need for food and eating, such as the search for food, the eventual storing of food, and so on. These activities serve to make possible the more direct function of need satisfaction and the avoidance of distress. We may designate this large group of functions as supporting or auxiliary activities. Many of these activities, such as the building of bees or termites and migration of birds, are highly standardized in certain species. In man, on the basis of physiological need satisfaction and the standard methods for the avoidance of distress, a complex structure of subsidiary activities has developed. However, they lack standardization almost entirely.

We disagree with those lists of instinctual behavior which consider activities such as homing and curiosity as among the original functions in man. Curiosity may be defined as the exploration of the environment in order to determine what opportunities and contraventions it presents to the other functions of the organism. Homing is again not a direct function but one which is subsidiary to the avoidance of a great many distress situations and also to the satisfaction of a number of need situations.

In man the superstructure of auxiliary functions is very complex. There are a great many training, occupational, and other forms of activity which are first-line means for getting one's bread and butter. Even more complex is the group of auxiliary functions concerned with sex, such as courtship, care of the young, and family life. The pattern of the auxiliary functions in man is highly variable and does not allow for generalization. One could, of course, attempt to make an approximately complete inventory of these functions. Its value, however, would be quite questionable. The complexity is augmented by the fact that a great variety of secondary meanings may be attached to the direct and auxiliary activities.

We may then classify the structurally or physiologically defined functions of the organism in the following way:

- I. Vegetative and reflex functions
- II. Complex standard reactions
  - A. Standard reactions to standard need situations
    - 1. Food behavior (hunger, thirst, and, under certain conditions, air hunger)
    - 2. Primitive sex behavior
  - B. Standard reactions to standard distress situations (coughing, blinking, excretion, sleep, rest, etc.)
  - C. A group of activities which are auxiliary to the standard need satisfactions and to the avoidance of standard distress situations. The group of these auxiliary functions is not highly standardized in man.

FREELY SET OR "CHOICE" FUNCTIONS

Behavior cannot be reduced to physiological need satisfactions, to reactions to physiological distress situations, and to the auxiliary functions built around these primitive functions. Man may frequently set goals and ideals for himself which are quite independent of physiological need and distress conditions. If one regards the physiological necessities as the only realistic basis of human behavior, one is forced to admit that a great part of human behavior consists in striving toward "fictitious" goals. What physiological need could possibly be satisfied by getting a golf ball into the hole or pushing billiard balls around? Nevertheless, people often engage with considerable zeal in such activities. The utilitarian theories of play seem to be rather forced. It is true that the strength and skill which one acquires in playing games may be useful for satisfaction of the needs of the organism and for coping with physiological distress situations. This is, however, only a by-product and not the primary motivation of play activities.

Many other activities which are not considered as play have equally "fictitious" goals, that is, goals which are independent of physiological necessities. Play and work differ from each other mainly in respect to their integrative features. Play is a relatively separated activity, relatively closed within itself, something which is done for its own sake, while work has to lead to results useful for other activities; although these other activities may again be of a fictitious character. When it becomes easy and simple to take care of the physiological necessities, behavior is concentrated in the pursuit of non-physiological issues.

When we speak of strivings toward freely set ideals, this does not mean that everything may become the object of man's pursuits. It should be understood that man chooses only such ideals as are in accordance with human nature. Whatever man will do will be some form of specific expression of the basic trends toward increased autonomy and toward homonomy.

The free choice of "ideals" is further limited by personal experience and by the personal situation of the individual as well as by culture—both in the narrower sense of the family culture and culture at large.

It is possible to make a more or less adequate inventory of the main types of choice activities. Such an inventory has, however, several limitations. Only general groups of activities can be listed because the most specific expressions show so much individual variation that any generalization would be too forced. The list which we propose is not complete. Furthermore, some of the general fields of activities which we list may play a leading role in one person's life and may not be important at all in another person's life. In other words, we cannot enumerate the generally valid, but only the frequent, forms of behavior. We claim general validity only for the statement that the two main human trends are in some form expressed in everybody's life and that there does not exist any human striving which does not fall into one or both of these general categories.

We may classify the principal fields of activity into those which are chiefly expressions of the trend toward increased autonomy and those which are chiefly expressions of the trend toward homonomy. We may add a third group of activities which do not have any specific goal, but are subsidiary activities which facilitate the various expressions of the basic trends. Thus we have activities subsidiary not only to the structurally defined, but also to the freely set, activities. Such groupings of activities have only a limited validity. Human behavior, as a rule, is multiply motivated: a given activity may express more than one tendency at the same time.

A. *Specific Expressions of the Trend toward Increased Autonomy.* 1. Drive for action: The trend toward increased autonomy has been defined as a tendency of the organism to impress its autonomous determination upon a possibly large realm of events. Perhaps the clearest and most direct expression of this trend is the drive to do things, to make things happen, without any ultimate purpose, but for the mere joy of action (*Funktionslust* of Bühler[2]) for the sake of experiencing oneself as the cause of changes. Such activities can be observed even in the infant. When the child's physiological needs are satisfied and no physiological distress is present, he will move his limbs or manipulate an object. He likes to make noises, later he likes to scribble or to make things happen in some other way. When he begins to learn language and exercise symbolic activities such as imagination, he will use them in a similarly playful fashion. He also learns "word magic," that is, that with words he can make the adults do what he wants and he does so untiringly.

[2] K. Bühler, Die geistige Entwicklung des Kindes, 4th ed., Jena, Fischer, 1924.

As development proceeds most of this type of activity is soon largely replaced by more meaningful maneuvers. It will no longer satisfy the child to do things for the sake of mere action or to produce in order to experience himself as the cause of changes. To be satisfying, the activity has to lead to some more or less useful result. With the exception of play activity, one finds relatively few forms of behavior in adults which express mere drive for action. This, however, does not mean that such a tendency is rare in adults. On the contrary, it is very common, although it seldom occurs in "pure culture," but is attached as one component to many forms of behavior. One may carry out a given piece of work with a definite practical purpose in mind and at the same time enjoy the activity, the production, the achievement for its own sake. Such a tendency is the desire to conquer the environment for the sake of conquest and to achieve greater efficiency to do so (skills). The practical usefulness of activity is in many cases of little significance. One may observe feverish activities in persons who may have no use for the results (for instance, money) of their activity. Such fervor may indicate that the person is pressed by some personal need, but occasionally it indicates only the mere drive for action. The most unpleasant aspect of confinement consists in the lack of the possibility to act.

2. Drive for superiority: Similar tendencies may be directed not only toward environment but also toward

one's fellow man, and appear as a tendency to dominate, to compete with or to gain superiority over others. These tendencies again seldom occur in pure form. Interpersonal relationships involve a great many different tendencies. The trend toward dominance, however, is a very common aspect of interpersonal behavior.

3. Drive for acquisition: A common expression of the trend toward increased autonomy is represented by the drive to acquire and accumulate property. To possess goods, of course, has a very practical purpose for the satisfaction of direct physiological and other needs. It is also an efficient means of obtaining security. One aspect of such activities, however, is a more direct expression of the trend toward self-expansion. One's property differs from other objects of the environment in that one can do with it, to a large extent, whatever one wants. To own something means conquest, a greater possibility of dominance.

4. Drive for exploration: Curiosity, the eagerness to explore and to know the world, is another manifestation of the trend toward increased autonomy. That which one knows is to a certain degree conquered. To know about the properties of objects and about the laws of various processes offers a basis for efficient management and for prediction. When information is collected one tries to establish regularities, one tries to simplify and to reduce the facts, to establish non-obvious connections, and the like. Knowledge may serve practical purposes,

but it may also be pursued merely for the sake of knowing, as an expression of the self-expansive tendency.

5. Drive for integrity: While one seeks in these various forms of behavior an expression for one's self-expansive tendencies one will resent and resist every form of intrusion into one's activities. One will resist being dominated by others and resent any intrusion into one's property and any disturbances of one's privacy.

The trend toward self-expansion is a tendency toward an egocentric organization of the world. It roughly corresponds to what one calls "will to power" or "aggression." In all its manifestations the person's individuality is stressed.

B. *Specific Manifestations of the Trend toward Homonomy.* The trend toward homonomy is directed toward something larger than one's individual self and manifests itself in the tendency to participate in and unite with such larger units. Although this field has been one of the chief concerns of philosophers, theologists, and literary writers, it has been little explored by scientists. We can add little to what has already been presented in the previous chapter.

One of the main fields of expression of the trend toward homonomy is that of interpersonal relations. This does not mean that social behavior is a pure manifestation of this trend. The wish to dominate, to gain superiority, completely permeates the whole social life. Equally important or even more important for interhuman relationships are, however, the expressions of the trend toward homonomy. This can be well observed, for instance, in certain mass phenomena. It has frequently been said that people go to war because they are forced to do so, or because they have an opportunity for a release of their aggressive tendencies. If one has occasion to observe the behavior of people in mass demonstrations, as, for instance, at the beginning of a great war, one is impressed by still another fact. Such mass demonstrations give people the opportunity to experience that they belong to a group. This is probably the most important factor. It is quite possible that "extraverted" Western culture which places the main emphasis on power and achievement does not offer sufficient opportunity for the expression of the basic human need for "belonging"; hence the drive for its expression readily flows into whatever channel is opened for it. Paradoxically people may go to war because they are starved for love, for "belonging," in brief, for homonomy.

The need to share and to participate in and to belong to a larger unit is expressed not only in such rather diffuse mass phenomena, but also in more specific interhuman relationships such as loyalty to the family, the gang, or any other small group, as well as in friendship and love.

It is difficult to enumerate the manifestations of the tendency toward homonomy not because they are rare, but on the contrary because they are present everywhere, especially—though somewhat obscurely—in the field of interhuman relationships. On the whole, one can say that every human craving is colored by social motives. We dress ourselves and eat, not only for physiological reasons, but also to express our social status. Similarly we desire to possess material goods, not only to provide for material necessities and for the sake of self-expansion, but also because of the social status which they give.

The wish to be appreciated and recognized by others, to have a good reputation, to have a good social standing, is only partially motivated by the will for power. It definitely implies also the appreciation of social values. One's social integration involves a nice balance between the wish to be one with the group and the wish to be different from the group. Men almost dread to deviate too much from the group in any respect: to be considerably shorter or taller than the average, to have a very deviating color of skin, and so on. People who have some difficulty or defect of which they are ashamed are usually considerably relieved when one assures them that they are not the only ones with such difficulties, that they do not stand out as monstrosities, but share the same difficulty with many other people. Yet, on the other hand, people usually do not want to be just one of the mass, but want to excel, to be in the limelight, or at least to be noticed. One can frequently observe much "exhibitionistic" effort made by people to call attention to themselves when they suffer from the feeling of being unnoticed. The desire for attention can be clearly seen in hysteria. It is difficult to tell whether the wish to dominate or the wish to be loved is the more important one in the craving for attention.

Homonomous cravings are not directed exclusively toward human beings. We have already said that the wish to possess material goods is essentially an expression of the tendency toward increased autonomy. Quite frequently, however, a person identifies himself to a large extent with his property and is bound to it by a feeling of belonging. One may keep an estate where one lived for a long time, where one spent one's childhood, or which has been owned by one's ancestors, even if it would be more practical to sell it. One holds to it because of a homonomous emotional attachment.

The homonomous tendency may express itself in the love of nature in general, and this manifests itself in what is spoken of as the feeling "to be one with nature" and "empathy" into various happenings in the world around us. Such tendencies seem to be present at quite an early age. The child in his play activities imitates and places himself in the role, not only of human personages, but also of a horse or a locomotive. Much study would be necessary to understand the motivation of such behavior. It is, however, probable that one of the motives is to feel oneself as one with something outside of the narrower self: to be oneself and at the same time to be somebody or something else, too.

We also mentioned that one seeks knowledge mainly for the sake of a theoretical and practical domination of the world. Knowledge, however, also offers a basis for the satisfaction of the need for homonomy. The knowledge of history connects the happenings of the day with the past and promotes the experience of continuity and unity, as well as the experience of one's life as a part of a larger historical process. The study of other sciences may also promote the experience of oneself as a part of larger units.

Art, religion, and ethics offer numerous opportunities for the expression of the trend toward homonomy. These fields have been studied mostly in relative isolation and by highly specialized students. Research directed toward these fields from the point of view of personality organization is greatly needed.

Western culture places the main emphasis on domination and achievement. This handicaps the expression of homonomous tendencies, but cannot entirely obliterate that which belongs to the fundamental nature of man. Religion is definitely in discredit for the "enlightened" man, although his dislike for religion is probably not directed against the essence of the religious attitude—that is, against the attitude of participation in a meaningful cosmic order—but against the quite extraneous or adventitious elements in the historical religions. The ethics of Western culture are largely utilitarian. It would be of value to investigate how far religion and ethics still represent channels for the trend toward homonomy. If it were found that such channels are largely obstructed, the possibility of other channels through which this trend expresses itself would need to be investigated.

C. *Subsidiary Tendencies.* The freely set types of activities are supported by a number of auxiliary or ancillary functions in a manner similar to the physiological need satisfactions and the warding-off reactions of physiological distress situations. Auxiliary functions have no other role than to promote and facilitate the other activities of the organism. Among the auxiliary or ancillary functions the most important are the *drive for security,* the *drive for orientation,* and the *drive for integration.*

1. The drive for security: This drive has no primary goal. It is based on anticipation of situations which could interfere with the satisfaction of one's needs and with the free expression of the various tendencies of the person. One wishes economic security, security from the dangers of the environment, security for one's family, occupational security, assurance that one is accepted by the group, security in the love of others.

The wish for security is probably genetically rather a late acquisition since it presupposes the ability to anticipate. It is often difficult to judge from a single outward manifestation whether a person is driving at security or at some other goal. As previously emphasized, to acquire money may be motivated as much by the wish to conquer as by the wish for security. In the continued observation of a person's behavior one can usually detect the main source of motivation. Some people will in almost all their activities follow the principle of "playing safe" while other more adventurous natures "stick out their necks," and are "looking for trouble." The drive for security is a rather conservative one: it tends to preserve the status quo and is not inclined to new adventures.

In some instances insecurity is based on the real or assumed inadequacy of the person to cope with the various requisites of life. In such a case one may speak of *insufficiency*. When insufficiency is relative, namely, in comparison with other people, one may speak of *inferiority*.

2. The drive for orientation: The term "insecurity" has also a somewhat different connotation. It may not so much refer to the anticipation of danger as denote uncertainty about "just where one stands." This may be called "lack of orientation" and the tendency to overcome it is the "drive for orientation." One may be uncertain of the goals and ideals which are worth following, or one may be uncertain about oneself, one's abilities, whether one is better qualified for one or another type of profession, and one may also be uncertain about one's relationship to others and about the attitude one should take toward them. Much of the current un-

rest in Western civilization seems to have its cause in this lack. It is not infrequent that children are troubled with doubt about their parentage. Inconsistent behavior on the part of the parent is frequently the cause of such uncertainties. A capricious change from expressions of affection to brutal severity is certainly not beneficial for the child's sense of security and orientation.

Lack of orientation is a much more serious affair than insecurity. Even though one feels insecure, one is better equipped to cope with dangers when they can, to a certain degree, be foreseen. Attempts can then be made to prevent them or to cope with them in some other fashion. The outcome of the fight may appear doubtful, but one knows at least what to fight for. On the other hand, lack of orientation handicaps every planful action or univocal attitude. It either paralyzes the person or expresses itself in an inconsistent, scattered type of behavior.

A person has to have some guiding points in his behavior. The factors which seem to be the most important components of one's orientation will be summed up in the following paragraphs.

a) The person has to have some picture of himself. He has to answer the question: Who and what am I? Strangely enough, the person may have doubts and uncertainty even with regard to those questions about himself which might seem most obvious. Uncertainty as to whether one is in actuality a male or a female exists not only in children but it is also not rare in adults. Such uncertainty usually does not appear to be consciously formulated, but rather manifests itself in the ambiguity of one's attitude in assuming the male or female role with all its implications. To be a man or a woman has much broader implications than the strictly sexual one. In the older type of Western culture the man is expected to earn the living, the woman to take care of the home and children. There are differences with regard to political, legal, and domestic rights and duties. One set of rules of etiquette applies to men, another to women. A greater degree of aggression is permissible for man than for woman. Certain overt manifestations of emotion, such as crying in the presence of other people, is permissible for women, but is very unmanly for a male. Different forms of behavior and personality traits are expected from the two sexes. They clothe themselves differently. Briefly, very different kinds of taboos and privileges are valid for the two sexes.

The acceptance of the male or the female role, respectively, means the acceptance of rather definite modes of behavior in a large field of human activity. Thus it is evident that a whole-hearted acceptance of one or the other role contributes a great deal to one's orientation. It restricts, but at the same time it also defines rather concretely, how one should behave. On the other hand, insufficient identification with one of the sexes is often the basis of uncertainty and lack of orientation. Over-compensations such as the so-called "masculine protest" are common reactions to this personality constellation.

The bodily characteristics, such as stature, attractive or unattractive appearance, color of hair and eyes, physical health, are also important for the picture which a person makes of himself. The person's evaluation of such characteristics is seldom entirely objective. People of definitely short stature often refer to themselves as of medium height; the color of the eyes may appear to one as blue when everybody else sees them as gray. I knew a man with flaming red hair who consistently referred to it as "blonde." With regard to the quality of the singing voice, persons almost generally misjudge themselves. Variations in such bodily characteristics have little physiological significance. On physiological grounds a man can be equally happy whether he is a few inches shorter or taller than the average or whether he is red-haired or black-haired. Such bodily characteristics, however, may play an extraordinarily important role in the person's life through the social symbolism attached to these characteristics. Tall stature, for instance, is a conventional symbol of superiority, adulthood, and masculinity, and short stature is a symbol of the lack of these features. The importance of this factor becomes evident when one observes the great variety of compensatory behavior seen in short people. They may continuously compare themselves with others in this respect. There is a saying that "a short fellow is happy only when he sees one shorter than himself." Compensations may take the form of aggressiveness, for instance, intellectual bullying of the tall people. Occasionally one observes that short men dislike to have a tall person stand in their presence, and they seem ill at ease before the other is seated.

In the picture which the person makes of himself, personality features and psychological capacities, such as courage, will-power, intelligence, and memory, are also included. Such an evaluation of both bodily and psychological characteristics is essentially of a social nature. One is tall or short, strong or weak, beautiful or ugly, clever or stupid by comparison with other people. Thus self-evaluation determines to a large extent one's social orientation.

b) Another fundamental component of one's orientation is the establishment of one's place in the social group. One needs clarification as to where one belongs. Belongingness to family, national, racial, and other groups and more intimate relations like friendship or love are essential for one's orientation. Uncertainty about one's belonging to the group or belonging to a disadvantaged group are frequent sources of human problems. Certain convictions as to what to expect from other people and what one wishes to be for others also contribute to one's social orientation. The emotional attitudes of trust, distrust, friendliness, misanthropy, and so on are indicators of one's social orientation.

c) Another group of factors which define one's orientation are the basic attitudes which one has with regard to the major issues of life. We called this group of factors axioms of behavior and we have mentioned that they form the person's philosophy of life. The topics to which these basic attitudes refer are not identical in all persons. There are, however, certain problems inherent in the nature of living which are most likely to become major issues for every person. Thus, for instance, death and love are major issues for practically everybody. The attitudes toward such issues are very different from person to person and are highly characteristic for the individual. There are persons for whom life is essentially a coping with adversities in a world full of dangers and uncertainties. For other people the world is a place of opportunities, something which has to be exploited to the utmost. For others, again, life is a transitory affair which matters but little as compared to the after-life. Others experience life as a treasure, as a unique event which will never recur. Some people experience life rather as a punishment, while for others it is an expression of a wise and benevolent cosmic order. Some people feel that life is fundamentally dull, commonplace, and they are frequently excessively attracted by anything which is different from the routine mode of living. For some people to love and to be loved by others is the all-important thing. The fact that one has to die may be taken in a rather matter-of-fact way, considered as the natural end, but it may also be considered as a most dreadful fate and one may be haunted by a fear of death throughout one's life. Such attitudes may be transitory, but more often are characteristic and permanent features of the person.

The picture which one makes of oneself, of one's place in the world or social group, and certain basic convictions and attitudes toward the major issues of life are the fundamentals of one's orientation which give a definite direction to one's actions.

3. The drive for integration: Another group of auxiliary functions is concerned with the integration of the multifarious activities of the personality. The great differentiation of human trends into manifold channels of expression would lead to disintegration without unifying, integrating functions.

For the integration of the various activities broad superordinate goals and perspectives are needed. These represent the ideals of what one wishes to accomplish in life and also self-ideals, that is, what one wishes to become. Such ideals are shaped by many factors such as personality make-up, cultural influences, personal experiences.

The self-ideal undergoes characteristic changes with age. The child's self-ideal is to become a grown-up, which is usually specified as to be like the father or the mother or some other older person of one's environment. The wish to become an adult manifests itself in many different ways. A great part of the child's play consists in the imitation of the activities of adults such as playing soldier, doctor, shopkeeper. Boys often anxiously wait for every sign of growing up, such as the increase of stature, hair growth, signs of sexual maturation, and other bodily signs of adulthood. Certain activities which are tabooed for the child, and hence are symbols of adulthood, such as smoking, drinking, sex activity, and certain modes of dressing, may appear especially attractive to adolescents. There is sufficient evidence for the assumption that the fear of never becoming an adult is quite common in children and sometimes not without serious consequences. Such fear is especially intense when there is an actual retardation in bodily development; it may become fixed and persist into adulthood. We have mentioned the concern of people with short stature about their body height. Since a full-sized body is a symbol of adulthood it is not unlikely that the great concern about short stature may often be a persisting fear of not growing up. Adult males not infrequently complain about the trouble which the heavy growth of beard causes. Frequently they are, however, not really complaining, but rather bragging, that is, they are proud of this symbol of adulthood. The beard, of course, is also a masculine symbol and may have important significance for those who are insecure about their masculinity. Many other examples could be mentioned which seem to indicate the persistence of the fear of not growing up into real adulthood.

In childhood the self-ideal is most frequently shaped according to the example of the parents, whose place is later taken by other heroes or other desirable characters. The formation of the self-ideal is accomplished essentially by a series of successive identifications. Conformity of one's actions with one's self-ideal is the basis of self-respect. Loss of self-respect is one of the most destructive changes which a person may suffer.

The specific *ideals of personal accomplishment* may greatly differ from person to person, but for happy personality integration a more or less clear experience that one is using one's life correctly, that one is doing one's share in life, is needed. This is a rather curious aspect of personality. Why should a person worry that he will die without having done the right thing and that his life will be wasted, even if he is intellectually convinced that with death everything will be over? This brings the aspect of duty, of some kind of metaphysical obligation, into one's life plan. The person may formulate such obligation in terms of religion or ethics, but even when it is not formulated in any manner it is probably felt somehow by most people. This expresses the need to serve with one's life a superindividual cosmic order. We had occasion to refer to this type of need in discussing the principle of homonomy.

The feeling of obligation may have a more restricted social significance. It is then experienced as a duty to live up to one's reputation, to fulfill the expectations of others. This may become a very heavy burden. Parents frequently considerably overrate the capacities of their children and show them in words or behavior that great things are expected from them. Such persons may develop an excessive drive for power and may overstrain themselves to fulfill the expectations of others, although on their own account they might have been content with more moderate accomplishment.

The behavior of people is greatly influenced by the wish not to disappoint the expectations of others. This also hinders changes in one's behavior. One may from time to time come to the conclusion that one needs to change and reorganize one's mode of living. This is, however, very difficult as long as one remains in the same social environment. People cast us in certain roles, expect consistent conformity to the roles, and we respect such expectations. One may otherwise be ready for a change in the mode of living, but may not dare to undertake it, because of "what other people might think"—one does not want to disappoint others in their expectation.

FURTHER POSSIBILITIES OF GENERALIZATION WITH REGARD TO BIOSPHERIC DYNAMICS

In the preceding discussion we have enumerated some factors in biospheric dynamics which seem to be fairly general for the human personality, even if we cannot claim completeness. There are also certain other aspects of personality dynamics concerning which generalization could probably safely be made. One group of these factors are the *methods* with the aid of which one attempts to achieve the various goals which one desires: methods of self-defense, methods of obtaining superiority, of excelling, of gaining security. The number of such methods is not unlimited, and by observing human behavior one could single out typical patterns.

Further generalizations would be possible with regard to typical and fairly general biospheric situations. The "Oedipus situation" of the psychoanalyst might be a case in point. Once I read an essay which was concerned with the interpretation of a report in the newspaper of a man committing suicide at the dead end of a blind street. The essayist attempted to argue the point that this constellation was not incidental, but had a symbolic significance: the man got into a blind street in his life and reached a dead end from which there was no escape for him. Such "blind-alley situations" actually do occur. Other biospheric constellations may show the characteristics of a vicious circle. The following dynamic situation is not infrequent: one may make a relatively insignificant mistake and in trying to prevent possible consequences one gets into an even greater difficulty which may grow like a snowball and may soon reach gigantic proportions. Such "snowball situations" in a milder or more severe form occur in almost everybody's life. It may be a useful task for personality research to single out typical situations and study their structure. The knowledge which could thus be gained might offer considerable aid in dealing with individual cases.

In addition to what has already been mentioned there are presumably other aspects of personality dynamics where generalizations may be possible. The possibility of generalization is, however, definitely limited. We cannot hope to establish dynamic laws concerning man with the completeness that is possible with regard to the behavior of other species. This is due not alone to man's greater complexity, but also to certain specific characteristics of human behavior. One of these characteristics consists in the much more extensive use of substitutes by men than by animals. The use of money, for instance, influences considerably the dynamic structure of personality. The satisfaction of many needs is not aimed at directly, but by means of acquiring money, which, having an exchange value, readily opens the way for the satisfaction of these needs. This means in a certain sense the concentration and reduction of many drives to one. These reduced drives do not appear then in such a clear-cut, elemental form as in animals; instead, the drive for money becomes one of the most pronounced tendencies.

Another closely related factor is the high specialization of occupational activity. Man does not acquire directly the various necessities of life. A great part of his activities consists in a rather one-sided, specialized occupational activity; the surplus value which is thus acquired allows by exchange a short cut to the satisfaction of many other needs.

The use of substitutes is responsible also for a kind of fragmentation of human activity. Animals achieve various goals by continual direct attendance to a given activity. Through the use of substitutes man does not need to attend directly and continually to his multitudinous affairs. A person living in New York may run his business at the same time in New York, San Francisco, Shanghai, and Cairo. Activities and processes, once set up, run on with only occasional and mostly substitutive attendance—for instance, giving orders by letter—from the person who operates them. These activities go on undisturbed even when the person is attending to some other affair or is doing nothing. Men's activities take place prevalently in such indirect operations. Since this type of operation does not require continual attendance, man's direct activity becomes very fragmentary. Suppose a man goes to another city on business. The time between his departure and arrival will be filled with a number of operations, many of which have nothing to do with his present goal. While waiting for the train he may make a few telephone calls; on the train he may read, eat, write letters, and send out telegrams. The successive activities may have no connection among themselves, but belong to independent series of operations. The actual time-space configuration is composed of fragments which belong to widely different fields of activity. Through such facts the sphere of influence of the person and the number of operations which run parallel are greatly increased. The management of such complex operations necessitates a special organization of behavior, and requires a special kind of memory in order to know where one has to act, an increased capacity to shift from one activity to another, and increased ability for integration. This represents a great part of the strain and burden of modern living.

SUMMARY

The basic human trends (toward increased autonomy and toward homonomy) are expressed through a great number of specific channels. These specific expressions are so diversified and show so much individual variation that the attempt to make a complete and generally valid inventory would be futile. All we are able to do is to point out the fields wherein a certain degree of generalization can be achieved.

First, we pointed to the structurally defined functions of the organism. Under this heading we included: I. Vegetative and reflex functions; II. Complex standard reactions. The latter have been divided into 1) standard reactions to standard need situations (food behavior and sex behavior); 2) standard reactions to typically recurring distress situations (as coughing, blinking, excretion, rest, sleep); and 3) auxiliary functions (as homing, migration, exploration) which have only goals auxiliary to other goals and serve as an aid to the functions mentioned under 1) and 2).

Not only with regard to structurally defined functions, but also with regard to freely set or choice activities a certain degree of generalization is possible. This type of activity can be divided into two groups: specific expression of the trend toward increased autonomy and specific expression of the trend toward homonomy. Under the first heading we have included: the drive for action, for superiority, for acquisition and possession, for exploration, and for integrity. Under the specific manifestations of the trend toward homonomy we have included activities which aim at participation in the social group; the desire for social status; the wish to be noticed, but not to deviate too much from others; certain forms of emotional attachment to the environment; love of nature; artistic, religious, and ethical expression.

Among the tendencies which are subsidiary to the freely set activities we have included: the wish for security; the wish for orientation (as elements basic to one's orientation, we have mentioned the picture which one makes of oneself, of one's place in the world and in the social group, and the attitudes toward the major issues of life); the tendency toward integration which requires certain ideals (self-ideal, ideals of personal accomplishment, the feeling of obligation).

Further generalizations were possible also with regard to typical methods of behavior and with regard to typical biospheric situations.

The possibility of generalizing with regard to human activity is definitely limited. One of the limiting circumstances is represented by the extensive use of substitute activities which extraordinarily complicate the process of living.

Brief and more or less preliminary definitions of the concepts which have been proposed for the description of specific dynamic features of the biological total process were given. We feel that in this chapter little more than the compilation of a list of topics for the study of specific personality dynamics has been accomplished. Such a list may be useful as an outline for empirical studies.

VIII. THE PROBLEM OF INTEGRATION

THE STRUCTURE OF WHOLES

The problem of the integration of part processes in the total organism is the most important and at the same time the most difficult problem for a science of personality. The difficulty lies not alone in the paucity of usable factual data, but to an even greater extent in the inadequacy of our logical tools. Such a handicap is felt not only in the study of personality, but in the study of wholes in general. An attempt will be made to develop some concepts which may be useful for the understanding of the structure of wholes.

Our scientific thinking consists prevalently in the logical manipulation of relationships. That the structure of wholes cannot be described in terms of relationships has, however, been repeatedly pointed out by many writers. While accepting the premise that holistic connections cannot be resolved into relationships, some authors have implied that the pattern or structure of wholes does not lend itself at all to logical manipulation. We suggest, however, that the structure of wholes is perhaps amenable to logical treatment after all, that, though it may not be described in terms of relations, it may be described in terms of some more adequate logical unit, representing an entirely different logical genus. Here the attempt will be made to demonstrate that there is a logical genus suitable to the treatment of wholes. We propose to call it *"system."*

The ideal would be to develop a logic of system to such a degree of precision that it might offer the basis for exact mathematical formulation of holistic connections. A. Meyer states, "The mathematics which would be needed for the mathematical formulation of biological laws does not exist today. It has to be created by the new biology."[1] To construct a logic of systems which would be the counterpart of the conventional logic of relations is in itself a gigantic task and cannot even be attempted here. It may be true that a substantial advance in the study of wholes, and specifically in the study of personality, will come from the development of a logic of systems. We must, however, content ourselves for the present with the clarification of some aspects of the logical properties of systems and with the application of the insight thus gained to our specific subject-matter.

In order to demonstrate some of the logical characteristics of systems we may compare them with better known logical forms, namely, with relationships. As an

[1] A. Meyer, Ideen und Ideale der biologischen Erkenntnis, Leipzig, Barth, 1934, p. 35.

example of a relationship we may take a quantitative one (Figure 6), and as an example of a system we may

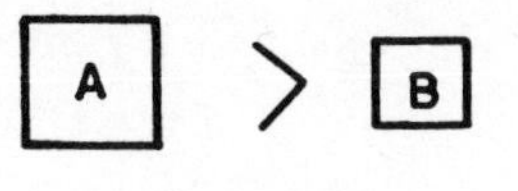

FIGURE 6

take a simple geometrical one (Figure 7) in which the points *a, b, c,* and *d* are parts of the simple geometrical system, the line A–B.

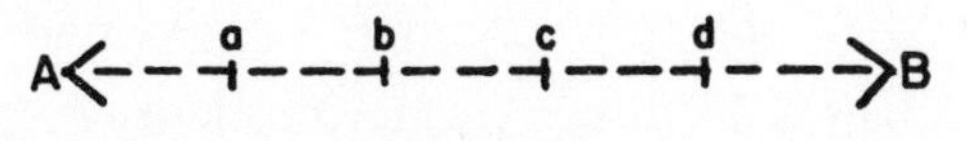

FIGURE 7

The differences between relationships and systems may be formulated as follows.

1. A relation requires two and only two members (relata) between which the relation is established. A complex relation can always be analyzed into pairs of relata, while the system cannot be thus analyzed. A system may involve an unspecified number of members. A system is not a complex relation. It is impossible to say what the relation between *a* and *b, b* and *c, c* and *d,* etc. should be in order to form a linear system.

I am aware of the fact that the restriction of the term "relation" to cover only two-term connections deviates from the contemporary usage of this term. Usually the term is employed also to include logical connections that involve more than two terms. Such connections, however, seem to fall into the following two categories.

a) Compound relations, which can be reduced to two-term relations. One or both of the relata may be groups involving a more or less large number of members. Group A may include *a, b, c,* and *d,* and group B may include *e, f, g,* and *h.* When, however, group A is related to B, or to one member of B, the group is taken as a totality, that is, as *one* unit. A compound relation may involve also a chain connection, for instance, a "causal" sequence: *a–b–c–d.* It is clear that a compound relation can easily be resolved into two-term relations: *a–b, b–c, c–d.* A more complex relationship would be the following:

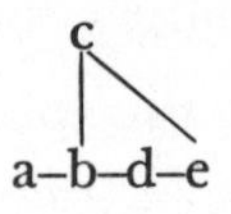

which consists of the two-term relations: *a–b, b–c, b–d, d–e, c–e.* The complexity may be even greater and yet a reduction to two-term relations still is possible.

b) There are also connections which involve more than two terms and cannot be reduced to two-term relations as, for instance, *b* is between *a* and *c.* It appears, however, that those compound connections which cannot be reduced to two-term relations exhibit all those qualities which are set forth in this discussion as the characteristics of systems. One may, of course, use the term "relation" in a very broad sense as is commonly done, but then one must admit that one subsumes two very different logical genera (two-term relationships and complex connections which are reducible to two-term relations on the one hand, and complex connections which cannot be reduced to two-term relations on the other hand) under the same term.

The term "system," as used in this discussion, is also at variance with the common usage. Usually one designates by system any aggregate of elements considered together with the relationships holding among them. It will be shown in the following discussion that the type of connections in a whole is very different from the connections which exist in an aggregate. The term "system" is used here to denote a *holistic system.* Further, in using this term we abstract *constituents* ("elements") and refer only to the *organization* of the whole. Thus "system" for our discussion is holistic organization.

It might seem desirable in the present discussion to substitute other terms for "relation" and "system"; however, it seems to me equally desirable to avoid the coining of terms. Since I have pointed out the differences between my usage and the common usage of the terms I may hope that the argument will not become obscured through this terminology.

2. A relation requires an aspect out of which the relationship is formed. Two objects can be related to each

other, for instance, with regard to their color, size, or weight. Therefore, before a relationship can be established it is necessary to single out some aspect of the relata which serves as a basis of the relation. The attribute of the relata on which the relationship is based is an immanent quality of the object, like size, color, or weight. The object enters into a relationship with another object because of its immanent qualities. Most relationships are based upon "identity," diversity, or similarity (partial identity with partial diversity) of the object, that is, on immanent attributes. The members of a system, on the contrary, do not become constituents of the system by means of their immanent qualities, but by means of their distribution or arrangement within the system. The object does not participate in the system by an inherent quality but by its *positional value in the system.* It is immaterial for a linear system whether points or stars or crosses or circles or any other objects be the members, if only in the arrangement the positional values remain the same.

Between the constituents of a system, after they gain a positional value from the system, further relations may be established *in a secondary way* which are not based on the immanent properties of the relata, but on their secondary positional value. Such relationship is, for instance, *A* is below *B*. Such relations are secondary: it is presupposed that the members have a positional value in a system of coordinates.

3. In establishing a relationship between objects and in arranging objects in a system, the separation of the objects is presupposed. Multiplicity of objects is only possible in some kind of *dimensional domain* (a manifold). The clearest examples of dimensional domains are space and time, which have been reorganized by philosophers for a long time as *principia individuationis,* that is, domains which make possible a multiplicity of individual objects. We cannot speak of *two* objects unless they are placed in different points of time or in different points of space or unless a distance between them is not established in some other kind of dimensional domain.

Although the dimensional domain is a necessary condition for both relationships and systems, the function of the dimensional domain is different for these two logical genera. The role of the dimensional domain for a relationship is merely disjunction of the relata. But the role of the dimensional domain ends here. The domain itself does not enter into the relationship. For instance, if two colors are separated in space a comparison between them can be made without any further reference to space.

The dimensional domain is more intimately involved in the formation of systems. Here the dimensional domain not only separates the parts, but it participates in the formation of the system. The system itself is dimensional. *A system is a distribution of the members in a dimensional domain.*

4. In a relationship the connectedness between the

relata is a *direct* one. The connection goes without any mediation directly from *a* to *b* and vice versa. The connection between the members of a system is, however, of a more complex type. Although there is a connection between the points *a, b, c, d* when they form a straight line, this connection is not a direct one in our sense. It is impossible to say what relationship should connect *a* with *b,* and *c* with *d,* and *a* with *d,* etc., to form a linear arrangement. In this example the members of the system which are points are linearly connected only by forming a whole. System-connectedness of the parts cannot be expressed as *a–b, b–c, a–c,* but as

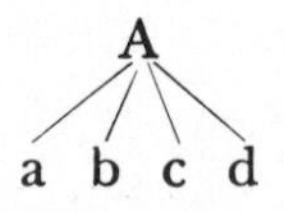

In a system the members are, from the holistic viewpoint, not significantly connected with each other except with reference to the whole.

The constituent parts of a system are not considered separately but with respect to a superordinate, more inclusive factor, the system in and by which they are connected. An interesting example of this state of affairs is given in the fact of geometrical symmetry. Such an arrangement involves two figures which are identical in shape and size, and show a special kind of correspondence with regard to their positions in space. The identity of geometrical figures can be demonstrated by bringing them together in space, in which case they must coincide. Symmetrical figures, however, can coincide only under special conditions. Taking one-dimensional geometrical figures such as those in Figure 8, it is clear that

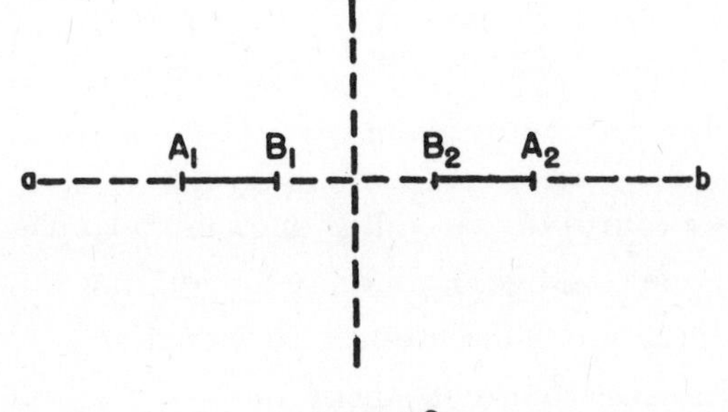

FIGURE 8

such figures cannot be made to coincide by moving them in a one-dimensional space, that is, along the line *a–b*. A_1 will not coincide with A_2 and B_1 with B_2 at the same time. To make them actually coincide they must be rotated within a two-dimensional space with respect to the axis of symmetry. Thus the position of the two lines is analogous, not in a one but in a two-dimensional space. Taking two-dimensional symmetrical figures such as those in Figure 9, it can easily be seen that they cannot be made to coincide in any way in the concrete if one shifts them within a two-dimensional space, but only within a three-dimensional space. Three-dimensional symmetrical objects again cannot be made to coincide in a three-dimensional space. That would require in the

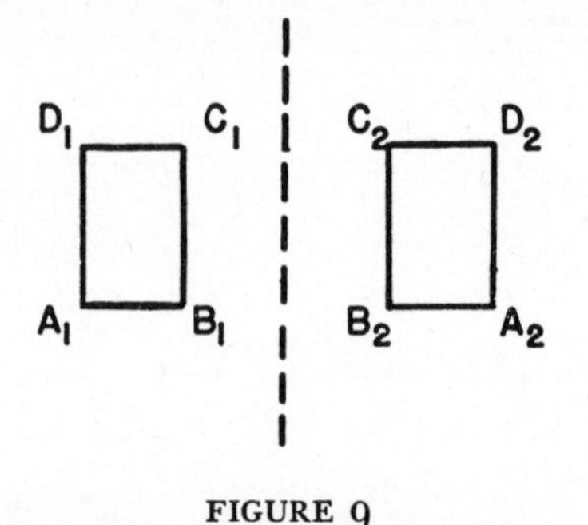

FIGURE 9

concrete a fourth dimension. If one's mirror image were real and one could go beyond the mirror, one still could not step into one's mirror image and completely coincide with it, because the right side of the person would be on the left side of the mirror image and vice versa; a right-hand glove cannot be made into a left-hand glove; and so on. For the coincidence of symmetrical figures, a space which has one dimension more than the number of dimensions of the symmetrical figures is required. Thus the congruence of one-dimensional symmetrical figures is brought about in a two-dimensional space, and that of two-dimensional figures in a three-dimensional space. Symmetry seems to be psychologically a kind of system-connectedness, that is, a connectedness of parts, not between themselves but in a superordinate whole.

Up to this point we have considered only one type of relations, namely, comparative relations based on "identity," diversity, and similarity. Another type of relationship which is of great significance in science is the causal relationship. Causal relationship can be expressed as follows: if *a* occurs, *b* follows. Causal relationships may be in many respects different from comparative relationships, but they are alike in that they represent direct connections between one member and another. Even complex causal relationships can be analyzed into two-membered relationships. Where such analysis is logically not possible, we deal with system-connectedness.

On the basis of the foregoing discussion the differences between relations and systems can be summarized in a preliminary fashion as follows. 1) Relationships involve two and only two members (relata). Complex relationships can always be analyzed into pairs of relata. Systems may involve an unspecified number of components, not analyzable in certain respects into pairs of relata. 2) The relata enter into a relationship by virtue of their immanent attributes, while the constituents enter into a system-connection, not through their immanent attributes but through the positional value which they have in the system. Secondary relations which are based on positional values of the relata can be established also between members of a system. But the system itself cannot be described even in terms of such relationships. 3) For the existence of systems a dimensional domain is necessary. Systems are specific forms of the distribution of members in a dimensional domain. 4) In relationships the connection between the relata is a direct one. The members of a system, on the contrary, do not need to be directly connected; they are connected within and by the whole.

Dealing with relations and dealing with systems involve two different logical manipulations to which two psychologically quite different processes may correspond. In the recent past there has been much rather inconclusive discussion concerning the possibility of two different processes of knowing: explanation and understanding. I am referring here to the discussion of the problem, *erklärende und verstehende Psychologie*. The difference between the two concepts, as they have been used in the aforementioned discussion, is probably that explanation refers to relational thinking, understanding to system thinking. Relational thinking aims at the establishment of the direct connection between two objects. For instance, in the study of causation one has to find for member *a* (effect) a second member *b* (cause) with which it is necessarily connected. In causal research the task is to single out from a multiplicity of data pairs of facts between which there is a necessary connection. In system thinking the task is not to find direct relations between members but to find the superordinate system in which they are connected or to define the positional value of members relative to the superordinate system.

The preceding discussion is far from being complete and adequate, but it is hoped that our main thesis at least, that relations and systems are two different logical genera with distinctive characteristics, has been given a measure of plausibility. It is still an open question whether relations and systems are *absolutely* different logical genera, or whether the one may be a subtype of the other. The latter possibility cannot be excluded and there are certain arguments in favor of it. One thing, however, seems clear, namely, that systems cannot be deduced from relations, while the deduction of relations from systems still remains a possibility. If that is the case then the more general logical genus would be "system," while "relation" would be a reduced, simplified system which is adequate only for the logical presentation of very simple specialized constellations.

SYSTEM AND GESTALT

In the course of the past two decades it has been almost generally recognized by biologists and psychologists that the clarification of the problem of wholes is essential for progress in the study of the organism. The increasing awareness of the problem of wholes led to the discovery of certain general principles, best formulated perhaps by the Gestalt psychologists. It will be useful to examine briefly these formulations in the light of the previous discussion.

The most generally known thesis with regard to wholes is the following: "The whole is more than the sum of its parts." This is not a very felicitous formulation since—contrary to the concept of Gestalt psychologists—it may suggest that a summation of parts takes place and that, besides the summation, a new additional factor enters into the constitution of wholes. In Ehrenfels' *Gestaltqualität* such an additional factor actually has been suggested.

Wholes, however, cannot be compared to additive aggregations at all. Instead of stating that in the formation of wholes something more than a summation of parts takes place, it would be more correct to state that summation does not play any part whatsoever in the formation of wholes. In summations the parts function because of their inherent qualities. When, for instance, linear distances are added to form a larger linear distance, the first distance, as such, is directly joined (*und-Verbindung*) to the second distance and this to the third, and so on. On the other hand, when a number of parts constitute a whole, the parts do not enter into such a connection by means of their inherent qualities, but by means of their position in the system. The formation of wholes is therefore not additional to the aggregation of parts, but something of an entirely different order. *In aggregates it is significant that the parts are added; in a system it is significant that the parts are arranged.*

It should also be kept in mind that "part" means something different when applied to aggregate from what it means when applied to wholes. When the single objects *a, b, c, d,* are bound together in an aggregate they participate in that aggregation as object *a,* object *b,* object *c,* etc., that is, as lines, distances, color spots, or whatever they may be. When, however, a whole is constituted by the utilization of objects *a, b, c, d,* the parts of the resulting whole are *not* object *a,* object *b,* object *c,* etc., but α, β, γ, δ, that is, *the positional values of the objects a, b, c, d.*

I would suggest that the principle "the whole is more than the sum of its parts" be modified in the following way: Aggregation and whole formation are processes of an entirely different order. And we may also formulate this statement more specifically: In an aggregation the parts are added, in wholes the parts are arranged in a system. The system cannot be derived from the parts; the system is an independent framework in which the parts are placed.

That the whole is, to a large extent, independent of the individual parts has been frequently pointed out. We may transpose a melody a few octaves higher or lower and it still remains essentially the same melody, although this transposition may be such that the two variations of the melody have no single individual tone in common. If we recall that the system is a kind of arrangement in which the parts do not participate by means of their inherent characteristics but by means of the positional values, the above-mentioned relative independence of the whole from the nature of the individual parts will be understandable.

The above statement needs, however, some qualification and restriction. The parts may need to have certain attributes which enable them to fill the positions which are required for the system. In a triangular geometrical arrangement the parts have to be *lines,* although their other properties (for instance, their absolute lengths) are irrelevant. Thus certain properties of the constituents are relevant, that is, they are necessary to permit the occupancy of a given position, while other properties are irrelevant. A similar distinction has been made also by J. von Uexküll, who differentiates between "leading" and "accompanying" properties.[2] The greater the organization of the whole, the more the inherent properties of parts are utilized as co-determinants of positional values. The human organism, for example, is highly economical in this respect: it carries a minimal load of irrelevant properties of parts; most of the properties of parts are "utilized," that is, are co-determinants of the positional value of the part.

"Wholes are never undifferentiated but always a *unitas multiplex.*" Let us place the emphasis first on the multiplicity. If one keeps in mind that the system is a way of arranging parts, the logical necessity of a multiplicity becomes evident since a single factor in itself cannot be arranged.

The term "whole" is frequently used with a very confusing double meaning. Sometimes the concrete organ-

[2] J. von Uexküll, Theoretische Biologie, 2d ed., Berlin, Springer, 1928, p. 87.

ized *object,* other times the *organization* of the object is called a whole. The term is used in this latter connotation, for instance, when one states that a circle may be small or large, drawn in red or in green color, and still remain the same whole, the same Gestalt. I propose that the term "whole" be reserved to designate the concrete *organized object,* while the *organization* itself, the way of arrangement of parts, should be called system.

The logical formulation of a given system states the construction principle or the *system principle* of the whole. Every system has one and only one construction principle. This is the meaning of the first term in the expression, *unitas multiplex.* The particular system principle may be perfectly or only approximately realized in a given whole. There are wholes in which all the significant positions of the system are occupied in perfect accordance with the system principle, but there are also wholes in which only a limited number of positions, sufficient to suggest the system principle, are occupied while other members are *out of position.* This is the difference which among Gestalt psychologists is somewhat vaguely referred to by the terms "good" and "bad" Gestalt. The various degrees of *Pregnanz* which a Gestalt may have express the degree of conformity of the positions of the parts with the system principle. There are also instances where in a whole a sufficient number of positions are occupied to indicate the system principle, while the other positions *are not filled.* These are "open" Gestalts in contradistinction with "closed" ones, wherein all significant positions are occupied.

Certain relations, as, for instance, comparative relations (*a* is larger than *b*), could be called static, while others could be called dynamic. The prototype of the latter is the causal relationship. In the same fashion one could distinguish between static and dynamic systems. We hope that we have demonstrated the existence of the static forms of systems. The question, however, as to the existence of dynamic systems still remains open. In static systems the whole imparts to its constituents a positional value which the given constituent does not have in itself, but only when it forms part of the given whole. With regard to dynamic wholes, one would expect that a given part *functions differently* depending on the whole to which it belongs. We would also expect that the whole has its own characteristic dynamics. Certain principles of holistic dynamics have already been formulated, as, for instance, the "tendency to closure" and the "tendency to *Pregnanz.*" Up to the present such dynamic principles have been satisfactorily demonstrated only within the psychological realm, which is generally characterized by great plasticity. That such principles hold true also in realms of greater rigidity is strongly suggested by certain facts, but it has not been satisfactorily demonstrated as yet. Such an assumption is a working hypothesis—and in the present discussion it is taken as such; a convincing demonstration remains a problem for future inquiry.

The possibility of the dynamic action of a system would probably be rejected a priori by many students. Although in the last analysis causality is just as inexplicable as a system action, still many students would feel more comfortable and would be willing to give credit for greater scientific validity to the formulation of the dynamics of a given happening in terms of causality than to its formulation in terms of system action. Causal thinking has been used in science for such a long time and, in certain fields, with such success that it is almost generally considered as *the* scientific thinking, although it may well be only a subvariety of it. Relational thinking is so firmly rooted a habit that the transition to system thinking is at least as difficult as the transition from a three-dimensional to a four-dimensional geometry.

This brief discussion of some holistic principles and concepts suggests the possibility of the logical formulation of some principles and concepts. Only a strict logical formulation can dispel the vagueness and obscurity which have been so common in the early holistic theories.

THE MATERIAL FOR PERSONALITY INTEGRATION

The preceding analysis of the structure of wholes has definite bearings on the problem of personality integration. Our task now will be to apply the results of the logical analysis specifically to personality integration. In order to do this, one has to consider first the nature of the material which is organized in the personality structure. We have dealt with the material previously and it will therefore be sufficient to recapitulate briefly our main points.

The subject of study for the science of personality is the biological total process. This is a unitary organization of part processes which we called biospheric occurrences. Biospheric occurrences are bipolar processes. The two poles are the subject pole and the object pole respectively. Biospheric occurrences, when considered from the subject pole as a point of reference, appear as manifestations of various dynamic tendencies. These can be traced back to more general tendencies, leading finally to the most general trends, that is, the trend toward autonomy and the trend toward homonomy. The ramifications and interconnections of organismic tendencies represent the subject-dependent organization of the biosphere.

Biospheric occurrences are influenced also by the connections which exist between the objects of the environment. The biological environment is a constellation of positive and negative valences. This can be expressed even better perhaps in simple language by stating that the environment is a constellation of opportunities and contraventions.

We cannot speak of subjective and objective "components" but only of biospheric occurrences the aspects of which have no independent existence. It is not sufficient to state that the biosphere is organized in accordance with certain organismic patterns, but it must also be added that at the same time such organization takes place *with regard to the objective setting*. And similarly the objective aspect of biospheric occurrences, the environment, is not merely a subject-independent constellation of external factors, but also a subject-independent connection of external factors which are *significant for the subject*.

From the unity of organism and environment in the biological total process it follows that the material which is integrated in the process of living consists not only of cell processes, muscle contractions, nerve impulses, drives, wishes, and so on, but also of environmental factors which function as opportunities and contraventions. In the course of biological activities not only organismic parts but also objects and happenings of the environment are arranged in certain patterns. In the activity of writing not only muscles and nerves are involved but obviously also paper, pencil, desk. The activities of a director in an industrial plant do not consist only in the coordination of his psychosomatic functions, but also in the coordination of the various activities going on in his factory. Although such a state of affairs is quite obvious, it is not superfluous to point to it specifically. The problem of personality integration is dealt with usually from an entirely subjectivistic point of view. Within certain limits such subjectivity has its justification. The subjective pole of the biospheric total process is the source of the organization; the subject is the centralizing, organizing factor. The material for this organization, however, involves both organism and environment. Thus, when we wish to study *organization,* the system formation as such, we may assume a subjective point of view. When, however, the *material* which is organized in the process of living is in question, we have to consider also the objective aspect of the biological total process.

We may conclude that the materials for personality integration are the biospheric occurrences. The meaning of this concept has been briefly indicated here and has been discussed in greater detail previously.

THE DIMENSIONAL DOMAIN OF PERSONALITY ORGANIZATION

It has been pointed out that a system may be defined as the distribution of parts in a dimensional domain. Every system implies some kind of dimensional domain which makes the multiplicity of parts possible and at the same time serves as a matrix for the arrangement of parts into definite patterns. Thus the question arises as to the nature of the dimensional domain in which the biological processes are arranged.

1. The first biological dimension to which I wish to call attention is what is occasionally called the *"vertical dimension."* The two poles of this dimension may be

called the depth and the surface. In daily parlance, too, we frequently characterize personality manifestations as deep or superficial, and we understand to some degree what is meant by such expressions. For scientific purposes we must, however, strictly define the meaning of these terms.

We have pointed out previously that all forms of human behavior originate from two general tendencies: the trend toward autonomy and the trend toward homonomy. These trends divide and subdivide into various branches. The first ramifications of these general trends are the personal axioms of behavior with their corresponding axiomatic values. These ramify successively into more and more specific attitudes toward more and more specific values and finally manifest themselves in concrete needs or drives which seek expression in actual behavior. The depth of the personality is formed by the basic human trends. Going from there toward the surface we meet first axioms of behavior, that is, very general attitudes referring to the major issues of life; then follow attitudes of increasing specificity until we reach the surface which is formed by the actual manifest behavior.

The connection between neighboring personality factors, arranged along the vertical dimension, is such that a factor closer to the surface is an expression and concretization of another factor which is closer to the depth of the personality. An aggressive act, for instance, may be the expression of hatred toward a given person. This in turn may be the manifestation of a more general attitude of aggressiveness which eventually may be traced back to some even more general attitude. In the vertical structure the more superficial factor is a part of the immediately deeper factor. The relationship between part and whole in this dimension is that the part is a concretization of the whole in some specific form.

Depth and surface differ from each other in many respects. Only the very surface of the personality, that is, manifest behavior, is accessible to direct observation. The depth has to be inferred from the surface manifestations. The depth is the more enduring, more permanent region of the personality, while the surface is more changeable. That is, modes of expression are changed rather easily, while a change of one's fundamental attitudes is much more difficult. This, however, does not imply the genetic priority of the depths of personality. The person in his development not only acquires more effective ways of expression, but may acquire also greater depths. The personality grows—so to say—from a middle position both toward the depths and toward the surface. The depth is more essential and represents what one is, while the surface is more accidental and represents only what one does. Surface and depth are to each other as actuality to potentiality.

2. When general trends originating from the depths of the personality reach the surface through a process of

successive specifications in the form of actual drives, needs, wishes, they have the tendency to concretize themselves in some form of actual behavior. The goal of such behavior is to create a biospheric constellation which represents the satisfaction of a need or the fulfillment of a wish. As a rule this constellation cannot be achieved at once, but only through a series of successive phases. The dimension along which these successive phases are arranged could be called *"the dimension of progression."* The initial biospheric constellation C_1 goes over to the final constellation C_2 through intermediary stages $c_1, c_2, c_3 \ldots . c_x$. Thus the whole activity may be represented in the following way: $C_1–c_1–c_2–c_3 \ldots . c_x–C_2$. Organization along the dimension of progression is a teleological one.[3] It is a means-end organization, each phase being the means for the following phase, and the end for the preceding phase. Later we shall see that the line $C_1–C_2$ cannot be divided arbitrarily into any number of phases as a geometrical distance can be divided into any number of smaller distances, but the number and place of the *caesurae* which divide the series of occurrences into phases are determined by the internal organization of the process.

It is important to keep in mind that the various phases of the means-end series are biospheric constellations.

[3] In the dimension of progression, besides the teleological structure, the genetic form of organization also takes place. Because of the great importance of this aspect, a special chapter will be devoted to it.

Very frequently ends (goals) are regarded as objects (for instance, food). Tolman[4] made an improvement when he defined goal not as an object but as a physiological state ("physiological quiescence"), thus placing the emphasis on the subject. In distinction, and at the same time in partial agreement with these two formulations, it is here claimed that the goal is a biospheric constellation which the organism tends to achieve. It does not seem necessary to repeat the reason for this statement, since it is implicit in the entire previous discussion.

The position of every single behavior can be defined both with regard to the vertical dimension and with regard to the dimension of progression. A given activity may be looked upon as an organization of means and ends, but at the same time this activity represents the satisfaction of some need which in turn is the surface manifestation of deeper tendencies. The course of a biospheric occurrence may then be traced in the following way: a general tendency, through a series of successive specifications, reaches the surface in the form of an actual drive. This is a linear course which leads from the depths to the surface. Reaching the surface a change in direction takes place by spreading out of the activity along the dimension of progression in the form of a means-end organization. This may be visualized as perpendicular to the vertical dimension.

[4] E. C. Tolman, Purposive Behavior in Animals and Men, New York, Century, 1932.

3. The two previous dimensions do not define sufficiently the dimensional domain of the biospheric organization. A multiplicity of personality factors is possible also in other ways than the distribution of items in the vertical dimension and in the dimension of progression. The items then are not distinguished as expression and expressed (surface-depths) or means and ends (progression), but exist side by side, forming the *dimension of breadth* or, as we may call it, the *transverse dimension*. As we go from the depths to the surface the tendencies of the organism become not only more specific, but also more numerous. The same general tendency may seek expression in a number of ways. The various specific expressions of the same deeper tendency are not subordinated or superordinated to each other, but exist side by side. They are distributed in a transverse row, "perpendicular" to the vertical dimension.

The transverse dimension is "perpendicular" also to the dimension of progression. When one is writing a letter this activity may be a means toward some goal. In the movement of writing several muscles are involved simultaneously. The simultaneous muscle contractions do not stand to each other in a means-end relationship but exist side by side, that is, in a transversal arrangement. The organization of parts into a whole along the transverse dimension can be called synergesis, or simply coordination.

The position of each behavior may be defined in

terms of three dimensions. The following illustrates this. A person wants to leave the house and is just reaching for his hat. This movement is composed of a number of coordinated muscle contractions (transverse dimension). This activity at the same time is a phase in a means-end organization (dimension of progression). Furthermore it is a concrete expression of some tendency of the organism which can be traced back to more and more general tendencies (vertical dimension).

One could raise the question whether the dimensions described in this section can properly be called dimensions or so designated only in a metaphorical sense of the word. If dimensions are defined as *principia individuationis,* then there is no doubt that what we have dealt with falls into the category of dimensions. It would be an interesting task to investigate whether there is any relation between the aforementioned dimensions of the biosphere and the space-time of physics. We have stated (page 108) that physics derives its field of study from the biosphere through a number of parenthetic exclusions. It is very probable that the physical dimensions may also be derived from biospheric dimensions through a process of exclusion. Thus the question would be: What features does physics exclude from the biospheric dimensions when it arrives at the concepts of time and space? Although the problem is a very interesting one, we cannot enter into its discussion because it would lead us too far afield.

This section may be summarized by stating that the domain for personality organization has three dimensions: 1) The vertical dimension. The items are so arranged along this dimension that one of them (the more superficial) is a concretization of the other (the deeper one). 2) The dimension of progression. The arrangement of items in this dimension forms a means-end organization. 3) The transverse dimension. The items of this dimension form a synergetic organization or coordination.

It remains a question whether these three dimensions define completely the domain for personality organization, or whether the domain has additional dimensions. The latter possibility cannot be excluded. The three dimensions which have been mentioned may not be the only ones, but they are certainly very important.

THE DIFFERENTIATION OF WHOLES

An important characteristic of wholes is the degree of their differentiation into parts. A part may stand out, have an individuality of its own, or it may be imbedded in the whole. When a person is crossing a brook where a few stones are above the water surface, every step has to be individually planned and stands out as a separate act in the total process. On the other hand, in ordinary walking the single steps have much less individuality, and are more imbedded in the total activity. Wholes in which the parts are deeply imbedded appear more homogeneous and diffuse, while wholes with individualized parts are more articulated and distinct.

In a diffuse system the total function is more or less evenly distributed over the entire whole. When, however, more complex functions are required from a given system a kind of division of labor takes place whereby to each part a more specific function is assigned. This has been very well demonstrated, for instance, in the work of Coghill[5] who has demonstrated that the more primitive form of motor behavior consists of generalized mass movements, while independent movements of single limbs and the single reflexes develop later. Similar phenomena can also be observed in the motor development of the human child, generalized mass movements preceding the phase at which the differented use of single limbs is achieved. Somewhat later the child grasps first with the whole hand, before the use of single fingers in a differented fashion is established. Such differentiated functioning may be lost in certain pathological conditions (Head, Rivers), when instead of responding to stimulation with individual reflexes the patient responds with generalized mass movements, with the so-called mass reflexes. In the field of perception, too, we may distinguish between various degrees of differentiation. In ordinary reading the total picture of the words predomi-

[5] G. E. Coghill, Anatomy and the Problem of Behavior, New York, Macmillan, 1929.

nates and one pays little attention to the design of the single letters. Thus the visual material is less differentiated than it is in proofreading. One may look at a flower bed and perceive it as a color pattern, or one may perceive single flowers individually. One may have a diffuse gustatory perception of some food, or a more differentiated one where the individual ingredients are singled out. In thinking, there are very marked differences according to the differentiation of the thought system. We may have a vague impression, for example, that an argument is correct or fallacious without being for the moment able to point out why, while in a better differentiated stage we spot the error. Learning is a good example of successive differentiations. Superficial acquaintance with a subject gives first only a diffuse impression, a "feel" for the subject, while after greater familiarity with the material the subject gains sharpness and distinctness.

The organism tends to be economical with respect to differentiation. Diffuse functions become differentiated only when there is a pronounced need for individualized, specific functions. The vegetative functions, for instance, can be carried out efficiently in a comparatively diffuse manner while functions which the sensory and neuromuscular organs have to carry out require a much higher degree of differentiation into specific part functions.

The parts of a system may be differentiated in various degrees according to functional requirements. For instance, the differentiation of the motor system is not evenly distributed throughout the whole body. The movements of the hand and fingers are much more differentiated than those of the feet and toes. Such differences manifest themselves also in the degree of morphological articulation. Considering only their morphological structure the feet have much greater functional potentiality than it seems. They are not differentiated functionally because there is no need for it. They have been specialized for a limited number of functions. However, with training some people acquire a considerable skill in using their feet and toes for other purposes. The difference is even more marked if one compares the motor functions of the hand with those of the muscles of the back. One is able to move one's fingers individually, but on the back one can move only large groups of muscles. This is not due to differences of innervation. There are persons who are able to contract separately almost every single muscle of the back. The difference is rather in the nature of the functions which are required, which necessitate in one case a slight and in the other case a high degree of differentiation. Through training the degree of differentiation may be developed considerably. Compare, for instance, the motor articulation of the hand of a pianist with that of a laborer who uses his hands mainly in handling a pick and shovel. The differentiation of vocal functions also varies greatly. Examples which illustrate various degrees of differentiation could be multiplied almost ad infinitum.

In a highly differentiated whole the parts are more individualized and have a greater relative autonomy, a greater independence from the whole. Thus in the process of differentiation there is a distinct tendency toward the breaking up of the unity of the whole, that is, the danger of disintegration. This tendency is normally counterbalanced by the whole through its integrating function. In this case the whole exerts its influence not by opposing differentiation but by coordination of the differentiated part functions under the general system principle. When this latter phase is successfully accomplished the whole reaches a higher degree of efficiency and becomes capable of more adequately differentiated functioning. The evolution of wholes is itself accomplished in steps of successive differentiation and systematic reintegrations. The potential danger of disintegration implied in every form of differentiation, however, should not be minimized.

In every biospheric constellation one may distinguish a more differentiated component which, at a given moment, stands in the foreground ("figure") and the rather diffuse remainder of the biospheric constellation which forms the background. This applies to the subjective as well as to the environmental aspect of the biospheric constellation. Each biospheric occurrence is differentiated out from a background of diffuse organismic tendencies toward a diffusely perceived constellation of environmental opportunities and contraventions. From the diffuse organismic background a more definitely shaped drive emerges for which, from the diffuse environmental background, some definite factors are singled out and drawn into the foreground. A general sketchy plan may then arise with regard to the means and ends for the satisfaction of the drive. The plan becomes more articulated, and specific opportunities which fit into the plan and specific obstacles which interfere with it are singled out from the diffuse environmental background. The solution of intellectual problems and muscular activities may be needed which are differentiated out of a diffuse background of ideas and a diffuse background of the tonus pattern of the body, respectively. The process of differentiation may be a slow one or may occur almost instantaneously.

If a given part is differentiated out of the whole and enters into the foreground, although its relative autonomy increases, it does not function entirely independently of the rest of the whole. A given occurrence is not defined solely by the happenings in the foreground, but is influenced also by the background. A single biospheric occurrence is determined not only by the directly involved factors, but also by the more remote personality background and the broader, more remote environmental setting.

The status of differentiation of the biosphere is continuously changing. Occurrences emerge into the foreground and soon retreat into the diffuse background of life, making place for new occurrences to emerge.

The concept of differentiation has the possibility of a wide application in the whole field of personality research. Thus, for instance, the conditioned-response phenomena gain a new interpretation in the light of the concept of differentiation. This conception implies that the organism originally does not respond to a separate stimulus, like food, but to the total situation in which food occurs: conditions of light, sound, temperature, the state of the organism itself, briefly, the whole objective and subjective setting. When a situation, for instance, the situation of feeding, is repeated, the composition of the total environmental constellation varies from time to time and only a group of factors which are closely associated with the food remain constant. Such factors are the visual appearance of the food, its odor, taste, and so forth. Thus, by repetition, from the total situation a group of constant factors is differentiated out, factors serving as indices of a situation which brings satisfaction for the need while the rest of the situation is pushed more and more into the background, although it still retains a somewhat remote influence on what happens in the foreground. If now we arrange the situation in such a way that some normally variable factor becomes constant, this will also be included in the differentiated group of indices. A new "figure-background" formation takes place, with a new element included in the "figure."

If this view is correct, then the problem involved in the phenomenon of conditioning is *not* how conditioned responses arise by a hypothetical concatenation of simple reflexes. Rather the problem would be: How do differentiated, local responses to differentiated items of stimuli develop from the original total reaction to the total situation? Moreover, according to our point of view, in the situation of experimental conditioning, no concatenation of reflexes takes place, but a new sort of figure-background differentiation.

The concept of differentiation is a very important one for the study of the biological total process. Significant investigations have already been made on the basis of this conception. The work of Coghill, Head, and Rivers has already been mentioned. Driesch's[6] investigation in genetics and his theory of *harmonisch equipotentieller Systeme* are based largely on the concept of differentiation. The central idea of the *Entwickelungspsychologie* of the school of Leipzig has also been the concept of differentiation. The concept has been best formulated theoretically by W. Stern.[7] However, in spite of these important studies, the concept of differentiation has not yet been as fully exploited as its significance would justify.

[6] H. Driesch, Die Maschine und der Organismus, Leipzig, Barth, (Bios, vol. 4), 1935.

[7] W. Stern, Studien zur Personwissenschaft, I: Personalistik als Wissenschaft, Leipzig, Barth, 1930.

THE PROBLEM OF INTEGRATION

HOLISTIC INTERPRETATION OF THE STIMULUS-RESPONSE PATTERN

One of the principles formulated with regard to the structure of wholes in an earlier section of this chapter was that a given constituent functions as a part of a whole not due to its intrinsic properties as such, but due to the position which it occupies in the system. Intrinsic properties are relevant only in so far as they impart to the given constituent features which qualify the constituent to occupy a required position in the whole. Thus, for instance, the chemical properties of hemoglobin relative to oxygen are significant in this context because they qualify this substance to occupy a significant position in the total economy of the organism. Certain other properties of hemoglobin, on the other hand, may be biologically entirely insignificant. We may then conclude that any constituent becomes part of a whole through the position which it occupies in the system; immanent properties of a constituent are relevant for the whole only when they are relevant to the constituent's positional value.

This notion has important bearings on various problems of personality organization. We may analyze with profit its implications concerning the stimulus-response problem. According to the above point of view an object acquires the property of being a stimulus not by any immanent qualities, but by the particular position which it occupies in the system of the total organism. In order to evaluate the significance of this statement we have to clarify first what is meant by "occupying a position in the system of the total organism." A system can be defined by what we called "system principle." The main task in the previous chapter was exactly the discussion and definition of the system principle of the organism. According to the theory propounded, a double pattern, the trend toward increased autonomy and the trend toward homonomy, represents the system principle of the total process of living. The position of any factor within this system is characterized by the role or function which the given factor has within the frame of the general dynamic pattern of the organismic total process. The position of a given factor is dependent upon whether it promotes or handicaps the realization of the basic pattern (autonomy-homonomy) of the total process and upon the specific way in which it promotes or handicaps it. The totality of all factors organized by position in the general pattern of the organismic total process forms the structure of personality.

Stimulus implies either the appearance of a new factor which occupies a significant position in the biosphere or the change of a part from one position to another. In the first case one usually speaks of "external," in the second of "internal," stimuli. Examples of external stimuli are, for instance, the appearance of a factor from the outside which threatens to break up the system of the organismic total process (contravention) or a factor which lends itself to be constructively built into the pattern of the organismic process, to fill a gap in the system or offer the possibility of expression for the basic trends of the organism in some special way (opportunity). In general, external stimuli can be defined as contraventions and opportunities, that is, as situations which either have to be warded off or can be utilized for the realization of the system principle of the organism.

The position of many of the external stimuli is not very clearly defined. Many data, for instance, the greater part of our perceptual world, are simply registered and their position may be defined as being in reserve. Such data are registered and kept in the background as factors of potential significance in the organismic scheme.

Internal stimuli arise from the organismic activity itself. They create changes of constellation which necessitate a rearrangement of the system. Thus, for instance, the organism using up foodstuff creates a change, the state of hunger, which functions as a new internal stimulus.

The distinction between external and internal stimuli is somewhat artificial. Tolman is right when he claims that for the initiation of activities both stimulus (external stimulus) and an initiating physiological state (I would say instead "an initiating constellation of subjective factors") are needed. The first phase of an activity is stimulation; this is a biospheric constellation in which an object pole and a subject pole can be distinguished but not separated.

Stimulation in general can be defined as a positional value change in some part of the organism which causes a change of constellation of the whole. Such change of constellation calls for some kind of rearrangement which is effected by certain positional value changes of one or more parts of the organism. The positional value change aiming at some kind of rearrangement is what one calls "response." The response is determined by and is in accordance with the system principle of the organism, that is, the response serves to assert the organism's basic trends (autonomy and homonomy) in some of its more specific ramifications.

That our assumption is basically different from the conventionally assumed stimulus-response pattern will be clear from the above discussion. Usually it is implied that the stimulus-response connection is a part-to-part relationship, while according to the theory presented here the stimulus-response connection is a system action which proceeds from the part to the whole (positional value changes in one or more parts—change of total constellation) and from the whole to the part (rearrangement of the total constellation according to the system principle of the organism—effected by positional value changes in one or more parts).

An example may illustrate this. The first results of a recently initiated experiment may impress me as highly improbable. Hence I will put the data aside on the assumption that there is some error in the experimental technique which is to be checked later. Then I chance to read a scientific report in which another investigator, working with an entirely different technique, obtained results similar to mine. The positional value of my data in the scheme of my endeavors changes immediately. They may no longer be viewed as the result of technical error but perhaps as indicators of some important new fact. Thus the data gain new significance and value for me. Their apparent improbability even adds to their stimulus value. This change of positional value induces a reorientation, a change in the momentary constellation of my interests and attitudes with regard to the particular problem. This rearrangement of emphasis in the total constellation means a redistribution of tensions in the system which find an outlet in some specific response, such as an immediate resumption of the experiments in question. The stimulus-response connection can be expressed in a shorthand fashion in the following way: $part_1$–whole–$part_2$.[8]

The change of constellation in the whole induced by the stimulation is either a disturbance in the arrange-

[8] This theory is not to be confused with the conventional pattern: receptor → central-organ → effector. The middle term in our scheme is not a central organ or central process, but the total personality constellation. One of our previous statements (Chapter II) that the stimulus does not *cause* a reaction but prompts the organism to respond to it in its own characteristic fashion, has now gained a sufficiently clear meaning.

ment of parts, that is, the formation of a "bad" Gestalt or the rise of an "open" Gestalt. We have defined as "bad," or Gestalts with little *Pregnanz,* those wholes in which only a limited number of positions sufficient to suggest the system principle are occupied, while other members are out of position; and we defined "open" Gestalt as being such wholes where a sufficient number of positions are occupied to suggest the system principle while other positions are not filled. Gestalt psychologists have demonstrated that among open Gestalts there is a tendency toward "closure" and also that there is a tendency toward greater *Pregnanz,* that is, "bad" Gestalts tend to become "good" ones. These tendencies could be regarded as subvarieties of one more inclusive tendency: the tendency *toward a complete realization of the system principle.* This is accomplished in the case of closure by filling in unoccupied positions, and in the case of the tendency toward *Pregnanz* by a rearrangement of positions in such a way that outlying points are moved toward positions corresponding to the system principle. System dynamics—at least *one* basic principle of system dynamics—would then consist in a movement toward a greater approximation of the system principle. The response phase of the stimulus-response process (rearrangement of the constellation of the whole which is accomplished by positional changes in one or more parts) can best be understood as a manifestation of the trend toward the greater approximation of the system principle.

It is possible that on the basis of specific investigations this principle may be formulated in greater detail. Certain facts would, for instance, indicate that the more nearly complete is a whole, the stronger is the tendency toward perfect completion. If this possibility could be substantiated, new light would be thrown on those phenomena which Hull attempted to explain on the basis of his hypothesis of goal gradients.[9]

In the rearrangement of a constellation, the response may take place either by positional shifts close to the object pole of the biospheric occurrence or by positional shifts close to the subject pole. In this latter case, which is a sort of "change of attack," one speaks of *adaptation*. Behavior, as a rule, involves in various degrees both the manipulation of environmental factors and an adaptive rearrangement of the subjective factors, for the purpose of meeting the situation adequately.

THE RANGE OF VARIATION OF THE POSITIONS IN A SYSTEM

Against the holistic formulation of the stimulus-response pattern the objection may be raised that in many instances the total organism does not seem to be particularly involved in the stimulus-response processes. On the surface the latter often seems to be a rather segmental affair which may take place even in relative isolation

[9] C. L. Hull, The goal gradient hypothesis and maze learning, Psychological Review, 39:25–43, January 1932.

from the total personality. Such would be the case, for instance, with simple reflexes. One could attempt to answer this objection by stating that the isolation of part processes is never a complete one and in most instances at least a modicum of dependence upon the whole can be actually demonstrated. This statement, however, would only avoid the real issue. The objection has sufficient basis to demand serious consideration. One has to admit relatively isolated part processes and one has to examine whether the fact of relative isolation is compatible or not with the holistic theory of stimulus-response processes.

Personality can be regarded as a hierarchy of systems. In the larger personality organization the significant positions are occupied by constituents which themselves are also systems; the constituents of the secondary system may also be systems; and so on. Thus personality may be considered as a hierarchy with the total personality organization at the top; below it follow the subsystems of first order, second order, third order, and so on.[10] When one studies the connections in such a hierarchy from the

[10] The bottom of the hierarchical order is represented by physicochemical processes. Whether these, too, have a system character is difficult to decide. Although not entirely convinced, I am in sympathy with the theory of A. Meyer (the German biologist), who regards the biological happenings as the prototypes of all events. He considers the laws of physics and chemistry as a "*modellmässige Vereinfachung*" of the biological laws. If we translate such a point of view in terms of my theory, it would mean that relational connections and system action are not fundamentally different. Causation would be an extraordinarily simplified and reduced form of system action.

dynamic point of view, it is useful to distinguish the dynamics *within* a given subsystem and *between* systems of different orders. We maintain that the dynamics within a system is not a relational one; that is, it is not based on direct connections between the constituent parts, but is a system action which takes place in the previously defined fashion. The fact of the relative isolation of certain stimulus-response processes would not be in contradiction to the system character of the process. The stimulus-response process may still be considered as following the pattern: $part_1$–whole–$part_2$, only the middle term would not refer to the total organism but to a subsystem.

Besides the internal dynamics of a given subsystem we have to consider also the dynamic connections between systems. Does a change within a subsystem influence the other systems of the organism and, if so, to what extent and under what conditions?

The part functions which make up the biological total process differ from each other in that some of the functions have a rather fixed position while others have rather variable positions in the system to which they belong. The function of a part may be uniform and may show little variation, while the functional variation of another part may have a wide range. Thus, for instance, the salivary glands have a restricted range of functional variation as compared to the range of variation in functions of the cerebral cortex. Part functions which have a broad range of variation are sensitive to changes in the constellation of the whole. The given part function is determined by the momentary constellation of the whole; that is, it depends upon the constellation of the whole which of the various functional possibilities of the given part should be realized. Other parts, on the contrary, function in a rather constant and uniform way. The latter types of function take care of some constant, uniform need of the organism. The uniform function is, so to speak, entrusted to the part once and for all. Such functions are relatively uninfluenced by the momentary constellation of the superordinate whole.

The following diagram illustrates the difference between fixed and variable positions in a system.

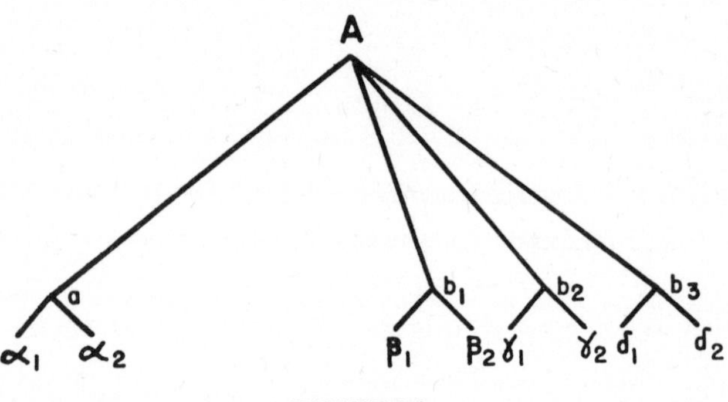

FIGURE 10

A is a system which is formed by a subsystem of fixed position (*a*) and by another subsystem of variable position (*b*); *a* always occupies the same position in A, while *b* can occupy the positions b_1, b_2, b_3; α_1 and α_2 are parts of *a*, β_1 and β_2 of b_1, etc. We may now compare the stimulus-response process in the subsystems of fixed and of variable positions. The given stimulus in subsystem b_1 consists in a positional change β_1, which changes the total constellation of b_1; the constellation of the subsystem will be rearranged by means of the response β_2. The stimulus-response pattern will in this case be β_1–b_1–β_2. We stated, however, that the position of this subsystem depends upon the constellation in A, its position being in one case b_1, in another case b_2 or b_3. Thus in a response the stimulus in the subsystem goes not only through the immediate whole (b) but also through the superordinate whole A. The position of the subsystem b in the superordinate system A varies from time to time.

On the other hand, in the case of the subsystem a, which has a fixed position, the pattern of the stimulus-response process is: α_1–a–α_2, where a has a fixed value and does not vary. This gives the impression that the stimulus-response process is entirely independent of A. However, strictly speaking such is not the case because a represents a positional value in A; a implies A. The position a is system-adequate to A; that is, function a is in accord with the system principle of A. The difference is only that the system-adequate position a is fixed, so to say—it is a preestablished arrangement defined once for all, while in the case of a plastic subsystem the system-adequate position is defined from time to time in accordance with the momentary constellation of the superordinate system.

The fixity of a position in a system is usually only relative. Similarly the variation of a position is not without limits. The organism in its various regions has different degrees of positional variability of its part functions. The range of positional variation has several implications. 1) Small range of variation means great uniformity of functions. 2) Uniform function can be adequate only there where the environmental conditions are fairly uniform. The greater the homeostasis (Cannon) of the environment, the greater is the uniformity of function of the corresponding biological part process. 3) The variability of position is further correlated with the degree of automatization: the smaller the variability the more automatic is the function. Automatization means that a given part function is little influenced by those changes of constellation which take place in the superordinate system. 4) Further we may note that the greater the variability of the function the more it can be directly influenced by conscious processes.

In order to exemplify the differences between part systems with a small range of variation and those with a broad range of variation of position, we may roughly distinguish two regions in the organism, the one being characterized by a great, the other by a small, range of variation. In the first group we may include (A), sensory-neuromuscular functions, in the second (B), the functions of the viscera.

A. The sensory-neuromuscular functions take place

essentially in the extrasomatic section of the biosphere. The corresponding organs also form topographically the outer regions of the organism. Sensory data give us information mainly with regard to the conditions of the external environment. Although there are sensations informing us of our body functions, these are diffuse as compared with the sharp, object-forming external sensations. The functions of the striped muscles similarly serve mainly to manage the external environment. 1) Conditions in the external environment are highly variable and homeostasis is slight. We may and actually do increase the homeostasis of our external environment, but it never approaches, for instance, the homeostasis of the blood. 2) A broad range of variations of the organismic functions corresponds to the high variability of conditions in the external environment. No fixed functions, however precise and complex they might be, would be adequate to manage situations in which such a large range of changes takes place. Functions must be plastic in order to be adequate to cope with a changing world. Since the changes in the external environment are almost unpredictable, these functions must be highly sensitive to the total constellation. 3) This circumstance does not allow to any great extent for automatization of functions. 4) Conscious activity has its sphere of direct influence primarily in this outer layer, while other functions may be influenced through conscious process only indirectly.

B. The environment with which the visceral functions have to deal is much more standardized and homeostatic. 1) The process of standardization of the environment is well exemplified in the transition of food from the external environment into the blood stream. The food is first carefully selected; then, by a series of processes, such as mastication, exposure to chemical influences of the secretions of the digestive glands, mechanical work of the stomach, it becomes more and more standardized. When the material gets to the blood stream its conditions become highly homeostatic. 2) This great uniformity and constancy of conditions allow efficient functioning by means of processes which have a relatively small range of variation. The variation decreases as it goes inward. Chewing is still quite variable; swallowing and gastric movement are already fairly uniform and rigid; they perform highly specialized tasks. 3) The functions become increasingly automatic. 4) Parallel with this, the direct influence of conscious activity decreases.

Functions which are partially visceral but have also reference to the external environment as, for instance, excretory functions, are midway between automatization and voluntary control. In the case of excretory functions such a middle position is also morphologically reflected in the double (voluntary and involuntary) sphincter.

Fixation of functions has a great economic value since it largely frees the organism from energy-consuming adjustments. Therefore the organism tends to establish such uniformities even in spheres of greater plasticity. This is accomplished through a standardization of the environment, the establishment of fixed habits, the routinization of daily life, and other similar arrangements.

In this section a distinction has been made between rigid systems in which the parts have rather fixed positions, and more plastic systems in which the position of the parts is more variable and greatly influenced by the momentary constellation of the whole to which it belongs.

Rigid and plastic systems differ from each other in various respects. 1) Processes which go on in a rigid system are rather localized happenings; the processes in plastic systems spread upward and downward to superordinated and subordinated systems respectively. 2) Rigid systems carry out highly standardized, uniform functions; plastic systems have a broad range of functional variation. 3) Rigid systems are associated with a high degree, plastic systems with a low degree, of homeostasis in the environment. 4) The functions of rigid systems are more automatic than those of plastic systems. 5) Plastic systems are to a greater extent directly influenced by conscious activity than are rigid systems.

The various part systems of the organism show different degrees of plasticity. On the whole, the sensory-neuromuscular functions are more plastic, the visceral functions more rigid.

THE CONTINUITY OF ACTION IN A HIERARCHY OF SYSTEMS

It has been pointed out that a change in some part system of the biological total process may take place in relative isolation or may have repercussions in other systems. We may now examine whether any law may be established concerning the manner in which a change in a given part spreads to other regions of the organism.

For this purpose it is desirable to clarify the concept of part from a new angle. The concept of part should be first of all distinguished from that of fragment. Fragments are results of an arbitrary division while the whole is articulated into parts by its inherent organization. Taking a process such as walking, for example, we may say that the parts of the act of walking are steps, while, for instance, the last fourth of the first step together with the first half of the second step would be an example of an arbitrary fragmentation of the walk. What is the criterion which allows us to tell where parts begin and end? Why do we not call, for instance, the lifting of one leg a part, the moving of the leg forward a second part, the placing it again on the ground a third part? We know that the part has a position in the whole, that it has a definite role for the realization of the function of the corresponding whole. The function of walking is to carry the body from one place to another. The total locomotion in this case is composed of a number of smaller units of locomotion. When the leg is only lifted, the body does not move into a new position yet; progression is made only if the foot reaches the ground again, that is, when the step is completed. An uncompleted step does not contribute to the total process of walking. Thus we may say that the part is characterized by being relatively complete in itself and by contributing *directly* to the realization of the function of the whole.

The concept of parts should be reserved to *immediate parts*. We have mentioned that complex wholes, like the organism, consist of a hierarchy of systems: a system of first order, systems of second order, third order, and so on. A given subsystem is part only of the immediately superordinate system, but not of a distant superordinate system. The restriction of the concept of part to mean "immediate part" is necessary if the concept is to have any significant meaning. It would not mean much, for instance, to state that the word "man" is part of a textbook of sociology, merely because the word occurs in that textbook. Similarly it would be incorrect to say that the sound "o" is a part of the sentence, "Man is a social being." These are not immediate parts. A sound cannot be a part of a sentence without being part of a word and the word cannot be part of a treatise unless it is part of a sentence. The concept of part has meaning only with reference to the corresponding immediate whole. In other words, part and whole refer to connections between neighboring systems. In a hierarchy of systems, a second-order system is part of the first-order system and at the same time it is a whole, the parts of which are third-order systems.

We may now conclude that a part has to have two characteristics: first, it has to be *relatively complete* in itself, and second, it has to occupy *directly* a position in a system without the mediation of intermediary systems.

The latter characteristic has important implications for the dynamics of wholes. System action goes either from part to whole or from whole to part. From part to whole: change of one or more positions (addition of new positions, disappearance of positions, or change from one position to another)—which results in a changed constellation of the whole. From whole to part: a change in the constellation of the whole—which is effected by changes in the positions of parts. Since a system action consists always of a change progressing from part to whole or vice versa, and since the whole-part relation always refers to the connection between neighboring systems, it follows that the *spread of change from any section of the whole is continuous.*

Changes cannot affect directly a distant region of the hierarchy of systems, but always spread across the intermediary systems. If some of the sounds of a word are changed, such change does not alter the meaning of the sentence except if the change of sounds affects the meaning of the word which then, in turn, may change the meaning of the sentence.

By the same token, we may state that such attempts

as, for instance, tying up *directly* some physicochemical changes with some complex form of behavior are very deceiving. If one neglects the intermediary steps one may bring into relationship members so distant that the connection between them remains entirely incomprehensible. The connections between the influence of a given drug on cell metabolism and some of its distant effects, for instance, a friendly, communicative attitude, cannot be understood if one disregards the various stages in the spread of influence through the intermediary systems. Correlations between processes in distant parts have, of course, a definite value from a theoretical as well as from a practical point of view. The establishment of such correlations should, however, be only a beginning. The next step is the tracing of the passage of change through the intermediary systems.

The continuity of spread in a composite system may be regarded as a basic law of system dynamics. Change in any part of a system spreads in a continuous fashion and may involve the entire whole, or also the range of the spread may be limited. We know that a whole can change also by a mere rearrangement of its parts without any change in the internal structure of the parts. Four straight rods can be arranged in many different geometrical patterns without "changing" the rods themselves, or, taking an example from biology, groups of "identical" muscle contractions may result in a variety of movements simply by changing the time sequence of the single contractions. Also the constituents of a whole may change without effecting any change in the system. Walking from one point to another may remain the same system even if the internal structure of the single steps varies considerably. A change in the whole does not necessarily involve changes in the structure of its constituents and similarly changes in the structure of constituents may take place without inducing changes in the structure or whole. The structure of the parts will be affected only by such changes in the whole as require a rearrangement in the structure of the part; and the whole will be affected only by such changes in the structure of the parts as involve a positional change of the part and thus change the constellation of the whole. Only this type of change spreads upward (from part to whole) or downward (from whole to part). Other changes remain localized.

We may now summarize the foregoing discussion in the following way. Parts are characterized by being relatively complete in themselves and by occupying a position directly in a system. The concept of part should be restricted to mean "immediate" part. System action spreads in a continuous manner upward or downward to the superordinate and subordinate systems respectively. It may spread over the entire whole or it may be limited to a certain region.

THE PROBLEM OF INTEGRATION

SUMMARY

The problem of integration is probably the most important and the most difficult chapter in the study of personality. Before much advance can be made in the study of integration, a system of logic adequate to deal with the problem has to be developed. An attempt in this direction is offered.

Relationships have been contrasted with systems and an attempt has been made to show that the structure of wholes cannot be described in terms of relation, but in terms of systems. The differences between these two logical genera can be summarized as follows:

1) Relations involve two and only two members (relata). Complex relations can always be analyzed into pairs of relata. Systems may involve an unspecified number of components. 2) The relata enter into a relationship due to their inherent attributes, while the constituents enter into a system connection not directly through their immanent attributes but through the position which they occupy in the system. Secondary relations which are based on the positional values of the relata can be established also between members of a system. But the system cannot be described even in terms of such relationships. 3) The existence of a system implies a dimensional domain. Systems are specific forms of distribution of members in a dimensional domain. 4) In relationships the connection between the relata is a direct one. The mem-

bers of a system, on the contrary, do not need to be directly connected; they are connected in and by the whole.

The logical formulation of a given system states the system principle of the whole.

Some of the most important formulations of Gestalt psychology have been interpreted as system characteristics.

The attempt has been made to apply the notion about systems to the problem of personality integration. The materials which serve as constituents for personality integration are biospheric occurrences. The parts are arranged in a specific domain. The domain for personality organization has at least three dimensions. 1) The vertical dimension leads from the depth to the surface. The items along this dimension are so arranged that the one (the more superficial) is a concretization of the other (the deeper one). 2) A second dimension is that of progression. The arrangement of items along this dimension forms a means-end organization. 3) A third is the transverse dimension. The items of this dimension form a synergetic organization or a coordination.

Wholes may be strongly articulated and have highly individualized parts or else they may be diffuse and have deeply imbedded parts. In every biospheric constellation one may distinguish a more differentiated component which stands in the foreground ("figure") and the rather diffuse remainder of the biospheric constellation which forms the background. The concept of differentiation has great significance for the consideration of various personality problems. As an example of the applicability of this concept to the interpretation of biological facts, the significance of differentiation for the phenomenon of conditioning has been tentatively suggested.

The notion of systems has interesting implications when applied to the problem of the stimulus-response process. The stimulus is a positional change of one or more parts of the whole. This changes the total constellation of the whole. To this the organism responds by rearranging the total constellation according to the system principle. The rearrangement takes place by positional changes of one or more parts.

The distinction has been made between rigid systems in which the parts have fixed positions and are little affected by changing the constellation of the whole, and plastic systems in which the position of parts is more variable and is easily influenced by the momentary constellation of the whole. Rigid and plastic systems differ from each other in various respects: 1) Processes in a rigid system are rather localized; the processes in a plastic system spread out to the subordinate and superordinate systems. 2) Rigid systems carry out highly standardized, uniform functions; plastic systems have a broad range of functional variation. 3) Rigid systems are associated with a high degree, plastic systems with a low degree, of homeostasis of the environment. 4) The functions of rigid systems are more automatic than those of plastic systems. 5) Plastic systems are to a greater extent directly influenced by conscious activity than are rigid systems.

Parts are characterized by being relatively complete in themselves and by occupying directly a position in a system. The concept of part should be restricted to mean immediate part. System action spreads in a continuous fashion upward and downward to superordinate and subordinate systems respectively. It may be limited to a small region or be widely diffused.

IX. DISTURBANCES OF INTEGRATION

ONE PART MAY BELONG TO VARIOUS SYSTEMS

If a given function has been identified as part of a larger system, this connection has validity only for the given occasion. The connection is usually not a permanent one. An individual function may participate in more than one system. Function *a* may be at one time part of the system A, another time of the system B, or C, etc. New functions can arise not only by addition of new part functions, but also by a rearrangement of the same part functions to form different total functions. Thus, an individual muscle contraction may be at various occasions part of widely different motor patterns. The field of symbolic activities is especially abundant in examples which show the multiple utilization of smaller units. The organism works in a highly economical way, forming from a relatively small number of part functions a great variety of larger functional systems. In a sense one may say that the organism is functionally overcrowded, that is, it carries out a great variety of functions with the aid of a relatively small number of individual items. This is possible only if multiple functions are assigned simultaneously or successively to a given part. The functional overcrowding manifests itself occasionally also as a morphological one. A good example of this is the anatomical combination of the urinary, sexual, and in certain degree also anal organs. The urethra in the male, for instance, is just as much a part of the urinary as of the genital system. Another example is the close association of the nutritive, speech, respiratory, and some minor functions which are carried out with the morphological structures of the "oral zone."

The functional overcrowding of the organism is greatly increased through the fact that secondary meanings may be superimposed on primary biological functions. Sex activity may function as an act of reproduction and at the same time, by a superimposed symbolic meaning, also as an act of aggression. Psychoanalysis places special emphasis on the fact that certain primary physiological functions, such as eating, excretion, and sexual acts, are overlaid with secondary meanings. The contributions of psychoanalysis on infantile theories and on "organ language" fall readily into this category.

Figures 11 and 12 visualize how the same part may belong successively or simultaneously to more than one system. Figure 11 shows that on a given occasion *a* is part of A; on other occasions it may be part of B or C. Figure 12 shows that *a* is part of A, B, and C simultaneously. In the first case we may speak of *vicarious functioning,* while in the second case of *cross-functioning.*

Cross-functioning is not an exception but the rule in

personality dynamics. In a previous section (page 131) we compared the ramification of the dynamic tendencies of the biological total process to the ramification of the branches of a tree. General tendencies ramify into primary, secondary, tertiary branches, the actual behavior representing the tip of each terminal branch.

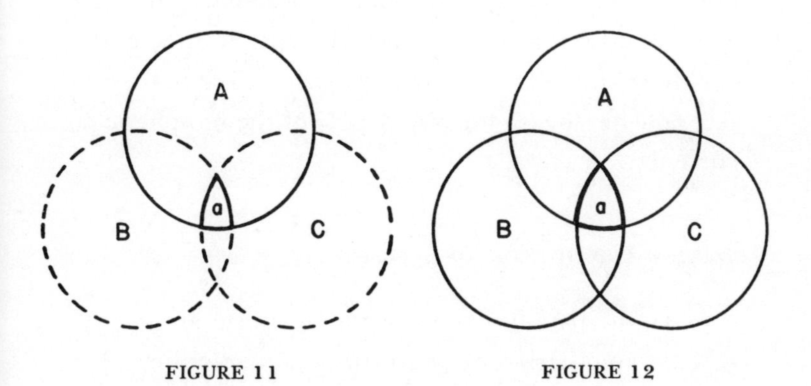

FIGURE 11

FIGURE 12

This, however, is only one side of the picture. We must add that a given sample of behavior seldom corresponds to a single terminal branch; it usually represents a confluence of many terminal branches. One speaks frequently in such a case of multiple motivation. An activity may be carried out, for instance, because it serves to earn money, but at the same time it may also serve to satisfy many other needs of the person, needs which may have entirely independent origins. As a rule we try to kill two birds—or many—with one stone.

The items involved in cross-functioning and in vicarious functioning are not only subjective factors but also environmental conditions. A given environmental factor may present opportunities for the formation of several systems. This is only the restatement of one basic feature of the present study, namely, that a biospheric occurrence always involves a subject pole and an object pole. We shall see that the conflict situations which frequently arise through the fact of multiple functioning may have their centers of gravity either close to the subject pole or close to the object pole of the biospheric occurrence.

SETTING AND SHIFTING OF SYSTEMS

Since the part functions of the organism are so little specific, an orderly way of organismic functioning is possible only by means of precisely working mechanisms which prevent interference between those systems which have an equal claim to utilize the same group of part functions. These mechanisms have already been referred to as the *setting* and *shifting of sets*. We have compared such mechanisms to the function of a typewriter. On the typewriter each key has a double function, namely, to write small or capital letters. We set the machine to write small or capital letters and thus we may determine in what way the part should function at a given moment and to the exclusion of the other functional possibility. This was, however, only an analogy and now we are in a position to define more exactly what the process of setting consists of. *Setting can be defined as the constructing of a system.* The parts have multiple functional possibilities, but after being arranged in a given system, they function in one definite way, namely, in accordance with the system principle. The other functional possibilities of the parts are excluded; they become activated only when the parts are rearranged in other systems and work in accordance with the new system principle. Shifting consists in the dissolution of a set system and the establishment of a new one whereby the parts of the previous system are re-utilized and made to function in accordance with the newly set system.

The biospheric total process is a complex system action. Given the functional multiplicity of parts, an orderly activity can be ensured only through the efficient functioning of the setting and shifting mechanisms. Setting and shifting may thus rightly be regarded as the key mechanisms for organized activity. The study of these mechanisms seems to be a fruitful field for the exploration of personality organization. They also have the advantage of being more easily experimented upon than many other factors of personality.

From among the numerous research possibilities which the study of sets offers, we wish to mention one example. In the previous chapter where the biological total process was described as a hierarchy of systems, almost nothing was said about the content of the single systems. This was not an entirely arbitrary omission, but was due mainly to the fact that knowledge in this field is almost completely lacking. Such knowledge cannot be provided by theoretic clarifications—such as the present study was intended to be—but by new facts derived from empirical investigations. The study of sets may offer an excellent method to determine which parts belong to a given system.

When an overt movement is carried out it is obvious that certain muscle contractions are directly involved as parts in the movement. There are, however, also factors involved of which it is not so obvious that they form part of the activity. Consider, for instance, the implications of the following well-known phenomenon. The subject is instructed to make continuous circular movements in a horizontal plane with his right hand and to move his left hand at the same time up and down. Such activity will show a definite tendency to disorganization: the left hand will tend to move in a circle or the right hand will tend to move up and down. The limited range of attention does not explain this phenomenon. We may substitute, for instance, the reading of a text for the activity of the left hand. Reading certainly requires more attention than a simple muscular activity and the movement of the right hand will not be greatly interfered with. This phenomenon demonstrates the well-established fact that the movement of a limb induces slight tonus changes in the opposite limb. These tonus changes are symmetrical to the tonus changes of the overtly moving limb. In our terminology one can state that the system of movement involves not only the muscles of overtly moving limbs, but also those of the opposite limb. That the opposite limb is also involved in this system becomes manifest through the difficulty, through the inhibition, which arises when one tries to use the muscles of the limb to form a system different from that in which it was involved.

Here we mentioned a phenomenon which is already known. Similar methods, however, could be used for the examination of widely different functions. The principle of such experimentation is to use the phenomenon of interference of contemporaneous functional systems as a criterion for the determination of the parts which are involved in a given system. The mutual facilitation of functions can also serve for a similar purpose. What we propose here is, of course, only one of the many ways that processes of setting and shifting can be brought to the laboratory for the investigation of highly significant problems.

INTERFERENCE OF SYSTEMS: SYMPTOMS AND SEQUELAE

In spite of the high efficiency of the setting and shifting mechanisms, the mutual interference of systems is inevitable in such a complex organization as the biological total process. The multiple utilization of part functions is a highly economical arrangement, but represents at the same time a serious vulnerability for the organism. The case where competition between two or more systems takes place is very important for the understanding of certain pathological constellations, as well as for that of many everyday phenomena. By competition of two systems we mean a configuration in which there is a tendency to utilize a number of part functions in a given system while another tendency simultaneously exists to organize the same part functions within the frame of another system. Frequently the constellation is such that one of the system-forming tendencies has a greater potency and becomes a leading system while the other system of smaller potency can be called the interfering system.

In such a constellation rather typical phenomena can be observed. We may assume that A and B are systems which have one part function or a group of part functions (*a*) in common (Figure 11). We may also assume that *a* cannot be simultaneously part of A and B—that is, we deal with the vicarious function. Suppose that there is a strong tendency for the formation of A and a weaker, but persistent, one for the formation of B. In such case part function *a* is under the influence of two interfering forces: the one which makes *a* function according to the system principle of A and another which tends to utilize the same part function according to the system principle of B.

The interfering system may not have sufficient power to displace the leading system or even to appear on the surface as such. It may become manifest, however, by *inhibiting* the leading function. The leading function in this case has to assert itself against the pressure of the interfering system. The phenomena which thus arise may be called *symptoms of pressure*. These may take the form of fatigue and tenseness and, under certain conditions, of anxiety.

Symptoms of Pressure. Fatigue is characterized by the slowing down of the leading activity or by an increasing difficulty in carrying it out. Fatigue frequently is interpreted as a lack of available energy. This explanation may be correct in many instances; the lack of available energy, however, is certainly not the only factor. An activity may be difficult to carry out and it may be slowed down not only because there is not sufficient energy available for the function, but also because the latter has to proceed against the pressure of interfering systems. The so-called "mental fatigue" seems to be prevalently of the latter type.[1]

Tendencies to behave in one or another way have to be suppressed continuously. In the course of the day many tendencies are activated, but they have to be suppressed because otherwise no orderly functioning would be possible. The activated but suppressed functional systems accumulate and exert an increasing pressure upon

[1] Muscular fatigue due to metabolic intoxication is another matter.

the leading functions which have to proceed in the dense medium of resistances. Thus fatigue arises and manifests itself in the increasing difficulty of carrying out the leading function. This can be well observed in the period preceding sleep which is characterized by the feeling of tiredness, difficulty in concentrating, and difficulty in following a trend of thought.

The interference with a functional system may cause not only uniform inhibition of the leading activity, but the balance of forces between the two systems may show oscillations. The interfering system may come close to the point of breaking through and may be repelled, then may again come close to breaking through, and so forth. Such oscillation may continue for a considerable period of time. We may say metaphorically that in such instances the interfering system does not exert a uniform pressure on the leading function but pounds at it. Such constellation of forces manifests itself in a symptom which is commonly called "nervousness." It consists in tenseness, restlessness, irritability, jerkiness of behavior, and, if it involves the skeletal muscles, occasionally in tremor.

Pressure symptoms which arise out of a competition between systems can be observed in many conditions. The pathological condition which used to be called neurasthenia is characterized mainly by pressure symptoms: fatigue, difficulty in concentrating, and tenseness. Similar symptoms may also indicate the beginning of more serious personality disorders, such as schizophrenia. The so-called "experimental neurosis," which is produced by the artificial setting of conflicting functional systems, manifests itself mainly in pressure symptoms: restlessness or fatigue-like phenomena, the latter leading occasionally to sleep.

In connection with pressure symptoms *anxiety* should also be mentioned although it probably does not arise directly from interferences, but is rather a reaction to certain kinds of interfering factors. The content of the interfering system may be such that it would be incompatible with the existing personality organization. When systems of such content are close to the point of breaking through, the organism anticipates the danger which would thus arise, and reacts to it with anxiety. Anxiety is a reaction to a real or hypothetical danger which threatens the personality from within. That is, the endangering factor is not in the environment but in the person himself. Anxiety is further characterized by the fact that the object of danger is not clearly perceived.

This formulation of the mechanism of anxiety is supported by common clinical experience. In some personality disorders in which, at the onset, anxiety predominates, anxiety usually disappears as the condition becomes worse and the interfering tendency breaks through in the form of various psychotic productions.

Symptoms of Intrusion. Symptoms of pressure arise when the balance of force between the competing systems is markedly in the favor of the leading system. When the interfering system is somewhat more forceful it still may not displace the leading system, but intrude into it at various points. The phenomena which thus arise may be called the symptoms of intrusion. The seemingly unmotivated appearance of compulsive and obsessive phenomena which intrude in the course of leading activities are good examples of this group of symptoms.

The interfering system may not appear as such overtly, but may only modify or twist the leading activity. Good examples of twisting are those phenomena which have been called *Fehlhandlungen,* and have been extensively studied by psychoanalysts. We do not regard such twisting as an intentional disguise, but rather as unintended products of the competition between systems. The "transference" of psychoanalysis may also be regarded as a phenomenon of intrusion: in one's attitude toward a person certain features are intruding which are "meant" for some other person.

Symptoms of Mutual Invasion. An even more severe form of system interference is present in those cases in which neither of the conflicting systems has a dominance over the other. This may give rise to such phenomena as retardation, indecision, ambivalence. In severe cases it leads to a mutual invasion of the competing systems. The mutual invasion of systems manifests itself in a chaotic constellation in which no leading function is present. The systems involved are disorganized and their fragments intermingled in a disorderly way. Since none of the systems dominates the scene for any length of time we may recognize in such a chaotic state only fragmentary and incipient activities which do not reach completion. Such a picture can be observed, for instance, in the various forms of confusional states. Confusion refers primarily to the mutual invasion of thought systems. This may be mild or as severe as the schizophrenic production of "word salads" which is characterized by a fragmentation of thinking and by a disorderly throwing together of unrelated fragments of thoughts.

Not only thought systems but also systems of psychomotor activity may mutually invade each other and result in a chaotic confusional picture. This can be observed in a mild form even in states of embarrassment, and it is quite marked in cases of panicky "catastrophic reactions" (Goldstein).[2] I have described an extreme form of disintegration of activity in a schizophrenic patient.[3] Mutual invasion of systems may take various forms according to the systems involved. I have, for instance, described certain forms of spatial disorientation and have considered them as states of confusion which result from the mutual invasion of contradictory orien-

[2] K. Goldstein, Der Aufbau des Organismus, Haag, Martinus Nijhoff, 1934, p. 23.

[3] A. Angyal, Disturbances of activity in a case of schizophrenia, Archives of Neurology and Psychiatry, 38:1047–1054, November 1937.

tation schemata.[4] The mutual invasion may take the form of a rather local affair, but may also involve the total personality.

There are also some instances in which the interfering systems gain in potency with the passage of time and push the leading system into the background. Thus the roles are changed; the interfering system becomes the leading one and vice versa.

The successive appearances of the various groups of symptoms which arise from the competition of systems can be well observed in many cases of schizophrenia during the onset of the illness. The early signs may be only *symptoms of pressure:* fatigue, inability to work, difficulty in concentrating, etc. Then restlessness may follow. The danger of intruding tendencies is frequently anticipated by the patient who reacts to them with anxiety. This may take the form of fear of death or fear of some other specific danger or else it may appear simply as a sense of some undefined impending danger. Isolated *intrusions* of interfering tendencies may then appear, frequently followed by a period of confusion, panic, or other form of *mutual invasion,* until finally the interfering tendencies break through, more or less twisted, in the form of frankly psychotic behavior.

Interference of systems is a very common phenomenon and is in itself not pathological. Inhibited functions may

[4] A. Angyal, Über die Raumlage vorgestellter Örter, Archiv für die gesamte Psychologie, 78:47–94, 1930.

be ventilated during sleep or disposed of in some other way. When they are not acted out, they may possibly fade away or deteriorate with time. *System interference becomes pathological only when the interfering system is persistent and when the personality mobilizes strong resistance against its expression.* The great persistency of certain pathological interfering sets indicates that they are in some way important for the organism, that they are nourished from some fundamental tendency of the person. Strong resistance, on the other hand, indicates that the inhibited tendency is in some way incompatible with the rest of the personality and hence means a serious menace for the existing personality organization.

Inhibited tendencies may seek expression in various ways. They may reach closure by a short cut, that is, leaving out intermediary steps and thus leading to the formation of a closed but incomplete Gestalt. A good example of short cuts is the phenomenon of precocious ejaculation which is not only a shortening of the phases involved in the process but a dropping out of intermediary phases. When the condition is advanced ejaculation may occur before complete erection and, in some instances, even without any erection. Such a condition involves, of course, also problems of a purely physiological nature, namely the physiological mechanisms which allow such short cuts.

Inhibited tendencies which cannot find an outlet in a reality situation and overt action may find an expression in phantasy productions. The most common examples of this are daydreams. Such phantasies can of course be of use to the individual only if they possess a certain degree of reality value, that is, if the person, at least at that moment, "believes" in them.

The fact that phantasy productions may gain a certain degree of reality value raises an interesting problem which is worth discussing briefly because it throws light on an important aspect of integration. That a given datum is factual is not a sufficient, and perhaps not even a very essential, condition for being convincing and real to the person. Things which one sees in the mirror are just as factual as any other visually perceived object. We call them unreal because they are not consistent with other—for example, tactual—experiences referring to the same object. We may give the following definition: *"reality,"* convincingness, belief is based upon an integrational constellation, namely, on *consistency of a partial item with the corresponding whole.* The lack of consistency is the basis for disbelief and unreality character. In science, and also in everyday life, it is always problematic when the factual evidence is sufficient to be convincing. Facts are of relatively little weight for beliefs. It is, for instance, questionable whether the phenomena claimed by occultists would be generally accepted even if more factual evidence could be offered. Probably not, because they seem to be inconsistent with scientifically established laws. Resistance to the acceptance of the psychoanalytic doctrine, especially in its earlier days, was not entirely on a factual basis. It was rejected because it seemed inconsistent with certain scientific convictions, on the one hand, and with the desires and wishes of the person, on the other.

When a person acts in a way which is not consistent with his usual behavior, for instance, under the influence of some powerful emotion or under the influence of alcohol, it may seem to him in retrospect that he could not have acted that way; he may feel that he "was not himself," that he was "beside himself." When factual evidences and inconsistency with the system come into conflict, it gives rise subjectively to *doubt* which may reach such intensity that it becomes distinctly pathological.

While a factual datum loses its convincingness because it is inconsistent with a larger system, phantasy productions, in spite of their lack of factuality, may become very convincing and realistic when they are consistent with a given personality constellation. Extreme examples of this are the delusions which are very convincing for the person in spite of having very meager factual basis, or no factual basis at all. A person may have an intense anxiety and not be aware of the true object of his anxiety. Then he may consistently complete this constellation by postulating some kind of danger which—because consistent with his mood—may have, for him, a strong reality value.

Probably hypochondriasis, too, is based on a similar mechanism. The imperviousness of pathological convictions (delusions) to reasoning is understandable on the basis of these considerations.

In cases of interference of systems certain symptoms may be observed not only in the systems which are immediately involved, but also in distant systems which seem to be only very remotely related to the competing systems. Certain somatic symptoms may be mentioned as examples. The nature of such symptoms depends only in part upon the content of the conflict. They seem to follow a pattern which is characteristic for the individual. In every stress situation some persons will have unpleasant epigastric sensations, others palpitations, others perspiration, and so on.

It is still obscure how such symptoms which often seem to be quite unrelated to the original conflict can arise. One may think of the following physiological analogy. When an arterial branch is obstructed the blood will flow in places of less resistance, with consequent stasis and hyperemia in the regions of the collateral branches. This is, of course, only an analogy and for a better understanding one has to study the phenomena themselves. In such a study, reference to the concept of differentiation may prove useful. Each biospheric occurrence grows out from a diffuse biospheric background through a process of differentiation. When the differentiation is prevented by an interfering system the organismic tendencies remain in a diffuse state, causing a state of "stasis," a diffuse tension of the background. This tension then finds an outlet through channels of least resistance. Such channels may be individually different, depending upon the organization of the given person.

There are many other symptoms and sequelae which arise from the interference of the systems and have not been mentioned here. They are topics for more specialized study. Our purpose has been only to give a few examples of the phenomena of system interference in order to shed some light on one aspect of the problem of disturbed integration.

SEGREGATION OF SYSTEMS

In the previous section have been discussed those integrational disturbances which arise out of an interference between systems. We wish now to discuss briefly those forms of disturbed integration which are characterized by the *lack of coherence and of regular communication between systems.* Such integrational constellation may be called *segregation.*

There is a normal feature of personality integration which facilitates the disjunction or segregation between systems. In connection with problems of differentiation we have pointed out that the stronger the differentiation of a system the more the parts are individualized and independent of the whole. Differentiation always involves the danger of too great an independence of the part functions, that is, a danger of disintegration. A whole may differentiate into so many specialized parts that their unification and their control may present a serious problem for the organism. The process of differentiation only facilitates and offers the occasion for disjunction, but probably is in itself not sufficient to cause a segregation of systems. Normally, through a process of synthesis the differentiated parts are again closely integrated into the whole. There must be certain influences which interfere with the process of synthesis to bring about segregation. For the present we may leave these influences out of consideration, since we are concerned here only with the structure of a disturbed integrational state, irrespective of its origin.

The segregation of systems shows various pictures according to the systems involved. It has been pointed out that three dimensions at least can be distinguished in the domain which serves as a kind of matrix for personality organization. One obtains a different picture of segregation if the structure of the biospheric total process is interrupted in the vertical or the transverse dimension from what one obtains if it is interrupted in the dimension of progression.

The vertical dimension extends from the depth to the surface, that is, from general trends through more specific ones to the actual behavior. When there is a break in the continuity of the vertical structure, depths and surface become disjointed from each other. Since the surface is the specific expression and concretization of the depth, the result of a break of continuity in the vertical structure will be an incongruity between the expression and that which is expressed. In such a case tendencies in the depths of personality cannot express themselves in concrete surface manifestations; they remain repressed. Another aspect of the break or impairment of continuity of the vertical structure is that the surface manifestations no longer express deeper tendencies and thus become more or less empty. In such a case we may speak of *superficiality*.

All observable behavior is, of course, on the surface. This does not mean, however, that it is superficial. Depth and superficiality of behavior depend upon the depth of tendencies which are expressed in it. An emotional expression may be superficial, shallow, one to which nothing much in the depth of personality corresponds, or it may come from the very foundation of one's personality. In behaving in a certain way one may be deeply involved or may just be acting, "putting on a show."

Segregation between depth and surface may often be voluntarily created and controlled by the person. Social contact often necessitates that deeper tendencies should not appear in surface manifestations. This is a kind of defense reaction. Such is the case in certain forms of detachment and reserve in social behavior. An example which points in the opposite direction is what one occasionally calls "emotional incontinence."

When the system is interrupted somewhere along the *dimension of progression,* that is, when the means-end organization is interrupted, the activity is aborted before it can go to completion. In such a case we may speak of *frustration.* Frustration does not bring about a segregation of systems, but merely prevents "closure." There are also disturbances of means-end organization which involve a segregation of systems. Subordinate goals may become independent and lose contact with the main goal of activity. This may result in a fragmentation and disintegration of the total function.

Segregation in the *transverse structure* may be called *dissociation.* This consists in a lack of coordination between the parts of a whole and manifests itself in a kind of dysplastic behavior. By lack of coordination is meant not only motor incoördination, but also a lack of coordination between the various tendencies and attitudes of the person.

Segregation in one dimension is usually followed by segregation in other dimensions. In cases of good integration the connections of a given biospheric occurrence extend over a wide range of systems, while in the case of segregation the biospheric occurrence becomes a more or less localized affair. We make such distinctions frequently in daily life, for example, when we say that one person is doing something half-heartedly and that the other is involved "body and soul." Activities, the connection of which with other parts of the personality are severed, are feeble, unenergetic. Segregated systems may occasionally draw energy from the organism and thus they may become parasitic. On the other hand, activities well integrated with the rest of the personality are more forceful, because they are supported, backed up, *reinforced* by many systems of the personality. Thus we see that the "amount of energy" which propels activity depends not only on the amount of raw energy, which in last analysis is derived from metabolism, but furthermore and to a greater extent upon the integrational status of the person.

The symbolic systems are especially apt to undergo segregation from the rest of the personality. The various forms of symbolic functions differ substantially from each other in this respect. Thinking is, on the whole, more detached than emotion. It makes a great deal of difference whether one merely thinks that an injustice was done to oneself, or whether one experiences it emotionally. William Stern made a distinction between *"Erlebniss"* and *"Lebeniss."*[5] These terms are difficult to translate into English, but one could say that in *Erlebniss* one experiences something psychologically, while in the case of *Lebeniss* one lives it through. In our termi-

[5] W. Stern, Studien zur Personwissenschaft, I: Personalistik als Wissenschaft, Leipzig, Barth, 1930.

nology we would say that in the first case we deal with a more or less segregated psychological phenomenon, in the second with a phenomenon which involves the total personality or large regions of it. Anybody who has attempted psychotherapy knows that it is relatively easy to convey a healthy notion to the patient, to make him accept it on an intellectual level, but it is often very difficult to induce a state in which such a notion really permeates the personality and influences the behavior. Another example which demonstrates various degrees of segregation and good integration is learning. It is one thing to acquire a detached knowledge of a fact, to memorize and to be able to recall it, and another matter to integrate and to digest it, and thus really learn. Two persons may have similar experiences which they may be equally able to recall. One person may actually learn from experience while the other may not.

We may now briefly recapitulate the main points of this section. Segregation consists in a lack of coherence and of regular communication between systems. The communication between systems may be interrupted along any of the three biospheric dimensions. Disjunction along the vertical dimension results in repression of deeper tendencies and superficiality of manifest behavior. Segregation in the dimension of progression may take place when means and ends are only loosely connected. Segregation in the transverse dimension may be called dissociation, and it manifests itself in lack of coordination. Segregated functions normally lack energy or lead a parasitic life in the organism.

THE CONCEPT OF BIONEGATIVITY

The discussion of the disturbances of integration leads us into the field of pathological behavior. This occasion seems to be opportune for a brief discussion of some concepts referring to personality disorders.

The subject-matter of psychiatry is usually defined as "abnormal behavior." At present two definitions of abnormality are current: the statistical and the normative. The criterion of abnormality in the statistical sense is deviation from the average; in the normative sense, deviation from a fixed standard.

The statistical concept of abnormality is of little use for the study of personality disorders, if only because it depends on averages which may themselves be pathological. In a population in which most people are afflicted with syphilis, an admittedly pathological condition will become a statistically normal one. Likewise, since a person without pathology, however mild, is practically never found, one may say that the occurrence of some pathology is statistically normal.

An unusually gifted person who deviates considerably from the average is statistically, but not necessarily psychiatrically, abnormal. Not all deviations, but only deviations in certain directions are considered abnormal.

To correct this situation some authors distinguish between subnormal and supernormal. Only the first would have pathological significance. Such reduction to quantitative differences is, however, not practicable, nor does it promote conceptual clarification. A heart rate of 40 beats per minute, for instance, could be called subnormal and a heart rate of 140 beats per minute supernormal, although both are equally pathological. Thus, it would seem that those who distinguish between subnormal and supernormal do not have in mind a purely quantitative difference; they mean by subnormal something which is "worse," less efficient, and by supernormal something which is "better," more efficient, than the average. Goodness or efficiency, however, can be measured only by certain standards. Thus this definition is not a clear-cut statistical one, but rather a normative one.

The difficulty in defining abnormality normatively lies in the necessity of establishing a legitimate norm, since arbitrarily set standards are obviously of no value. As a rule the standards of a given culture are accepted as the standards of normality. The relativity of such standards, however, has been sufficiently demonstrated by more recent studies in cultural anthropology.

The type of behavior which is vaguely referred to as abnormal has rather definite characteristics. This type of behavior can best be defined in terms of integration. In an ideally healthy organism the various part processes are integrated in such a way that they subserve and promote the total function of the organism, while in an "abnormal" condition the integration is impaired and one or more part functions impede or disturb instead of promoting the total function. Referring to such impairment of integration, it seems advisable to avoid the term "abnormality" and to substitute for it a better defined and more expressive one which is not burdened with the confusing ballast of hazy connotations. The term "bionegativity" is proposed. *Bionegativity may be defined as a personality constellation in which one or more part processes disturb the total function of the organism.*

What is meant by the total function of the organism has been discussed at various occasions in this study. We mean a twofold dynamic pattern tending both toward increased autonomy and toward homonomy with all its specific ramifications. In case of bionegativity some of these ramifications lose their integrative connection with the total function and cause destructive changes (invasion, segregation, etc.).

The definition of bionegativity which has been offered has various implications. Bionegativity is an integrational status, a specific relation between part and whole. Neither the personality as such nor certain part processes but only the relationship between the part and whole can be called bionegative. The total personality, even in the most sweeping personality disorders, tends to behave according to its inherent tendency, even if its expression in behavior appears distorted in consequence of severe bionegative constellations. A given factor may be bionegative in one personality organization, but perfectly biopositive in another one. This is especially true with regard to the symbolic organization, which is more plastic and variable than the physiological one. Within certain limits it is, however, possible to enumerate "abnormal" factors and traits. The personality organization has a limited range of variation and there are some factors which would be bionegative in any possible personality organization.

Against the concept of bionegativity one could raise the objection that it does not cover the whole field of "abnormality." Bionegative constellations are possible not only when a poorly integrated part function disturbs the total function, but also when some part function which is essential for the total function is damaged or lacking. This might be the case, for instance, in brain injuries and many other conditions. But although this is true, a modification of the concept of bionegativity does not seem to be necessary. The destruction of parts may be responsible for bionegative constellations, but in such cases the bionegative constellation in itself is manifested in the incongruency of the remaining functions.

The concept of bionegativity is more inclusive and more neutral than the concept of pathology. It applies to mild and transitory constellations from which nobody is free, as well as to extremely severe conditions as seen, for instance, in the major psychoses.

It is not likely that the term bionegativity would be misunderstood by the reader although the root "bio" could suggest a purely somatic phenomenon. We have, however, sufficiently stressed the point that such terms as "biosphere," "biological total process," do not refer in this study merely to physiology, but to the physiologically, symbolically, and socially integrated total process of living. Those bionegative constellations which are called personality disorders proper arise especially at the level of social integration. Such a point of view has been rightly emphasized by H. S. Sullivan, who considers personality disorders as disturbances of the interpersonal relations.

Although we have rejected the concept of statistical normality as inadequate for the definition of the field of personality disorders, such a concept has certain relations to the concept of bionegativity.

In recent anthropological literature one occasionally finds statements concerning the cultural relativity of abnormal behavior. It is said that a given form of behavior may be socially approved and regarded as normal in one culture, while disapproved and considered abnormal in another culture. Thus, it is perfectly normal for an inhabitant of Dobu to blame the sorcerer for his mishaps, while such behavior would be regarded as paranoid in our society. Likewise to a person from a foreign culture many of our customary actions would appear distinctly odd or abnormal.

We may disregard here the objection that such parallels may be very superficial, and that the behavior of our psychotics is probably widely different from the behavior of "primitive" people. It is, however, to be considered that the behavior which deviates from the average, from the customary, may occasionally be an indication of a bionegative constellation. The inhabitant of Dobu who would not accept magic would not only be regarded by his fellow men as odd but there is some probability that he actually might be an odd person, even in any other kind of society.[6] Unconventional attitudes may be an indication of lack of contact with one's culture, an inability for socialization, which creates bionegative constellations at the level of the person's social integration.

The behavior of persons whom one calls eccentric or odd is not necessarily foolish or impractical, but often only unconventional. Absence of conventionality in one's attitude is not infrequently a powerful means of progress. In reading the lives of great discoverers one often wonders whether they excelled their contemporaries in intellectual endowment, or whether they were merely less socialized and more detached from the sci-

[6] This statement does not imply a denial of possible differences between cultures in the sense that one culture may foster more than another the development of certain specific bionegative constellations.

entific and other conventions of their own culture. The absence of conventionality may be a laboriously achieved result, but more frequently it is an indication of an impaired ability for socialization.

Great deviation from the average in behavior, although not necessarily bionegative in itself, may frequently indicate a bionegative constellation. This is true not only of behavior, but also of the body structure. A great deviation from average body height, as seen in dwarfism and gigantism, indicates the presence of bionegative constellations in the physiology of the individual. But even if it were possible for a person with a body height of two feet or seven feet to have a perfectly integrated physiology, such marked deviations from the average would necessarily create bionegative constellations. Our doors, automobiles, chairs, and utensils in general are not made for either two-foot or seven-foot people. And such a deviating person would be even more handicapped in his interpersonal relations. Our world is made for the average man. Society does not approve of nor does it tolerate too much deviation from the average.

What is abnormal statistically is likely to become bionegative. The correlation between the two is, however, not high enough to make a distinction unnecessary. Our conclusion is that the concept of abnormality is inadequate for the definition of the subject-matter of psychiatry, while the concept of bionegativity as defined here seems to serve the purpose well.

CAUSATION AND SYSTEM ACTION IN STATES OF DISTURBED INTEGRATION

A given disturbance of integration may not remain isolated but may induce further disturbances, and the picture may thus become increasingly involved. It can be shown in many cases that the origin of such disturbances lies in the interference of some outside agent with the functions of the organism, that is, in a trauma. The causes of trauma can be gross physical or chemical agents, pathogenic microorganisms, psychological factors, and the like. The traumatic origin can be demonstrated for organic disease of known etiology. For congenital diseases one can reasonably assume some kind of trauma of the germ cell or a trauma in the ancestry. One could assume that some personality disorders have an endogenous origin such as insufficient integration or undue dominance of a part function. It seems unlikely, however, that a healthy organism would begin to malfunction spontaneously without the interference of some noxious agent. The question, however, is left open.

The organism is continuously exposed to traumata. Life itself, by its very nature, can be considered as a traumatic process. The self-expansive activity of the organism consists in an interaction between individual and environment. While the organism is governed by its inherent dynamic tendencies, the other factor in the question, the environment, follows the laws of the physical world without regard for the needs of the organism. Therefore, every contact with the environment involves a greater or less severe trauma. The accumulation of the minimal effects of traumata manifests itself in aging and leads finally to a so-called "physiological death."

One can distinguish two main types of traumata. 1) *Positive traumata:* the interference of an outside agent (physical, chemical, bacteriological, psychological, and so on) with the dynamic tendencies of the organism. 2) *Traumata of scarcity* which are due to certain inadequacies of the environment with regard to the needs of the organism. This kind of trauma arises when the environment is lacking in certain factors which are essential for the organism. For example, most organisms need oxygen and the scarcity of this substance in the environment means a severe trauma. The insufficiency of vitamins in food is a typical example of a trauma of scarcity. Certain psychological factors also belong to this group: the lack of certain important elements in childhood training, the lack of acceptance by the social group, the lack of affection and recognition on the part of others, and the like.

A disturbed integrational state manifests itself in a variety of symptoms which can be evaluated as indicators of the underlying disturbances. Not all of these symptoms belong to the same order of phenomena. Some symptoms can be understood in terms of causation, some others in terms of system action. For the analysis of a complex state of disturbed integration the following classification of symptoms may be used.

1. Symptoms which are causal effects of the interference of the traumatic agent with the organism. When, for instance, a sharp object is thrust into the body it causes a discontinuity of tissues and flow of blood. These symptoms are direct causal effects of a traumatic agent. Such effects are determined, on the one hand, by the properties of the traumatic agent and, on the other hand, by the physical and chemical properties of the organism. At this stage the organismic qualities of the individual are not as yet drawn into activity.

2. A second group of symptoms represents more or less planful organismic reactions and attempts to repair the damage caused by the traumatic agent. Following the previous example we can observe that the organism reacts to the discontinuity of tissues in its own way: from the walls of the wound, a proliferation of connective tissues and blood vessels starts which slowly seals up the gap with the formation of a scar.

3. The reaction of the organism to the traumatic damage is an unusual condition and as such it may act as a further trauma. In the previous example the original damage was repaired by the formation of a scar. The scar, after retraction of the connective tissues, may cause a second trauma. The scar on a tubular organ might cause stenosis, in the brain it might cause mechanical irritation, and so on. One deals here with a symptom

which is a *causal derivative* of an *organismic reaction.* The new damage calls for new adjustive reactions on the part of the organism. The second reaction may not bring the organism to a complete equilibrium, either. Further traumata may derive from it, calling again for new adjustive reactions. Thus we have, besides the first trauma, causal derivatives of the first order, of the second order, of the third order, and so on. Correspondingly, we have organismic reactions to the original traumata, and organismic reactions to the causal derivatives of various orders. The distinction made here is one between causation and system action.

Not every influence of one part of the organism upon another part can be regarded as system action. System action spreads from part to whole in a continuous manner following the paths of the intrinsic articulation of the whole. The influence of unrelated part systems upon each other (for instance, the influence of a pathologically segregated system upon other systems) should be thought of in terms of causation.

Some schools of psychopathology deal with every symptomatology entirely in terms of causation (mechanistic point of view), others almost entirely in terms of purposeful organismic reactions. Psychoanalysis may be classified in the second group. If a patient hallucinates the mechanist would ask, "What *caused* the hallucination?" and would explain it, for example, by the toxic irritation of a certain cortical area. The psychoanalyst would probably ask in such a case, "What is the organism driving at by hallucinating? In what way does the hallucination serve the patient?" In formulating such a question one should, however, keep in mind both possibilities, namely, that the symptom may be a causal effect or that it may be an organismic reaction. The inadequacies of a strictly mechanistic point of view have often been stressed. It is, on the other hand, also necessary to warn against the exaggerations of the purposivistic point of view.

The planfulness of the organism does not exclude mechanistic happenings. One may consider the following analogy. A rabbit is running through a field which is covered with snow and leaves his footprints on the ground. It would be obviously incorrect to ask in such a case what the rabbit intended by putting his footprints in the snow. The running of the rabbit through the field might have been a purposeful action, it might have had some goal (to avoid an enemy or to seek food). The making of footprints was, however, not purposeful, but the causal derivative of a purposeful action. Let us now modify this example. According to popular belief the rabbit, before he leaves his warren in winter time, makes a number of long jumps around the warren covering a rather large area with irregularly distributed footprints "in order to make it difficult for his enemies to find his trail." Suppose that this observation and interpretation are correct. In that case it would be entirely justified to ask what the rabbit intended by making footprints in the snow.

In bionegative constellations usually both types of symptoms—causal effects and organismic reactions—are present. To separate them is a necessary procedure in symptom analysis.

SUMMARY

The organism works in a very economical way; it carries out a great number of activities with the aid of a relatively small number of part functions. To do this is possible because the individual items may be arranged in different ways and can form a part successively (vicarious functioning) or simultaneously (cross-functioning) of more than one system.

Given the fact that the parts have multiple functions, precise working of the setting and shifting mechanisms is necessary to assure orderly organismic activity. Setting is the arrangement of parts into a system and hence a narrowing down of the functional multiplicity of parts to the one function which is in accordance with the given system. Shifting consists in the dissolution of one system and the re-utilization of its parts (or some of its parts) for the establishment of a new system.

The fact of inhibition and mutual facilitation may serve as a criterion for determining which parts are involved in a given system.

The competition between different systems for the utilization of the same part functions may give rise to integrational disturbances of various degrees of severity. In such competition the system of greater potency may be called the leading system and the system of smaller potency the interfering system.

The interference exerts a resistance against the leading system action. This causes "pressure symptoms" in the leading system: fatigue, somnolence, difficulty of concentration, tenseness. To the pressure of the interfering system the organism may react with anxiety.

If the interfering system gains in potency, it may intrude as a foreign body into the leading activity (compulsive, obsessive phenomena, and so on). The intruding part usually appears more or less "twisted."

Interfering functions may also invade each other with a resulting severe disorganization (confusional states, panicky reactions).

At the onset of psychoses (especially schizophrenia) the above-mentioned sequence of symptoms of increasing severity can often be observed.

Those tendencies, the expression of which is inhibited by strong leading systems, may seek expression by short cuts.

Daydreams and delusions may be considered as examples of short cuts. Such phantasy productions may appear entirely convincing and realistic to the person. Convincingness and belief are influenced only to a moderate degree by factual evidence; they depend to a much greater extent upon consistency with the rest of the existing personality organization.

In the case of system interference, too, symptoms arise which are not directly referable to the interfering systems. It is suggested that the mechanism of such distant consequences may be the following. Because of the obstruction of a channel of expression, a kind of "stasis," a diffuse tension arises in the little differentiated "background" of the biological total process. This diffuse tension may then find an outlet through channels of least resistance. These channels may be different from person to person.

Not only interference but also the segregation of systems disturbs the personality integration. Disjunction along the vertical dimension results in a repression of deeper tendencies and in a superficiality of manifest behavior. We may speak of segregation in the dimension of progression when means and ends are only loosely connected. Segregation in the transverse dimension consists in a lack of coordination.

In connection with personality disturbances the concept of "abnormality" was discussed. The statistical concept of abnormality was rejected as inadequate for the study of personality disorders, if only because averages also may be pathological. The difficulty of normative definitions lies in establishing legitimate standards. It was proposed to substitute for the concept of abnormality that of *bionegativity*. Bionegativity is defined as a personality constellation in which one or more part processes, instead of promoting, impede or disturb the total function of the organism. Neither a part nor the total organism can be called bionegative. Only the relation between the two can be so termed. The statistically abnormal is likely to become bionegative. The correlation is, however, not high enough to make the distinction unnecessary.

In the analysis of the symptom complex of a bionegative constellation one has to distinguish between the direct causal effects of a traumatic agent and the organismic reaction to this effect. The organismic reaction may have causal derivatives as a by-product and the organism may react to these causal derivatives with further adjustive attempts.

X. THE COURSE OF LIFE AS A GESTALT

THE TIME ASPECT OF PERSONALITY AND THE BIOGRAPHICAL METHOD

The dynamic nature of life necessarily requires the viewing of personality as it evolves through time. In modern personality research increasing emphasis is laid upon the necessity of studying the biography of the person. In psychoanalysis the past history of the person is of paramount importance. For the psychobiology of Adolf Meyer the study of a life history is the fundamental approach in which all data obtained by any other method finally have to be integrated. Among sociologists, W. I. Thomas especially has emphasized the importance of the case study method. Life history as a psychological problem has been receiving in recent years careful scrutiny by Ch. Bühler and her collaborators.

The biographical approach brings up a number of highly important theoretical questions. The time aspect of personality, the nature of historical-genetic connections, the relationship between past, present, and future, the practical problem of distinguishing the significant from the unimportant and accidental in compiling biographies, the problem of self-development and chance, the articulation of the life history into phases, and so on, are all problems which need clarification.

Nobody questions the fact that the present state of the personality is significantly determined by its past. The nature of interconnection and the mode of influence of the past upon the present, however, can be conceived in various ways. In general, it is assumed that each biological occurrence impresses itself on the more or less plastic personality, leaving permanent "traces" in it. According to such a view the person carries the past within himself in the form of traces or conserved impressions. This means that, strictly speaking, the whole personality is concentrated in the present, although in its passage through time it may change and shape itself.

Were this point of view correct the study of life history could be justified only on a methodological basis. It is frequently assumed that a complete cross-sectional picture would tell us everything about a person and it is only because we do not have a reliable method for obtaining complete information about the present state of the individual that it is necessary for us to go back into the past for such information. This point of view has been clearly stated by H. A. Murray: "If it were possible to examine directly all these traces, connections and readinesses in the brain, as well as all the contemporaneous physiological happenings, one could name every process that was functioning within the organism. Since this is not possible one must hypothesize the internal factors and substantiate the hypothesis with facts from the subject's past life."[1]

It is true that we do not have reliable methods for revealing directly all the factors which are operating in a person at a given time and that therefore the study of the life history may serve as a method for the detection of certain unknown factors in a given personality constellation. It is necessary, however, to point out that through the study of life histories we are able not only to fill the gaps in our knowledge with regard to the present status of the person, but to gain an additional insight which no other method can give. Even if we possessed a perfect battery of tests enabling us to survey all factors operating in the person at a given moment, the biographical method would still retain its value. The biography opens the way for a deeper understanding of the personality than is possible on the basis of a cross-sectional picture. It is desirable to elaborate this point somewhat further, because this discussion will serve to formulate clearly certain specific aspects of the biographical method.

Biography, like any other form of historical account, is more than a mere chronology, that is, it is more than a mere description of a succession of events. The historian as opposed to the chronicler tells us not only of events and their succession, but tells us also how the suc-

1 H. A. Murray, Explorations in Personality, New York, Oxford University Press, 1938, p. 284.

cessive events evolved from each other. The present condition obtains a fuller meaning because of the insight we are given into its genetic derivation. We may, of course, understand the behavior of the criminal, the psychotic, or that of any other person to a certain degree also from a purely cross-sectional point of view. His behavior may be analyzed as a result of a given constellation of forces, habits, wishes, motives, and tendencies. However, in viewing personality in such a manner too much has to be taken for granted and simply accepted as fact. We may state that the person's present activity is due to intensive hostile feelings or a strong wish for recognition, but what is left unexplained is why he has such strong hostile feelings or wish for recognition. Otherwise, the present state appears as a more or less random constellation of forces. Only historical analysis can reveal how one biospheric constellation leads to another and reconstruct the understandable succession of events, that is, give us an insight into how the person became what he is now.

One of the advantages of the biographical method over the strict cross-sectional analysis is that it permits a historical understanding of the present status of the individual. Another advantage of even greater significance must also be considered. The basic theoretical point of view, according to which the concept of personality is to be limited to the constellation of present factors and the assumption that the past belongs to the person only in so far as it is preserved and carried over into the present in the form of traces, requires serious consideration. The picture of a personality which at a given moment carries a load of twenty or fifty years of past experiences with the whole structure standing on the narrow basis of the present moment is too top-heavy, and not only esthetically unsatisfying but also of doubtful validity. Another point of view concerning the relationship between past and present in the course of life history would appear worth considering. This view does not reject the theory of traces but rather supplements it.

Instead of considering personality as a constellation of simultaneous factors, at any given moment we may view it as a temporarily extended whole or as a "time Gestalt." In time Gestalts or successive configurations the parts are distributed along the dimension of time. A sentence and a melody are examples of this. Similarly, life as a series of occurrences forms a time Gestalt. In any whole, and hence also in a time Gestalt, each part is significantly determined by the rest of the whole. The meaning of a word which concludes a sentence or the final part of a melody gains its significance from what went before without the last part carrying traces of the antecedents. In poetry there is a very definite connection between the rhymes, although they do not occur simultaneously but are separated in time.

To consider personality as a time Gestalt means to assume that personality exists not only at a given moment, that the person is not only what he is here and now, but that he is an organized process extending through time. Personality is not a plastic material which, though moulded by past experiences, can be completely defined by what it is now. Life could rather be compared to the tracing of a crayon moving along on the designer's sheet. The line drawn at any particular moment does not carry traces of what went before, but forms a meaningful structure in conjunction with the lines drawn previously. To consider personality as a time Gestalt means to state that it consists not only of present factors but also of such parts as exist in the more or less distant past or future. We assume then that the past functions not only as a trace, but that *qua past* it has an influence from a temporal distance upon the present. This implies the unification and dynamic togetherness of temporally distant factors.

Certain objections may be raised, however, against such a view. As far as physical happenings are concerned only such factors can act upon each other as occur simultaneously or as follow each other in a strict temporal contiguity. Even when we see, for example, a long extinct star, the light rays reaching the eye and the retinal processes occur in a strict temporal succession. Is it then possible that in the realm of personality processes the past—if not carried over in the form of traces—may influence a later happening?

There is a further objection to viewing personality as

a temporally extended Gestalt. The past is often considered as something fixed, immutable, dynamically immovable and irreversible, and the future as incalculable, "a closed book." The first does not exist any more, and the latter does not exist as yet. Thus the question arises whether any dynamically vital whole may include anything else than presently existing factors. In order to clarify this point, it is necessary to analyze the meaning of present, past, and future in relation to the life course.

Psychologically the person is in touch with his past through his memory. He is able to reach back from the present into the past and maintain connections with past events. Thus a whole is formed in which an intensive dynamic interaction between temporally distant parts takes place. One might object that in the process of remembering we do not establish contact with the real past, that we have only our memory traces and memory images which we have carried with us and possess at present. This objection is not quite valid. No one would seriously state that we remember memory traces or memory images as such. We remember by means of traces and images the real events which are located back in a temporal distance. A person who feels regret about an action which he committed ten years ago regrets the real deed in the past. The past is not carried over into the present but is only seen from the present in a time perspective, as the moon is seen in a spatial perspective and not in the eyes. We do not wish to deny the heuristic value of the hypothesis of memory traces. On the contrary, it is quite reasonable to assume that every experience leaves some trace which allows the organism to establish contact with the past. Dynamically active factors are, however, not these traces themselves but the past experience as such. A phobia, for instance, which has developed on the basis of an early traumatic experience is not caused by memory traces but by the traumatic experience which is exerting its influence across the dimension of time. Past is not synonymous with "absent" in the sense of "non-existent," but refers only to a particular location or direction within the dimension of time.

The point of view just presented may seem to involve a rather academic question. Granted that this is to some extent true, this point of view has at least the value that it permits a rather neat formulation of certain personality processes. The following may serve as an illustration. Psychoanalysts have traced certain modes of behavior to infantile phantasies or infantile theories. It is, however, difficult to conceive how a well-informed adult, let us say a gynecologist, could still believe in the theory of anal birth, even if certain features of his behavior, his dreams, his "free associations," and so on, seem to indicate it clearly enough. The difficulty of referring such beliefs to the unconscious mind has been indicated in an earlier chapter. The above-mentioned dilemma can be stated from our point of view in the following way. In such a case the person has at present a correct conception of the process of birth. Many years ago, however, he had a false and childish idea of this matter. This wrong idea —not carried over into the present, but existing in a distant past—exerts from this time an unmistakable influence on the person's present behavior. Why some of the infantile phantasies persist unchanged and continue to exert an influence upon the present behavior while many others are corrected with increasing knowledge and experience is a distinct problem which we shall have occasion to discuss later.

Another possible objection against viewing the personality as a temporally extended whole has to be met. This objection, as mentioned earlier, refers to the irreversibility and immutability of the past. A *dynamic* whole, a large part of which is unchangeable, is in fact contradictory. But is the past of the person really unchangeable? In a sense it is, because what once happened cannot be undone. However, in wholes in general, and in personality specifically, single events have significance only in relation to the whole of which they form a part and not as isolated items. Technically we would say—in accordance with the ideas expressed in discussing the structure of wholes—that single items do not participate in a whole by means of their intrinsic quality but by means of the position which they occupy in the whole. As life goes on and the life history as a whole shapes itself into new forms—although immutable if viewed as isolated items—these past occurrences gain new "positional values," new significance in the temporally extended changing personality. Since every experience changes the meaning of the life history as a whole to some extent and the single items of the life course gain in turn a modified positional value, a somewhat different significance or accent, we may rightly say that the past of the person is in continuous change.

The future also has a definite relationship to the present. It is not true that the future is entirely incalculable, a closed book. We are, to a certain degree, able to predict what a person will do in the future. Such a prediction, although not exact in details, is more frequently correct than incorrect as far as the broad features and general modes of behavior are concerned. The future is in a way active in the present as potentiality and disposition. It is that region of the personality which is not crystallized but still forming itself. Life, at any given moment, is unfinished, an "uncompleted Gestalt." Every uncompleted Gestalt has the tendency toward completion in accordance with some "system principle," which is already more or less clearly discernible in the incomplete whole. This determines to a certain extent the future course. Goal-directed activity, the experience of wishing, hoping, planning, anticipation, presentiment, and so on, necessarily implies the dynamic effectiveness and actuality of the future. This future is not complete and definite but, as A. M. Dunham aptly states, "rather a general direction . . . defining a range of possibilities which are only vaguely given."[2] This range of possibilities is not strictly enclosed in the present moment but is projected forward along the dimension of time, that is, it is projected into the future.

The following three points have emerged from the preceding discussion concerning the necessity and importance of the biographical approach to the problem of personality. 1) We may study life histories for methodological reasons as a technique for obtaining more information about the present state of the person. This is the least specific contribution of the biographical method. 2) Biographies may be studied in order to obtain a historical understanding of the person. A cross-sectional survey tells us only what factors are operating in a person at present. The present constellation is taken simply as factual. The historical analysis goes beyond this. It attempts to reconstruct how step by step, that is, in an understandable succession of constellations, the person became what he is now. 3) The most important and the most specific contribution of the biographical method is, however, that it presents the life history of the person as a temporally extended whole and thus gives the most adequate picture of the personality that we can have.

[2] A. M. Dunham, Jr., The concept of tension in philosophy, Psychiatry, 1:79–120, February 1938, p. 82.

THE COURSE OF LIFE AS A GESTALT

If one allows the life course of a person to pass before his eyes one sees him toiling to reach now one and now another goal. He is seeking some individualized expression of the basic tendency toward increased autonomy. Or else he is seeking to achieve a state in which he can experience himself as a part of superindividual units, most commonly reaching such a state in esthetic, ethical, social, and religious behavior. The latter are individualized expressions of the trend toward homonomy. Beyond the goals to be achieved and states to be reached the person has, however, the broader motivation of shaping his life into a coherent meaningful whole. The course of life is not entirely instrumental for achieving certain goals but has, so to say, an intrinsic or self-purpose. The course of life is, in a way, comparable to a work of art which one creates, shapes, and perfects by living it, and, if one is fortunate enough, one may even put the finishing touches to it. The person may be only vaguely conscious of this, but it still seems that the life history, the work which he creates by living it, is his greatest concern.

The intrinsic purpose in the life of the person—sometimes referred to as self-realization—is definitely connected with a feeling of responsibility. Life is regarded as a unique opportunity and it is felt to be a duty to shape the life course into something worth while. Failing to do this, the consciousness of having wasted one's life is experienced with remorse.

A very common human desire is to start life anew, to be again thirty or twenty or ten years old. This is not primarily a desire to prolong life or to relive that which has passed. Often it is not even the desire to be further advanced on the road of achievement when one should again reach one's present age. Rather it is born from the regret for certain things which one has failed to do or else which one has done, thus having caused gaps or introduced inharmonious elements into one's life history and thus disturbed the "composition" of his most personal creation. It is partly the same esthetic sense of unity with which we decline some new perspective of life: "No, I couldn't do that, not with my past." Death itself is not feared so much as the end of life, but rather as an arbitrary stop put to an unfinished work. Death, after a well-completed life course, is not a too disturbing thought; only the broken, uncompleted life is tragic.

The desire for self-realization, a tendency to shape one's life course into a meaningful whole, gives coherence and unity to the life history. *The personal development thus becomes a process of Gestalt formation.* Certain of our earlier considerations give some points of reference for the analysis of the personal development. It has been stated that the personality structure is being built along three main dimensions: progression, depth, and breadth. In biographical studies it would probably be useful to trace the course of personal development along these dimensions.

In the dimension of progression a structure of means-end relations is built. This is the most tangible aspect of the life course. It is the history of the person's achievement along lines of mastery, domination, production. This history does not lead in a direct line to a main goal. The path is usually marked by many deviations and frequent hesitancy. The main purpose to be achieved forms itself, as a rule, very gradually in the person's mind and actually many people never find it. A clearly defined and fully accepted purpose brings a definite concentration into the person's activity, and thus the means-end structure, being firmly organized, increases the efficiency, the energy output, and the productivity of the person.

In the dimension of depth the person grows from a median position toward both the depth and the surface. Development to greater depth means an increased metaphysical anchoring of one's personality, the formation of a philosophy of life and of a system of values giving a more or less clearly defined meaning to one's life. A person without sufficient depth is like a plant with weak roots. A well-organized person has to develop also toward the surface in this dimension. In our terminology this means the development of greater facility and perfection in expressing in actual behavior that which is in the depth of the personality. The development in this direction is a struggle for self-expression and sometimes the struggle is so prominent that it becomes the *leitmotif* of the life history.

To grow in the dimension of breadth ("transverse dimension") means to open up more channels for the expression of one's behavior tendencies. Defective development in this direction results in narrowness and is frequently associated with a rigidity of the personality. Growth in the dimension of breadth also implies a good coordination of the various channels of expression. When the person broadens out while the various channels of expression are but loosely coordinated, one has the picture of a kind of dissipation of energy, the person is "spreading himself thin."

The fullness of life depends upon a harmonious growth of the personality structure in all three dimensions. The course of life is essentially the development of a Gestalt from diffuse beginnings to greater differentiation. This process is governed by the same laws as any other Gestalt formation. Such laws are the tendency toward closure and the tendency toward *Pregnanz*—or, as we have expressed it previously, a "tendency toward the perfect realization of the system principle." In the last section of this chapter there will be an opportunity to discuss briefly the tendency toward closure in the life course. Here we refer only to some examples of the tendency to *Pregnanz*.

It is a common characteristic of the personality organization to build around defects and sometimes even around minor handicaps or "inferiorities" strong and intricate reaction systems. As is well known, this phenomenon is the central theme of the Adlerian psychology. It would seem at first sight rather peculiar and unreasonable that a single deficiency could become the main concern of the person and that this might become more important than all the excellent qualities and opportunities which he might also possess. This becomes more understandable, however, if one considers personality development as a Gestalt formation. The concentration upon every minor incongruous element in the personality organization is an example of the tendency toward perfection which is common to all Gestalts. It is a dynamic force which is known in Gestalt psychology as the law of *Pregnanz*.

The tendency of wholes toward perfection and thus reaction toward incongruous components of the total personality have significant bearings also upon those features of the personality dynamics, the knowledge of which we owe to psychoanalysis. As far as the purposiveness of those dynamic patterns or "mechanisms" is in question, they can best be regarded as attempts—successful or unsuccessful—to bring incompatible, incongruous elements into harmony with the rest of the personality and thus to approach a perfect Gestalt. It would be useful for the clarification of the nature of these phenomena to elaborate this, but that is beyond the scope of the present study.

COURSE OF LIFE AS GESTALT

In the first section of this chapter we touched upon a problem which we may discuss further at this juncture because it is related to the Gestalt dynamics of the life history. It was stated that past events in the person's life continue to exert an influence from a temporal distance upon the present behavior. The question, however, was left open as to how it happens that certain past experiences have an unusually strong and persistent influence upon later behavior, while others merge into a rather indistinct background.

If one examines concrete examples of biospheric occurrences which exert persistent and intensive influence upon subsequent behavior, one can state that all of them have one characteristic in common: they are occurrences which somehow have remained unsettled and have not been sufficiently assimilated by the person. In order to make the meaning of this statement clear it is desirable to recall that the evolution of any whole takes place in successive stages of differentiation and re-imbedding of the differentiated parts into the whole. Differentiation always involves a kind of disequilibrium because it is a stage which leads beyond the present status of the whole. The process of differentiation is normally followed by a process of assimilation or re-imbedding whereby the whole itself changes to some extent. In the phase of differentiation the connection between part and whole becomes looser and the part stands out distinctly and gains an individualistic character. In the process of re-imbedding the part again becomes deeply integrated into the whole; it becomes indistinct and loses its individual characteristics, because it is now entirely assimilated by the whole.

The imbedding capacity of the person is not unlimited, however. There are occurrences which are so sharply incompatible with the personality organization that no assimilation may be possible. Thus a personality constellation arises containing certain partial factors which are not integrated into the personality in any orderly fashion. The phenomena concerned with repression are good examples of this. The poorly assimilated elements which still draw upon the energy of the person like a cancer are the factors which have such persistent and often very destructive effects upon later behavior. Thus we see that the past exerts an influence either in an orderly or an un-orderly manner. In the first case a past biospheric occurrence becomes a well-organized but indistinct part of the temporally extended person, while in the second such assimilation does not take place and the part retains its individual characteristics and exerts, usually in a bionegative fashion, its influence upon later behavior.

No whole is entirely homogeneous but is always differentiated into more or less distinct parts. These parts are not the results of any arbitrary division but of the natural articulation of the whole. Tracing the intrinsic articulation of the life history as a whole, one finds that it is more or less distinctly divided into a number of phases which represent the parts of the life history. No single, arbitrarily chosen period of a life can be considered as a phase. A phase of life forms a relatively autonomous partial whole which—in spite of its dependence upon the total pattern of the life history—is relatively closed in itself. In each phase the person is confronted with some particular problem of life which forms the central theme of the given phase and gives to it its characteristic specific meaning. The life of a newborn child, for instance, is centered around food and sleep. The rest of the environment seems to be experienced by the infant as a disturbance to which it reacts by avoidance. Somewhat later, however, the opportunities of the environment and the possibilities of its own body are gradually discovered as means of exercising the self-assertive tendencies of the individual. At first the child does not recognize the heteronomous nature of the environment and attempts to deal with it in an arbitrary fashion in phantasy and play. When the limitations set by the heteronomy of the environment are discovered, a new phase sets in. The insight that changes do not occur by mere wishing and imagining, but by acting in accordance with the objective properties of the environment, brings an entirely new turn into the child's life which now becomes characterized by an insatiable curiosity and drive to explore the properties of the surroundings. Puberty, through the profound changes which take place at this time, stands out distinctly as a separate phase of the life course with its specific problems and meanings.

The man on the street also distinguishes certain phases in life such as infancy, childhood, puberty, adolescence, youth, adulthood, and senescence. The problem of life phases has been most carefully studied by Ch. Bühler who has traced the phasic course of life up to the age of adolescence[3] and has more recently projected it in broad outlines for the entire life course.[4] Whether the separation of the various phases proposed by Bühler is correct or not in all details is not very important from our point of view. Important only is it that the empirical data clearly indicate the phasic character of the life course.

The phasic course of life histories shows a certain degree of uniformity on the basis of which generalizations can be made. The uniformity is due to the fact that the psychobiological development follows in part more or less fixed pathways which are closely bound up with definite organic changes. Characteristic examples of this are puberty and involution. In addition, certain cultural factors also tend to make uniform the life course of people living in the same culture area. In our culture, for instance, there is a certain age when we send the child to school and, more loosely defined, an age at

[3] Ch. Bühler, Kindheit und Jugend, Genese des Bewusstseins, 2d ed., Leipzig, Hirzel, 1930.

[4] Ch. Bühler, Der menschliche Lebenslauf als psychologisches Problem, Leipzig, Hirzel, 1933.

which a girl is expected to marry and beyond which she is regarded as a spinster. Other cultures with their initiation ceremonies and other customs tend to direct and to make uniform to a certain degree the phasic course of life.

Study of life phases in general may serve as a valuable aid but by no means as a substitute for the analysis of phases in individual cases. In the first type of study one is interested, for instance, in the general characteristics of puberty. In a biographical study, however, the corresponding problem is to determine what direction puberty development has taken in the individual instance. Furthermore, the phasic differentiation of the life course is not entirely determined by general biogenetic and cultural factors. Significant occurrences in the personal life may superimpose an individualized phasic differentiation upon the generalized pattern of the life course.

Analysis of biographical phases may become a significant aid in the study of the pathology of the person. It is quite possible that certain forms of maladjustment may have their source in an abnormality of phasic development rather than in any deviation of separate personality factors. It is, for instance, a popular belief that one cannot skip stages in one's development without consequent deleterious later effects. On this ground a somewhat wild youth is frequently not regarded by popular opinion as bad; rather his behavior is frequently looked upon as a favorable prognostic sign for a peaceful and well-adjusted later life. This might be only a convenient rationalization, but our reasoning in practical psychiatric considerations is not very different from this. If, for instance, we find in a person's history that he never played as a child, we usually consider the omission as a dangerous sign. All that one can say at the present time about this problem is more or less a matter of intuition and hypothesis. It would, however, be not at all surprising if further biographical studies proved the importance of deviant phasic development for the pathology of the person.

The purpose of this section has been to point out that the life history has all of the characteristics of a true Gestalt. The life course, as any other whole, shapes itself in stages of successive differentiation and imbedding and is dominated by the tendency toward a perfect realization of the system principle. To make of one's life course a meaningful coherent whole, a work of art which one creates by living, seems to be the greatest concern of the person, although he may be only vaguely aware of such purpose. The course of life as a whole is intrinsically divided into a number of phases which function as its parts. The phasic differentiation of the life course is determined by general biological and cultural factors and other significant occurrences in the person's life.

COURSE OF LIFE AS GESTALT

HOLISTIC EVOLUTION AND CHANCE IN THE LIFE COURSE

A biographical evaluation can be most adequately carried out at the end of the life course. In practice, however, we have to make such evaluation while the history of the person is still in the making. For instance, in a psychiatric case study one aims to understand how a given personality constellation arose and to predict and modify the future life course of the person. Prediction, however, is only possible with regard to processes which are deterministic in nature. It is, therefore, desirable to examine in what sense and to what extent the life course is directed by deterministic principles.

According to all appearance the events of one's life are neither entirely random nor entirely predetermined. In order to single out those factors which enter as directive forces into the life course it is useful to recall a previous distinction. It has been pointed out that the biospheric total process is a resultant of two kinds of forces: autonomous and heteronomous determinations. The interplay of these factors represents the relationship between individual and environment. Viewing the individual-environment relationship longitudinally, the autonomous determinations take the form of an *organismic* or *holistic evolution,* while heteronomous determination appears as *chance*. These two factors have to be considered separately in the discussion of the problem of determinism in the course of life.

The term organismic evolution refers to all those phenomena which are determined by intrinsic factors in the person, that is to say, by biological laws in the broadest sense of the word. By chance, on the other hand, are meant those processes in the environment which—though they are relevant to the person's life—originate and proceed in independence of the organism. What we call chance are not random happenings. They are only beyond the control and foresight of the individual. Chance occurrences, in spite of the fact that they are strictly lawful processes, are practically incalculable factors in the life history, because it is impossible to know all those external factors which may become relevant for the person's life. Thus, if prediction is at all possible with regard to the course of life, it can be based only on the intrinsic laws of personality development. Prediction can, of course, even in the best case be only an approximation, because one group of those factors which are codeterminants in every biospheric occurrence, namely the chance occurrences, are incalculable.

The degree of predictability in the holistic evolution depends on the degree of lawfulness of personality processes. Without entering into the discussion of the age-old philosophical problem of determinism vs. indeterminism we may emphasize some points which are directly relevant to the present problem.

There is good reason to believe that the reliability of prediction in the biological sciences will always lag behind the reliability of prediction in physical sciences. One of the reasons for this lies in the difference in methods and practical aims of these two scientific branches. Prediction in physics is most reliable with regard to artificially arranged ideal cases. When physics has to deal with phenomena as they occur in nature, as for example in meteorology, the practical possibility of prediction largely decreases. Now, while physicists can accomplish a great deal by working with artificially arranged, relatively ideal cases, the biologist has to remain much closer to the study of phenomena as they occur in nature. This is partly due to the difference in the practical application of these two sciences. The main field of the practical application of physics is technology. Its task is to make some planful artificial arrangements and it is no disadvantage that the naturally occurring order of what is used as material is destroyed. In the practical application of biology, for example in medicine, the aim is to maintain the naturally occurring phenomena, modifying them only in some particular respect.

A more fundamental difference between biological and physical sciences with regard to predictability is based on the difference between the nature of the two fields. It is useful to distinguish between physical and biological determinism. Strict determinism, in the sense of classical physics, implies that if all the antecedent factors which enter into a constellation are given, there can be only *one* definite resulting effect. In biological processes, too, the effect is lawfully determined, but it is not narrowed down to a single possibility but to a *range of possibilities*. Only the *kind* of biological response is predictable from its antecedents. This statement is a logical deduction based on the structural characteristics of holistic processes. Part processes are determined by the whole in the sense that they take place according to the existing system principle. A part, however, is not defined in all its individual details by the whole, but only in so far as its position in the system is concerned. This allows a certain degree of individual variation in filling the positions which are determined by the system principle, that is, it allows a range of possibilities. Naturally, when the effect of the biological antecedents actually occurs, only one of these possibilities is realized. Which of the possibilities shall be realized is probably a matter of chance, meaning by chance a constellation of factors which are independent of the subject. Thus a biospheric occurrence is first broadly determined by organismic laws and is thus restricted to a limited range of possibilities. This range of possibilities is then further narrowed down by external influences to a univocally defined event.

Holistic evolution and chance are intimately interwoven in the person's life course and are practically inseparable. What seems to be a matter of chance may be largely determined by the personality structure of the individual and vice versa. If, for example, a man clashes with his employer and loses his job, that may be purely his bad luck in having happened to have an employer with whom he could not agree. But, if the situation of getting into conflict with his superior occurs in his life over and over again, one would suspect that such recurrence is not so much a matter of chance, but rather is based on some feature of his personality structure. Psychoanalysts would suspect in such a case the late effects of a poorly solved Oedipus conflict. To have an accident seems to be pure chance. However, it has been established beyond doubt that certain people have an unusually large number of accidents and that this is based on a particular personality organization.

The incalculability of chance makes life to some degree a matter of gambling. One never can be entirely certain of the later effects of whatever steps one takes in life. To take reasonable risks is absolutely necessary for a good adjustment; otherwise one would be doomed to inactivity. One may even develop a certain liking for the uncertainties of life and take a positive pleasure in "living dangerously." I remember that when I was beginning my practical work in psychiatry I was told by an experienced older colleague that the important thing in psychiatric practice was to have the courage to make mistakes. Taking reasonable chances seems to be an important prerequisite for any sort of practical activity.

As the life course proceeds it becomes more and more deterministic. At the early stages the person is a rather diffuse whole with many vague possibilities, but this whole becomes more and more crystallized and the range of possibilities decreases. The person becomes increasingly differentiated and the personality structure more and more rigidly patterned. To mention only a very simple example, at ten years of age a child may have just as much possibility of becoming an engineer as of becoming a physician, whereas a fifty-year-old man, if he is already an engineer, is very unlikely to become a physician. Every decision or choice definitely narrows down the possibilities of the future; and not only such important steps as the choice of a position or of a wife but even minor steps have in some degree similar effects. What a person does at any time not only has an immediate relevance but commits him to a future course to be taken. The mores and a kind of inner obligation to self-consistent behavior force a person to follow a course to which he implicitly committed himself by his previous actions.

The increase of determination with the progression of one's life course is based on a general law of Gestalt dynamics, namely, on the "law of closure." Every uncompleted whole tends to a kind of continuation which is in accordance with the system principle of that given whole. At an early phase of the life course only a few initial lines of the life Gestalt are given and the system-adequate continuation may take many different directions. The more the Gestalt approaches completion the less variation of a system-adequate continuation is possible. This is a general holistic law and the life course as a whole is not exempt from it.

Summarizing the preceding discussion, the course of life is a resultant of the interplay between holistic self-development and chance. Chance is every environmental object-dependent occurrence. Some of these occurrences can be foreseen, but most of them are practically incalculable. The holistic development is to some extent predictable and is governed by biological determinism. Physical determinism permits only *one* strictly defined effect of a given constellation of causal antecedents, whereas biological determinism defines the effect only as a *range of possibilities,* although this range is definitely limited. The course of life proceeds from lesser to greater determinism. The more the pattern of the life course has become crystallized, the less variation is possible in a system-adequate continuation of it.

SUMMARY

A theory of personality would not be complete without considering the evolution of the person in time, that is, his biography. The biographical study of the person may be pursued for methodological reasons: a cross-sectional picture of the personality leaves many gaps which one may attempt to fill by searching for significant factors in the person's past. Furthermore, only through a biographical study can we understand the person historically. A cross-sectional survey can reveal at the most only those factors which are at present operating in the person and the present personality constellation has to be taken simply as factual. In a historical analysis, however, one may attempt to reconstruct an understandable succession of constellations which lead up to the present state and situation of the person.

The life history, beyond giving a historical understanding of personality, gives us also a picture of the person as a temporally extended whole. We have offered a point of view according to which personality is not concentrated in the present but is a whole, the parts of which are distributed along the dimension of time whereby the person extends into the past and into the future. The hypothetical traces which past experiences leave in the organism are only the means which allow a communication with the past. The dynamically active factors are, however, not these traces but the past experiences as such, which from a temporal distance exert an influence upon the present.

The life history as a whole is a time Gestalt, the dynamics of which follow laws that are common to wholes in general, such as the law of *Pregnanz,* the law of closure, and an evolution in successive stages of differentiation and re-imbedding of the differentiated parts into the whole.

The tendency of the person to make of his life course

a coherent, meaningful whole is experienced as a desire for self-realization. This holistic development may be traced in the three basic dimensions of the person: progression, depth, and breadth. In the dimension of progression a means-end organization of widening scope may be built. Development in the dimension of depth creates, on the one hand, deeper metaphysical anchoring of the person's life, and on the other hand, a perfection in expressing one's deeper tendencies in actual behavior. Finally, development in the dimension of breadth means the opening of manifold channels of behavior and a good coordination of the various channels.

The life history is differentiated into a number of parts or phases. Each phase of the life course has its own central theme which lends a specific character and meaning to the given phase. The phasic differentiation of the life course is determined by general biogenetic and cultural factors as well as by certain specific significant occurrences in the person's life.

In the course of life, biological determinism and "pure chance" are intricately interwoven. Biological determinism has a specific meaning: while physical determinism permits only one definite effect from causal antecedents, biological determinism defines the effect as a range of possibilities. With an increased realization of the life pattern this range of possibilities decreases, that is, the further the life course proceeds the more deterministic it becomes.

EPITOME

This dissertation proceeded from an initial statement that a holistic theory of personality must fulfill three conditions. 1) There is imperative need of more specific and positive formulations with regard to the nature, organization, and laws of personality than are yet available. 2) Either the use of segmental data should be renounced and typically holistic facts be considered, or a method of synthesis for the unification of segmental data within a holistic frame must be formulated. 3) A set of new concepts which are appropriate to the holistic character of personality must be developed to permit discontinuance of the use of inappropriate concepts borrowed from the segmental sciences.

In conclusion we may examine briefly to what extent our theory has fulfilled these requirements.

1. What specific formulations have been given beyond the general statement that "personality is a whole"?

Having defined personality, dynamically, as the process of living, our first task was to determine the general pattern of the life processes. It was shown that life follows a double pattern, consisting of a tendency of the personality toward the achievement of greater self-determination (trend toward increased autonomy) and a tendency toward conformity with the superindividual wholes of society, culture, etc. (trend toward homonomy).

The life process as a whole, as well as its part processes, was interpreted as the resultant of two forces: the autonomous determination of the organism and the heteronomous influences of the environment. This was expressed by the ratio, $a:h$. The trend toward increased autonomy can be formulated symbolically as

$$\left(\frac{a}{h}\right)_1 \lessgtr \left(\frac{a}{h}\right)_2$$

This formula means that the organism tends to go from a state of lesser autonomy to a state of greater autonomy. In other words, the person has a tendency to master the environment, and, by conquest and achievement, to impose his intrinsic determination upon a widening realm of events. The concept of a trend toward increased autonomy is closely related to the technical concept of "aggression."

In the trend toward increased autonomy the biologically chaotic items of the environment are fitted into the structure of the individual's life. In the homonomous tendency the person seeks to fit himself into larger organizations. The trend toward homonomy expresses the tendency of human beings to share and to participate in, to fit into and to conform with, superindividual categories such as the family, the social group, a meaningful world order, etc. Characteristic examples of the trend toward homonomy are social, religious, ethical, and esthetic attitudes. Pure manifestations of these trends are rare but in combination with other trends they are practically constant co-determinants of behavior.

The general dynamic pattern of the organism flows into more specific channels of expression. The specific ramifications of the general dynamic trends form the skeleton of the personality structure. In man the specific expressions are so diversified that the attempt to make a complete and generally valid inventory would be futile. It was possible, however, to point out to a certain extent the fields in which generalization can be achieved. A preliminary enumeration and brief characterization of the more or less constant features of the dynamics of personality which may be useful as an outline for empirical studies were also given.

Supplementing our formulation of the general dynamic pattern of the personality and indicating the various ramifications of this pattern, we have attempted to give greater concreteness to the theory by an analysis of personality integration. We suggested that, in order to cope with this task, we needed first of all adequate logical tools. The basic category of a holistic logic, that is, the concept of *system,* was then introduced and the essential features of this concept were indicated. Systems were defined as certain types of order (determined by a unifying principle) which obtain in the arrangement of elements in a dimensional domain. In brief, we have introduced the concept of types of order in a field. With the aid of the "system" concept it was possible to analyze the various features of personality integration. Next we discussed the material for personality organization, characterized the dimensional domain of personality organization, and analyzed the various degrees of differentiation. The total personality organization was described as a hierarchy of systems and the dynamics of this hierarchy was thus exposed in terms of the laws concerning the range of variation of positions in a system, the continuity of action in a hierarchy of systems, and the setting and shifting of systems. The notions derived from the study of personality integration were applied also to a tentative interpretation of certain specific problems such as the stimulus-response pattern and the problem of conditioning. A separate chapter was devoted to testing the applicability of this theory of personality integration, especially in connection with the problem of the pathological disturbances of integration.

Finally the person's evolution in the time dimension was also considered. The life history was regarded as a temporally extended whole which follows laws that are characteristic of wholes in general, such as the laws of *Pregnanz,* the law of closure, and the succession of stages of differentiation. It appeared that the life history of the person is the result of an interplay between holistic self-evolution and chance occurrences in his environment. A more or less clearly felt desire for self-realization creates unity in the life history, while its division into phases provides articulation.

2. A holistic theory of personality further requires that one either renounce the use of segmental data and work with typically holistic facts or else formulate a method of synthesis permitting the unification of segmental data within a holistic frame. Certain data were characterized as typically holistic and it was stated that they constitute the basic material with which a science of personality has to deal.

On the other hand, we recognized that data offered by the segmental sciences such as physiology, psychology, and cultural anthropology can also be utilized in the study of personality. A workable principle for the synthesis of segmental data is one which relates them to the total personality instead of relating them to another set of segmental data. Thus, information offered by psychology can be utilized in a holistic theory of personality provided one does not relate it to physiological facts as such, but to the psychophysically neutral processes of the total organism. Psychological phenomena were interpreted as symbolic elaborations of processes which reflect the person's states and tendencies, as well as the ways in which the person is affected by his sensorial engagement with his environment. Psychological phenomena have biological significance only in relation to those primary processes *which they represent.*

The data of cultural anthropology can also be utilized in the study of personality, provided one is clearly aware of the relationship of such phenomena to the total personality. Culture is a socially inherited body of sanctions and directives which define the "proper" and "improper" ways of behavior. Culture has a twofold relevance for the personality. It is, on one hand, a complex of environmental factors forming a whole to which one has to adjust. On the other hand, culture is assimilated and modified by the individual and in part defines the personal standards of behavior. Culture, when assimilated, functions as that part of the personality which corresponds more or less to the concept of the super-ego in psychoanalysis.

3. The third requisite for a holistic theory of personality is to develop a new set of concepts which are appropriate for an understanding of the person. This prohibits by implication taking over concepts from the segmental sciences. The conception of "individual" and "environment" as morphologically separable entities has been rejected. Translated into dynamic terms, "environment" connotes heteronomous determination, and "individual," autonomous determination. Every life process is a resultant of these two factors. The life process does not take place solely within the body but it includes both intrasomatic and extrasomatic happenings. Every process which results from an interplay of organismic autonomy and environmental heteronomy is a part of

the life process, irrespective of whether it takes place within the body or outside of it. The realm in which life processes take place was termed the "biosphere." We urged the study of biospheric occurrences in their integral reality instead of the study of organismic processes and environmental influences as separate categories. The biospheric occurrences constitute the subject-matter of both holistic and segmental sciences. The segmental sciences, however, limit themselves more or less exclusively to certain selected features of biospheric occurrences and neglect such of the features as are not directly relevant to their restricted fields of interest.

The basic concepts which seem useful in the study of personality dynamics were defined. As a basic concept "tension" was selected. This term refers to specific instances of dynamic subject-object relationships. The tendency and potentiality of the organism to form a specific type of tension was labeled "readiness for tension." These tendencies, when viewed with the subject as our point of reference, appear as *attitudes.* The various attitudes of a person may be traced back to successively more and more general ones. In so doing one arrives at a limited number of very general attitudes, which are accepted as unquestionable and axiomatic for the given individual. These attitudes were termed "axioms of behavior." The same "readiness for tension," when viewed with the object as our point of reference, appears as an environmental relevancy which represents values for the organism and these can be traced back to a limited number of general axiomatic values.

Special effort was made to distinguish holistic concepts from the related psychological ones. Differentiation was made between the psychophysically neutral biological tension and the psychological experience of this tension in the form of interests; between the biological drive and the corresponding psychological experience of craving; between the biological subject and the psychological self; and so on.

The terminology used for denoting the various holistic concepts is not perhaps always a happy one. Only a few new terms were coined. Whenever possible generally accepted terms were used, but the difference between the conventional meaning of these terms and the specific meaning here assigned to them was pointed out. This terminology is provisional and, if one keeps in mind the definitions given, need not be misleading. The root "bio" occurs in several terms such as biosphere, biospheric occurrences, biological total processes, etc. They do not refer, however, exclusively to somatic processes but to the physiologically, psychologically, and socially integrated total process of living.

An attempt was made to lay the foundations for a science of personality. The usefulness of this outline for the formulation of more specific problems and for the interpretation of relevant data remains to be tested by empirical methods of inquiry.

INDEX

INDEX

INDEX

INDEX

INDEX